Celtic

The Supersonic 70s!

Gerard McDade is a writer, broadcaster, producer, stand-up comedian and hairdresser from the West of Scotland. Once he'd realised that he wouldn't be the first Celtic goalkeeper to play the part of James Bond whilst recording a duets album with Elvis Presley he decided to turn his attention to more attainable goals. In that capacity, he has worked extensively with Celtic FC, the club channel CelticTV, BBC Scotland and commercial radio amongst others whilst insulting audiences the length and breadth of the country with his half-wit wit. He still thinks the 1970s were fab, *groovy and sensational* and that Peter Latchford should have won more caps than Peter Shilton! Just like Elvis, he doesn't read reviews. Unlike Elvis, he's made it past 42!

www.gerrymcdade.co.uk

Celtic

The Supersonic 70s!

Gerard McDade

BLACK & WHITE PUBLISHING

First published 2009
by Black & White Publishing Ltd
29 Ocean Drive, Edinburgh EH6 6JL

1 3 5 7 9 10 8 6 4 2   09 10 11 12 13

ISBN: 978 1 84502 263 1

A CIP catalogue record for this book is available from the British Library.

Typeset by Ellipsis Books Ltd, Glasgow
Printed and bound by MPG Books Ltd, Bodmin

Contents

Acknowledgements

Okay, you've downloaded all those fab, solid silver '70s sounds on to your iPod/mp3 – you're propped up on your bean bag, bell-bottoms crossed, lava lamp on – there's a can of full-fat Pepsi sitting beside the *fave grub* half-eaten cheeseburger and you're just about to chew down on a Texan bar then crash out with the Olde English flavour Spangles . . . before hitting that supersonic '70s groove please give it up for the following: the Sensational Steve Mylles for his higher than Higher English skills; Joe 'Birthday Bhoys' Clark for coming up with the goods; Top Cat Tony Hamilton for the encouragement; Stevie 'Student Prince' Murray for his poptastic caricatures, as great an artist *off* the pitch as he was on it; Super Ali McBride; Cosmic Campbell, the man who puts the Brown in Black & White; Jock; Cesar and the Bhoys, of course, and, above all, Irene and the Boo for their patience and support . . . as Noddy Holder might have put it . . . Look Wot We Gon' & Dun!

THIS BOOK IS DEDICATED TO

THE DOUGANS:

CHIC, PAT AND JOHN (RIP)

The Mighty Cesar

King Kenny

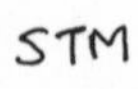

HoopsWearin'BadgeKissin'EuroDreamin'
KennyKingin'ConnellyPassin'9Winnin'CupLiftin'
JohnnyDoylein'ProvanProvin'GlavinGrabbin'
LatchSavin'JimmyJinkin'JockLeavin'CesarComin'
TenMenin'ShuggyShufflin'DannyLappin'BurnsLovin'
6Baggin'DixieLipsmackin'HailHailin' . . .
CELTIC!

Big Jock, the Don of Dons

1970
HoopsWearin'

Track list:

Simon & Garfunkel/Bridge Over Troubled Water; The Beatles/Let It Be; Christie/Yellow River; Edison Lighthouse/Love Grows; Dana/All Kinds Of Everything; Free/All Right Now; Badfinger/Come And Get It; Ricky Thomas/Love Of The Common People.

Had it been a movie, they would have shown this moment in slow motion: Alfred Hitchcock would have choreographed the arc of the ball from its primary thrust out of the midfield area high into the humid Italian night sky and downward into the penalty box; Buster Keaton would have happily directed the jocular image of that ball eluding the virile, handsome, lantern-jawed leading man who, in the effort of trying desperately to divert its path, stumbled backwards falling onto the pitch whilst pawing it into the path of the opposition attacker and Oliver Stone would have heightened the denouement by having the Celtic supporters, both in the stadium and beyond, in front of their television sets, rising as one and letting out a deliberate, slow, elongated *NOOOOOOOOOOOOOOO!* as if trying to stop a child from running into the path of a bus only to see Ove Kindvall of Feyenoord reach the ball first and toe-poke it beyond the despairing fingers of Celts' goalkeeper Evan Williams.

Celtic captain, he of the lantern jaw and the first British footballer to hold aloft Europe's top club trophy, Billy McNeill, could only watch on as helpless as a Morris Minor in the snow. The first European Cup of the 1970s had been secured.

Hmmmmm . . . late drama . . . victory for the spirited underdogs against more illustrious opponents . . . a side who had fallen a goal behind but had regrouped to outplay their adversaries in a 2-1 triumph . . . the first team from their country to lift Europe's premier silverware . . . and an outpouring of disbelief and joy from a healthy partisan support. Recognise *that* plot-line? Yup, you're right . . . Lisbon '67. But now it was Milan '70.

Tragically, of course, *had* this been a movie, the sequel to that famous Celtic European Cup victory three years previously, then the story would be about how the tables were turned on the bhoys from Glasgow. Only one man could have played the part of Jock Stein, the Celtic manager whose stature was revered throughout the game and whose no-nonsense gritty approach and shrewd tactician's brain had taken him from the danger-laden mining pits of his youth to the glamorous Hollywood heights of the football world. Even God called him . . . *The Big Man!* It would have taken John Wayne to capture the part perfectly and The Duke, having picked up an Oscar for his role in *True Grit* only weeks before the European Final, would surely have been Stein's choice.

But it wasn't a movie. This finale could not be changed by some alternative camerawork and the snip of a film editor's scissors. This was real life . . . real time . . . 6 May 1970 and Celtic had lost a match that they were overwhelming favourites to win. The game had finished 2-1 in favour of Feyenoord of Rotterdam and even the Dutch team seemed to sense that it might be the only time they got their hands on the trophy. Worse even than that; it had been the second major final in under a month when the silverware had been denied to the Celts.

Aberdeen's victory in the Scottish Cup Final of 1970, by a handsome 3-1 advantage, had been the talk of the pubs and clubs in Glasgow and beyond. Dons manager, Eddie Turnbull, had put together a young, attractive yet hard team who would joust unsuccessfully with Celtic for a couple of titles, but the Hoops were still the odds-on bet to win the Scottish Cup Final. Umbrage could possibly be taken at match referee Bobby Davidson who had awarded Aberdeen a penalty from which they scored, chalked off a Bobby Lennox 'goal' and waved away a Celtic spot-kick appeal, all in quick succession, but the truth was that, on the day, the Reds had over-turned the Greens.

The 1970s had barely begun and the rumour was that Celtic were losing their grip. A grip that had been established since that moment in 1965 when Jock Stein arrived to take over the stewardship of a football club that had under-performed for more than a decade. It had been eleven years since Celtic had won the Scottish First Division title and the Scottish Cup as well in that glorious double season of 1953-54 when the younger Jock was team captain.

Yes, there was that epiphanic 7-1 slaughter of the Ibrox innocents in the 1957 League Cup Final to which 'Tic adherents had clung onto like a Lourdes pilgrim with a miraculous medal, but that had been it for eight long years. Eight years when the trophy-polisher at Celtic Park was as usefully employed as Yul Brynner's hairdresser. Eight years when a succession of Celtic teams dubbed *Kelly's Kids,* after patriarchal chairman Robert Kelly, were about as productive as the Bash St Kids. Eight years when the only pot that avuncular first-team manager Jimmy McGrory got close to was the one in which he kept his pipe tobacco. And eight years when, it could be argued, Count Dracula had enjoyed a more intimate relationship with silver than the Celtic!

All that changed within weeks of Big Jock's arrival as Celtic edged out traditionally tricky opponents Dunfermline Athletic in the Scottish Cup Final of 1965 by three goals to two. It was the catalyst for a side that would go on to dominate the football scene both at home and abroad for the rest of the swinging decade with four titles, a further two Scottish cups, five League Cups and the biggest trophy of all . . . that European Cup in 1967.

Ironically, Jock Stein started the 1960s plying his trade fairly lucratively *at* Dunfermline Athletic. He'd even gone as far as beating Celtic in the Scottish Cup Final of 1961 with the Pars as well as a brief spell working at Hibernian. But, to a hopeful Celtic support, there was no question about it, Big Jock had, biblically speaking, emerged from the desert of the East. He had fasted for forty days and forty nights having survived on nothing but wild honey and locusts and all for one purpose . . . to lead his green and white flock into the Promised Land. Under his tutelage, Celtic had owned the second half of the 1960s as much as the Labour government had under Harold Wilson.

The question now was . . . would the Celts go the way of another famous act that had bossed the '60s but at the start of the '70s had imploded spectacularly replete with recriminations and memories of better days . . . The Beatles?

Paul McCartney had hauled the Fabs into court in April of that year wanting the judiciary to release him from his *Beatley* duties and the self-styled *four lads from Liverpool who rocked the world* were about to discover that *Love*, in actual fact, wasn't quite *All You Need . . .* a good lawyer helps as well!

Beatles fighting? 'Duke' Wayne winning a Best Actor Oscar? Celtic losing two Cup Finals in a row? What the hell was going on in this Age of Aquarius? How about a quick reality check then?

Celtic had also bagged their fifth League title in a row and retained the Scottish League Cup. They were now one season away from duplicating the achievement of a previous incarnation in Celtic jerseys that had famously picked up six consecutive League titles between 1904 and 1910. In Europe, there was no question that the humbling by the Dutch was a salutary lesson, but the shock with which the news was received worldwide was, at least, a measure of Celtic's position at the top table on the continent. They were still – and please don't belittle this you who are reading this book from outside the narrow walls of Scotland – the Kings of Glasgow.

Yes, yes, I know. It's only one city. There aren't even that many teams in the neighbourhood. Partick Thistle, Clyde, Queen's Park and that other lot from the Govan area. Our Celtic eyes have traditionally stretched beyond the football horizons of mere local dominance but, it has to be said, before there was anything . . . there was Celtic v Rangers!

Don't give me that tosh about narrow-mindedness either. We love beating them . . . they love beating us and if you want to dominate the world then you have to start with your own neighbourhood. And in 1970 we were the Boss Cats in the alley. TC kept his bin in the east end of Glasgow whilst our own Fancy, Spook, Brains, Choo-Choo, Benny the Ball et al were consistently outsmarting the collective Officers Dibble over at Ibrox.

So there was no need to over-react to more recent events. But the loss and perhaps, more importantly, the performance, in Milan certainly had to be addressed. What had gone wrong? As ever, there would be no one answer to that particular conundrum. It was an accumulation of factors. The Bhoys of 1967 had been the *parvenus* at this level. It was their first tilt at the European Cup and, at times, their Doris Day innocence was a considerable boon. The team that confounded noted opinion throughout a thrilling European campaign that culminated in a green letter day in Lisbon simply didn't know any better. Their very naivety, pitted against the sophisticated Euro-poseurs of Inter-Milan with their Mario Lanza hairstyles, manicured fingernails, olive oil suntans and football aristocracy, was a potent factor in Stein's ammunition.

The tooth situation appeared to outline the differences between the teams. Every combatant in the blue and black vertical stripes of Internazionale seemed to belong to some elaborate corporate dental plan that guaranteed the Italian champions' gnashers were fit to grace a Hollywood publicity shot. When Inter smiled in the sun it was like some huge solar panel had taken up residence on the middle of a football park. The Italians grinned the polished enamels of thoroughbreds.

Celtic, on the other hand, had asked goalkeeper Ronnie Simpson to store their *wallies* in his keeper's cap! Imagine, if you will, Celtic forward Bobby Lennox running towards you with that Olympic pace of his, the ball at his majestic feet, his face a study in determination and his toothless gums daring you to tackle him. It's little wonder that, after having taken an early lead through a penalty, Inter Milan opted to defend their precious lead against these unruly Glaswegian Picts.

Midfield schemer Bertie Auld struck the supreme psychological blow before a ball had been kicked when he decided, in one glorious, spontaneous karaoke moment, to belt out *The Celtic Song* at the top of his larynx as the bemused Italians lined up in the tunnel with their Scottish counterparts.

In a chamber designed to deliver artisans to the pitch but with the acoustical brilliance of La Scala opera house, Bertie's booming baritone had announced to the we've-seen-it-all-before-Italians that they were about to play a group of individuals the likes of which they had never experienced before.

The *Lisbon Lions* were being mid-wived to the world. History was made on a night when a mixture of Scottish gallusness, sheer disrespect and not forgetting the little matter of some outstanding football ability, destroyed the high priests of the European scene. It was 2-1 going on eight! 1967 . . . the Summer of Love and Celtic were learning to *looooove* the European stage.

There seemed little doubt that the Celtic side that arrived at their second European Cup Final in three years were a different affair. Yes, the famous Lisbon Lions still provided the backbone to the side and there were new faces in the shape of goalkeeper Evan Williams, full-back David Hay, wing-back Jim Brogan and the seasoned campaigner John 'Yogi' Hughes, who had been supremely unlucky to have missed out in the starting line-up of 1967, but to all observers it had seemed like a different Celtic squad.

Perhaps they had been complacently bloated by the wine of constant success and in mitigation they had disposed of English champions Leeds United in the so-called *final-before-the-final* only weeks before. In that encounter there had been the predictable pre-contest build-up by the press pack south of the border who had poured scorn on the very idea that Celtic would emerge victorious over an English team at the peak of its powers.

This was the Leeds United forged from the granite of their Scottish terrier captain Billy Bremner, streamlined by the wing-play of Eddie Gray and Peter Lorimer, also Caledonian extracts, and backed up by the hard men of Messrs Jackie Charlton, Norman Hunter and Mick Jones amongst others, the latter threesome a triumvirate who would have fancied themselves in a square-go with those other lions you tend to find at the Coliseum. Of course, the dossier-obsessed, dour Svengali who was United's manager, Don Revie, was a formidable leader. He had earned the respect of Jock Stein, but the Big Man knew that, if his charges played to their potential, then anything was possible.

Thus it was that the Celts took an early lead in the first leg away at Elland Road and maintained that advantage until the whistle had blown after ninety minutes. And *early lead* is putting it mildly!

Midfielder George Connelly had Celtic one-up within forty five seconds of the match! Intravenous injections take longer. Revie had barely had time to open his salt 'n' vinegar crisps never mind his tactical dossiers in the home dugout whilst the Celtic fans cavorted about barely registering that their favourites were wearing their traditional hoops, white shorts but with red socks on!

Maybe it was the sartorial disarray that disrupted the concentration of the Leeds back four. If it had, then it was a plan that had spectacularly backfired for it was the wily Revie who, at the eleventh hour, had pounced on the fact that both Celtic and Leeds United wore white socks, the distraction of which would be decisive for split-second refereeing decisions. As the home team, he demanded white sock satisfaction and suggested to Big Jock that the Celts could wear an alternative from the Elland Road laundry basket . . . red or blue! Celtic in blue socks? Yeah, right! You would see the Pope wearing Levis before that would happen!

The teams reconvened at Hampden Park two weeks after the Celtic Red Sox had crossed the border with that one-goal advantage. Celtic Park was undergoing major refurbishment that would have ensured a more miserly reduced attendance for a game that was being hyped up as the biggest event since the Woodstock concert the previous summer.

The Celtic directors decided to utilise the national stadium in a move that produced the highest ever attendance for a European fixture since Real Madrid had jousted with Manchester United at the same stage of the competition in 1957. For the record, 136,505 people turned up with tickets and although, this being Glasgow, there were a lot less Kaftans than Woodstock, the entertainment value was of the same high calibre premium.

The rest of the world was apparently becoming transfixed by the stricken American spaceship Apollo 13 which was trying to return to earth with the same sticky-back plastic technology that was normally the preserve of BBC's *Blue Peter* show.

NASA, having decided that a lunar policy of *been-there-done-that* was not quite the American way, had launched another rocket in the hope of re-visiting the moon-landing from 1969 only for the ship to become the victim of both its fate-tempting number, 13, and an explosion in the service module . . . whatever that was? On learning that the remit of the American Automobile Club did not extend to vehicular breakdown in outer space, there now followed a desperate race against time to return the three-man crew safely to earth. All of which, you would imagine, would be the primary concern of the world at large but not necessarily of the masses of football fans back in Britain who were consumed by the spectacle of Celtic v Leeds, Round Two as it kicked off at Hampden.

Billy Bremner, a man of whom it was rumoured would have *walked* from Leeds to play for Jock Stein and Celtic, renounced the faith in the most pronounced fashion in just under fifteen minutes when he stuck away a sweet, sweet drive from thirty-five yards. It's possible that Evan Williams in the Celtic goal was looking skywards for Apollo 13 as the ball swept past him with all the surprise of a meteorite, practically lacerating the net.

At 1-1, the game, the match, the tie, the overall bragging rights were well in the balance. Gradually, the Celts worked their way back into contention and when John Hughes nipped in horizontally like a trout ahead of Leeds centre-half and keen angler Jack Charlton to head the ball into the net two minutes into the second half, Celtic were back in front on aggregate and in command.

The imperious Bobby Murdoch adding the polish of a well-struck finish five minutes later only attested to the Celts' superiority. When it was all over, 2-1 on the night and 3-1 overall with Celtic the victors in both games, the players and supporters partied like it was Hogmanay in New York.

There were *less* heady celebrations two days later when the Apollo crew returned safely to earth and, let's face it, Americans aren't exactly reticent when it comes to doing a conga in times of national euphoria. And perhaps, therein, lay the problem.

Celtic were officially the Best in Britain. The team had seen off potential European Champions in Leeds United and now faced Feyenoord from Holland. To be frank, or perhaps Van Der Frank, very few people outside of the claustrophobic football world had heard of the Netherlands champions from Rotterdam. Arguably, even some of the inhabitants *of* that world were not exactly able to rhyme off the Dutch side's back four. Hell, did they even *play* with a back four?

Clogs? Yes. Edam cheese? Definitely. Finger-in-dyke boy? Read it as a child. Ajax Amsterdam? Yes, not bad but hadn't they been horsed 4-1 the year before by AC Milan in the European Cup Final? Feyenoord? Who? The feeling was that Randall & Hopkirk were more famous.

To be fair, that duo of detectives had been entertaining us on a weekly basis courtesy of ITV from September to March, which was almost the equivalent of a football season. Feature film *Butch Cassidy & The Sundance Kid* from the year before had introduced the concept of the *buddy-buddy* type partnership that could be light-hearted and funny yet with an underlying hint of danger. The Americans of course had fed directly off this idea when they brought cowboy coupling *Alias Smith & Jones* to television screens but the British took a slightly different take on the genre when melodramatic writer and producer Dennis Spooner introduced Detective Jeff Randall and his ghostly partner Marty Hopkirk (deceased) to us in the autumn of 1969.

The 1970s were to become the natural home for double acts both on screen and on the football pitch, as we shall see, but from a British television perspective, *Randall & Hopkirk* appeared to be a first. Every week brought fresh escapades for the down-at-heel-unlucky-to-be-alive Jeff as he sought to keep the roof over his head and the bailiffs from his door with a succession of seemingly far-fetched cases. Marty had more spiritual matters on his mind as he tried to help Jeff from the other side. This usually involved minor party pieces such as whipping up a sudden strong gust of wind capable of blowing a newspaper into the eyes of one of Jeff's assailants by merely puffing out his cheeks and blowing or scouting ahead of Jeff by closing his eyes and re-emerging in a room fraught with danger and bad guys.

Two things became obvious in this, our weekly entertainment drama; Jeff couldn't fight his way out of a playgroup (a considerable drawback in the murky world of private investigating) and Marty rarely seemed to fully utilise the considerable talents that he had acquired from beyond the grave. Somehow this mix of streetwise, earthbound grit and other-worldly hocus-pocus would win out in the end though and, for a six month period, Jeff Randall and Marty Hopkirk enjoyed a popularity that, whilst not quite Beatlemania, had raised the profile of the show and its stars, Mike Pratt and Kenneth Cope.

Feyenoord were probably only better known in Rotterdam. On the night, however, they would have their own version of Randall & Hopkirk in the pragmatic style of Wim Van Hanagem and the unearthly Ove Kindvall who had ghosted into the box to grab the winner and put a second European trophy in three years beyond Celtic's grasp.

Whilst the Celts appeared to be stung by the quality of their opponents and later judgement would have it circulated that Jock Stein had underestimated that quality, Celtic still had opportunities in the match. Indeed, although having been stretched for the bulk of the first half-hour, the Bhoys then snatched the lead from another Tommy Gemmell thunderbolt reminiscent of '67, albeit this time courtesy of a Bobby Murdoch back-heeled pass from a free-kick.

The joy was short-lived though as the intriguingly named Rinus Israel pulled back an equaliser minutes later with a looping header. Even as the match bore on into extra-time and with the Dutch seemingly marked with the stamina of the unfortunately named Grand National winner *Gay Trip*, Celtic, in the shape of John Hughes, had a late chance to go ahead and probably win the cup when the big forward latched onto a slack pass across the Feyenoord back four (ah, so they *did* play a back four!). He advanced one-on-one with goalkeeper Eddy Pieters Graafland like Gary Cooper as Sheriff Will Kane facing down ruthless gunslinger Frank Miller in *High Noon* but unlike big 'Yup', Yogi couldn't deliver the killer blow and his shot struck the 'keeper. Admittedly Coop had also struck Frank Miller but he did it with a lead bullet and not a stitched bag of leather and thus Miller was dead . . . just like Celtic's European Cup ambitions for 1970. For soon it was to be the turn of Kindvall and *his High Noon* moment was successful.

Immediately after the match, the recriminations arrived with the predictability of a Zsa Zsa Gabor wedding cake. Pre-match preparations had apparently been too lax. There was an air of casual expectancy around the Celtic camp. Feyenoord midfielder and ironically, future Celtic manager Wim *I-stopped-the-ten* Jansen's perm was so bushy that the ball appeared to eclipse when Wim headed it!

Probably most damaging of all was the story that described Celtic players at their training HQ in Varese negotiating sponsorship deals in an effort to cash in on the impending success. In the twenty-first century such negotiations are as commonplace as Victoria Beckham's pout, but in the far-off days of the early 1970s, the highly charged mix of football, money and middle-men was still viewed as an explosive cocktail.

Maybe, in the final analysis, on the night Feyenoord were the better side. It does happen and perhaps Celtic were at the vanguard of a dawning of new *total football,* given that Ajax Amsterdam would win the next three European Cups, Holland would unsuccessfully contest two World Cup Finals in the '70s and the finest player of this generation would be a Dutchman, Johann Cruyff.

All that however, would be in the distance. For the moment the job was to retain a perspective. Take a break from the pressures of life at the top. Perhaps, split up as a group, go away for the summer and then reconvene prior to the big kick-off of another enthralling season when the Celts would be looking to take their successive League titles tally to six. Probably the last thing a doctor would have recommended was that the entire Celtic squad headed off en masse to participate in a tour of North America.

1970-1971

JimmyJinkin'

Track List:

Elvis Presley/The Wonder of You; Freda Payne/Band of Gold; Jimi Hendrix/Voodoo Chile; Mungo Jerry/In The Summertime; Smokey Robinson & The Miracles/Tears Of A Clown; Matthews Southern Comfort/Woodstock; George Harrison/My Sweet Lord; Badfinger/ No Matter What; Ringo Starr/It Don't Come Easy; Rolling Stones/ Brown Sugar; T-Rex/Hot Love

Celtic's North American tour for 1970 must have seemed like a great idea to somebody at the club when it was first arranged. As fate would have it, there was a chance that the team would arrive across the pond as the Champions of Europe again although most Americans hadn't bothered to look at Europe since the end of World War Two whilst most backroom assistants would recall fondly the sheer bonding exercise that a previous trip in 1966 had engendered.

Celtic back then were a trophy-hungry squad of young men and the tour had forged friendships and a camaraderie that were essential ingredients for the side that swept all before them in the following season. The difference between that trip and this one would be as distinct as holiday packages organised by SAGA and Club 18-30. For a start, nobody really wanted to be there. It had been a long, hard season and although Celtic retained the League and the League Cup, the loss in the big one to Feyenoord was as painful as listening to Janis Joplin singing the blues. The fact that the Celts first match, against Manchester United in Toronto was only five days after the European Cup Final made it look like somebody had goofed on the organisational front.

Just to add spice to the notion that God had suddenly turned Dutch, there was a sixteen hour delay in the Celtic squad's outward bound flight. Sixteen hours to analyse *that* game for the millionth time . . . sixteen hours to question the logic of taking a tired outfit across the Atlantic Ocean to compete in the Toronto Cup (must have taken the Canadian organisers a few blue-sky thinking sessions to come up with *that* name!) and sixteen hours in which four million games of poker, gin rummy and hang-a-man just wouldn't cut it on the entertainment front. It would have been easier sitting through Des O'Connor's One-Man Show in, well, anywhere!

Arriving in what Winston Churchill once referred to as *the lynchpin of the English-speaking world* or, as we call it, Canada, merely one day before the Man United game could reasonably be considered as less than ideal preparation. It was, therefore, a lacklustre Celtic side that took on the Red Devils that Monday and little surprise that they were to go down by two goals to nil. Did I mention that nobody wanted to be there? Well, it showed.

In actual fact, the squad was bereft of one famous face when it was made clear that Jimmy Johnstone had been spared the agony of the tour. The wee man had a fear of flying that was to last an entire lifetime and seeing Salman Rushdie on an aeroplane would be a more common sight in the late twentieth century. Whether it was this phobia or a popular theory that wee Jimmy was playing poker for a new improved deal from the Celtic Park mandarins, his absence was noted with some chagrin and bitterness within the Celtic ranks. That certainly wouldn't have helped when the Celts lined up for their next two matches which were back-to-back encounters with the Italian side Bari.

Bari weren't exactly *la crema* of Italian football, but they could play a bit. However, their conduct over the double-header would prove too much for the Celtic squad and, in particular, the normally ice cool Jock Stein. The initial 1-1 draw in New York had been an ill-tempered affair, but this was merely the support bout for a second match in which the violent conduct wouldn't have looked out of place in a spaghetti western. Ominously, the game was held over for one extra day due to a spectacular electric storm . . . that force of nature, of course, was nothing to the thunder and lightning that was about to go off in the Exhibition Stadium, Toronto.

The Bari players indulged in over-the-top tackles that were *so* over the top that a cultured midfielder such as Bobby Murdoch could smell Italian leather up his left nostril. The up and coming Celtic forward, diminutive Lou Macari, was, despite his Italian pedigree or perhaps because of it, punched so many times that he should have changed his name to Lou Marciano. At half-time, Jock Stein had seen enough and decided that this version of an offer that could not be refused from the Cosa Nostra of Bari was answerable in only one way. When the referee (yes, there was one, although he'd been as conspicuous as the main character in Where's Waldo?) blew his whistle for the break, it was the cue for Big Jock to throw himself into the Italian dugout and administer a sound thrashing to the Italian coach.

In retrospect, perhaps it was his pent-up anger from the missed opportunity in the European Final that was finally to be released or maybe it was the cynical acceptance by his opposite number of the tactics employed by his thugs on the field, or perchance the Big Man's boiled eggs had simply been overcooked that morning but, whatever the reason, Jock Stein shifted into gear quicker than Jackie Stewart at Silverstone! Jock's physical presence was intimidating enough but a stream of expletives as the punches rained down from those meaty Burnbank fists forged in the rough-hewn hardness of a coal-mine must have been a terrifying combination for the beleaguered foreign coach.

Then, just as quickly as he launched this brute force, Jock stood up, grabbed his overnight bag and left the stadium as though he'd merely been teaching the Italians the intricacies of basket-weaving. It transpired that the Big Man had a flight to catch that would take him back to Scotland. No-one would suggest that his sudden departure was due to the notion that he could possibly have woken up with a horse's head in his bed! But then, in 1970, that movie was still to be made.

He would therefore have been oblivious to the outcome of the match which ended 2-2 even though Celtic were awarded a penalty in the last minute and a chance to win the game. Difficult to take a penalty though when the opposition decide to leave the pitch en masse and in a huff the likes of which you could possibly expect from your teenage son when you've grounded him for reading Playboy magazine . . . *your* Playboy magazine.

Lou Macari had won that penalty. Well of course he had. He'd already gone fifteen rounds with most of the Bari players and been rugby-tackled by the Italian goalkeeper. Given his treatment, it wouldn't have been a complete surprise if, wrapped in a carpet, he'd been bundled out of a fast-moving sedan onto a sidewalk that night as the Celtic party relaxed at their hotel.

Eventually the Bari boys were coaxed back out onto the pitch, presumably with the promise of a bottle of Chianti and a night out with Gina Lollabrigida thrown in as well, but even the referee had seen enough and blew for full time. He'd presided over a match that had descended into a mini recreation of the Second World War, seen an entire team walk off the pitch in a sulk and virtually refuse to come back on, missed the fact that, having reduced the Italians to ten men by sending off the goalkeeper, Bari then poured on so many substitutes that they seemed to be playing a 5-5-4 formation, awarded Celtic a penalty that they were never allowed to take, and generally proved himself to be the most inept judge of character since Pontius Pilate!

Thankfully, he had little time to reflect badly on himself as he received a telegram the next day from the SFA requesting that he take charge of the next Celtic-Rangers Cup Final! Okay, I made that bit up. Got a bit carried away with myself. How could he have been awarded such a prestigious occasion as a Scottish Cup Final if he was prepared to award penalty kicks to the Celtic?

Meanwhile, in Scotland, various theories were cooking as to the reasons for Big Jock's return. The Jinky situation had to be addressed as a few top clubs were sniffing around, interested in securing the wee fella's signature. Jock had a lot of paperwork to catch up on. His lawn needed cutting and he didn't trust the wife to trim it to his exacting standards. Or maybe he enjoyed the cut and thrust of the political hustings which seemed appropriate since Prime Minister Harold Wilson had announced a General Election to take place on 18 June. Whatever the reason, Jock Stein was detached from an active Celtic unit and that happened as frequently as a lunar eclipse.

The tour itself was less than thrilling for the not-so-happy party left across the ocean. Trusted Lieutenant, Sean Fallon, was left in charge of the group but, without the *Heidie*, the pupils were bound to get a little distracted. Sean was steeped in the traditions of the club and had a gentlemanly way with everybody he met. He also possessed a rich, velvet brogue reminiscent of warm summer nights in his native Sligo, an accent that never loosened despite the many years he'd spent living in Scotland in service to Celtic both as a player and a first-team coach.

He was not cut out for being a strict Commandant in charge, however, and when Messrs Gemmell and Auld decided to blot their copybooks by pushing the boat out on a trip to a supporters club, Sean decided that club discipline had been broken sufficiently to warrant their removal from the tour. A heady cocktail of boredom, frustration and the fanatical elements of the Kearny Celtic Supporters in New Jersey, who would willingly have bought drinks all night for Big Tam, Ten-Thirty Bertie and anyone else who had donned a hooped jersey, conspired to the popular duo's downfall.

In some ways, i.e. from the Celtic squad's perspective looking out from within a tour that appeared to be unravelling, the banishment of the two Lions could have been viewed as comparable to those stiff-upper lipped Johnnys during the war who would combine to vault over the barbed wire fence of the prison camp and make a bid for freedom. That said, those escapees only had to face the might of the German Army. It couldn't have been any kind of a picnic sitting wedged into the first available transatlantic flight in the knowledge that Big Jock would be waiting for you at the other end, demanding an explanation. It's highly unlikely that the buccaneering Tam and Bertie, the jester in the pack, ordered much from the in-flight buffet.

The sixteen hour opening delay, a freak electric storm, the Battle with Bari, Jock Stein's sudden disappearance and now the embarrassment of placing two icons of the Celtic cause on a flight home due to misbehaviour, all in all, it would be fair to say that Buddy Holly had had more success when *he* toured America, and look how that worked out!

Back home, the nation was getting excited and gearing up for the forthcoming World Cup Finals in Mexico. The England squad had a number one single with a raucous tune actually called *Back Home*, a selection that ranked right up there with other outstanding chart-toppers from the year such as Lee Marvin's *Wanderin' Star* and new Irish pop sensation and Eurovision winner Dana's *All Kinds Of Everything.*

As ever, when the word *nation* is invoked by the media, it tends to mean *England.* The other home nations were preoccupied buying West Germany flags, taking Brazilian samba lessons and learning to love pasta. In other words, getting right behind anyone who could stop this potential two-in-a-row by the then world champions.

Lee Marvin was a better actor than he was a singer in the same way that Lassie was better at scratching fleas than reading a newspaper and Dana's new found status wasn't giving Jimi Hendrix cause for concern. Only in this kind of environment could a song by a football squad expect to be at the summit of what the BBC still referred to as the Hit Parade.

And if we thought that Celtic's travails in The Americas were hard to behold, it was time to check out England captain, golden god from that golden summer of 1966 and all-round personification of British decency, Bobby Moore as he was escorted from a jeweller's shop in downtown Bogota, Colombia, accused of stealing a bracelet. Four days of intense diplomatic coming and going ensued as 'Our Man Out There' worked harder than a Colombian drug mule to pull levers and push buttons in an effort to free Mooreo for England's first game of the prestigious tournament, which was against Romania.

Eventually, the main man was released on bail and eligible to play whilst it emerged that other prominent sporting *celebs* had passed through tranquil, law-abiding Bogota and been subjected to the same charges. Understanding the rules of South American engagement they had paid a fee to have the bogus claims settled quietly whilst Bobby M had rightly challenged their veracity.

England and Brazil had faced off in the *final before the final* (copyright Celtic-Leeds United 1970) at the group stages when the Latin American champions-in-waiting had triumphed 1-0. Brazil would go on to win the championship in thrilling style by defeating Italian cattenacio (copyright Inter-Milan 1967) in the final that *was* the final by four goals to one. They were, without question, the finest team ever to have walked the turf. And yet, would Jimmy Johnstone have looked out of place amongst their ranks?

Admittedly there weren't that many ginger-heided five-footers in the Brazilian line-up and Jinky's idea of beach fitba' was tied into Celtic's Seamill training camp, but, on his day, the wee man was capable of unlocking any defence on the planet. It was, therefore, satisfying to realise that he still walked amongst us lesser mortals when Celtic opened their campaign for 6-in-a-row at the start of season 1970-1971.

Evidently Big Jock had smoothed out any ambiguity that Jinky had about remaining a Celt. He'd also taken it in hand to come down hard on the dynamic duo of Gemmell and Auld by imposing a fine in public and retribution in private. There would be no repetition of their American adventures on his watch.

There were unsubstantiated rumours that Manchester United had made less-than-discreet moves to take Jock Stein to Old Trafford but this seemed to belong in the minds of lazy journalists who, on Jock's abrupt departure from the American tour coupled with the fact that the two teams had played against each other in the ill-fated Toronto Cup, had put two and two together.

United were going through a period of change that started in the summer of 1969 with Sir Matt Busby's retirement as first-team coach. Wilf McGuiness stepped up from being assistant trainer to the big job as coach and then manager in June 1970 but there were reservations over his capabilities that led to the fevered excitement regarding the possibility of Jock Stein waving to the Stretford End before taking his seat in the home dugout at Old Trafford.

The thought was almost as unbelievable as Ted Heath and the Conservatives winning the General Election and forming the next Government. Labour was so far ahead in the polls that Harold Wilson hadn't bothered to cancel the milk and morning papers at 10 Downing St. When defeat came to Harold and the party in the early hours of 19 June, Britain realised that anything was possible. The sight of Ted Heath grinning from a set of gnashers that the aforementioned Inter-Milan squad would have been proud of as he stood waving to the crowds outside Downing St., reinforced the belief that stranger things could happen . . . even Stein in a Manchester United tracksuit.

As we were to see, it was a story that would be revived throughout the coming season.

It sure was a bizarre June and the type of month summed up by Mungo Jerry topping the charts with *In The Summertime*; a song that prescribed drinking and driving as an acceptable way to cruise the highways and byways. As the pre-season phoney war subsided, the only real issue on the agenda for the Celtic support was, how would the team react to the previous season's reversals? Would there be the first real dismantling of the Lisbon Lions and would there be the chance to view some of the other Celts who had been knocking on the first team door?

The faithful had seen glimpses of Harry Hood, Lou Macari, George Connelly, David Hay and Jim Brogan in previous games but there were also murmurings from those devotees who followed Celtic reserves about such starlets as Vic Davidson, Danny McGrain and one Kenneth Mathieson Dalglish. Would they get their chance?

The season started in traditional manner with the negotiation of the League section of the Scottish League Cup. It wasn't the League title and it wasn't the Scottish Cup, it was the League Cup and although, through time, it would become either the valuable first bauble of a potential treble or a throwaway cup if it was all the Celts or indeed, the Rangers won in a season, in the early 1970s, the League Cup still enjoyed a fairly healthy status.

Celtic were the holders of the trophy and remarkably had been since Stein had arrived. In many ways, it had become *our* cup. At the summation of the opening section which Celtic topped with victories over Hearts (twice), Clyde (twice) and two end-to-end 2-2 draws with Dundee United, it seemed clear that Jock was tinkering with his team. For every one of the games, Celtic had taken to the field with a different line-up, although he returned to more traditional ways when the League season opened with a 2-0 victory over Morton at home with Bobby Lennox claiming both goals.

The team were up and running; well, all except Tommy Gemmell who had picked up an injury in that first League game that was destined to keep him from those swashbuckling runs from left-back for a few months. This little deterred the Celts from underlining their superiority and, in particular, in the first derby match against Rangers when they had the luxury of a missed penalty by Jim Brogan but still ran out comfortable winners by 2-0.

As Elvis crooned *The Wonder of You*, a classic from His Highness's Las Vegas play-list and his first UK number one for more than five years, it seemed that the King and Celtic were well placed to handle whatever new fads the 1970s could throw at them. Indeed, after three games played in the new League season, the Celts were still to concede a goal.

That ended the following week when disaster struck at Easter Road although, arguably, the real disaster had happened in London the day before when Jimi Hendrix had finally succumbed to an excessive mix of alcohol and drugs and the greatest guitar player on the face of the earth had choked on his own vomit. A gruesomely graphic thought and I can only hope you're not eating your breakfast as you read this. Still, if you are, you're one up on the unfortunate Jimi; he didn't make it through the night and you did!

No-one really recorded Hibernian striker, Joe McBride's thoughts on the late Hendrix but the ex-Celt turned out to be the real *Voodoo Chile* when he put a spell on his former employers in a superb one-man exhibition of strike-play at Easter Road by bagging both goals in a 2-0 victory. It was like an episode of Randall & Hopkirk as the ghost of McBride returned to haunt Jeff, sorry, Jock Stein, and perhaps remind the Big Man that he had possibly dispensed with the injury-prone Joe's services too quickly.

Celtic couldn't even blame the famous European hangover as their opponents in the first round in Glasgow only three days before the Hibs encounter were called Kokkola from Finland and the Celts ran out 9-0 winners. Jimi Hendrix sweated more on stage than Celtic did in this bizarre opening game. If only Jimi had stuck to Kokkola himself rather than the lethal permutations of other substances then perhaps he would have been around for the second leg in Finland when Celtic disgraced themselves by only winning 5-0.

Between those matches the Celts had advanced to the semi-finals of the League Cup at the expense of Dundee who had put up a manly performance in the first leg to draw 2-2 but had run out of ideas in Glasgow when Celtic beat them 5-1. Both teams could make a case for being fed up looking at each other as they met, overall, three times in the month of September. Warren Beatty didn't date as often as that! Twice in the League Cup and once in the League with Celtic also winning that encounter 3-0.

Into the semis then where Celtic found themselves facing Dumbarton from the second division and Rangers had to measure themselves up to the mettle of Cowdenbeath. Rumours abounded of course that the semi-final draw had been *fixed* to secure the tie that everyone wanted to see in the final . . . Dumbarton v Cowdenbeath.

The Sons of the Rock up against the Blue Brazil would have been a fitting finale to the glories of the League Cup but that pesky old derby duo got in on the act as Rangers despatched Cowden with ease and Celtic provided the intrigue when they struggled balefully to get past Dumbarton. A missed penalty in extra-time at Hampden was the 0-0 epitaph to Celtic's weary attempt to win the tie at the first time of asking and it took a harassed 4-3 replay victory, again in extra-time, to eventually book a day out at Hampden for the final.

Janis Joplin had already become the second big rock casualty of the year when she died in Los Angeles from a drug overdose on 4 October. First Hendrix, now Joplin . . . is it any wonder that The Beatles wanted to split up before the grim reaper came a-calling down

Abbey Road way? Janis thus missed out on the chance of witnessing the fourth Celtic-Rangers League Cup Final in seven years.

Rangers won that first one back in 1964-65 when Jock was still fasting in the wilderness of Hibernian and they must have looked back on those days wistfully given that since that 2-1 triumph, they had only added one other notable trophy, the Scottish Cup in 1966, to the Ibrox trophy room. Such was the shadow of Big Jock that stretched across Glasgow and then onwards throughout Scotland and into Europe. It was, therefore, Celtic, as five times consecutive holders of the League Cup and with those three defeats of Rangers in their subsequent Final meetings, who were regarded as the favourites to continue the run.

I mean, who was *Derek* Johnstone compared to Jimmy Johnstone? It turned out that DJ was to be the difference in the match when the hitherto unknown sixteen-year-old Dundonian out-jumped Billy McNeill five minutes before half-time to grab the only goal of the game. Celtic had their chances, most notably towards the end of the ninety when Willie 'Wispy' Wallace had failed to convert a peach, but it just wasn't to be. The Rangers supporters celebrated like it was the World Cup but, then, it had been a long time since trophy-winning had been habitual for them whilst Celtic symbolically turned up their collective collars and walked off into the cold autumn night. I mean, come on, it was only the League Cup.

However, nagging at the back of our minds, and presumably at Big Jock's too, was that in line with Aberdeen and that Dutch outfit, this was the third surprising and consecutive defeat for a Celtic side in a major final in six months.

If there was a fall-out from all of this, it appeared to manifest itself four days later in a home League match against Hearts when the Bhoys found themselves 2-0 down after fifty-three minutes. The moment was pivotal: Celtic had lost their third final on the trot;

Aberdeen, the Scottish Cup holders, were being touted as the League contenders, having defeated Rangers at Ibrox one week before that League Cup Final; and now a further shock was on the cards with the Jambos apparently cruising to victory in Celtic's own backyard. You could almost sense the shamrock crest being ceremoniously cracked for publication in the following morning's tabloids.

At that moment the considerable frame of Bobby Murdoch grabbed the game by the collar and single-handedly inspired a Celtic comeback. They always said that *when Murdoch played, Celtic played* and on that night when Stein required his maturity and considerable ball prowess, he roared Celtic back into a seemingly lost cause with gusto and skill. His inspiration was such that, within a remarkable ten minute period, two goals from Willie Wallace and one from the man who would go on to be top scorer for the season, Harry Hood, had turned around the match 3-2 in Celtic's favour. From this point, Celtic could kick on in their quest for that historical six-in-a-row.

However Aberdeen, managed by Eddie Turnbull, captained by the much-admired Martin Buchan, were living up to their reputation as that season's challengers. Although the top three at the start of November were Celtic, the Dons and Rangers, the men from the Granite City ascended to pole position by early December courtesy of a 1-0 victory over the Celts at Celtic Park. Joe Harper struck the all-important winner and, with two scalps in their pouch from visits to Glasgow within a couple of months, Aberdeen had every right to feel that this could be their year. Celtic bounced back like champions to finish the year with two consecutive victories, although in the final fixture of 1970 against Morton in Greenock, the shock news was that Lisbon Lions Cesar McNeill and Jimmy the Jink had been dropped.

The 3-0 scoreline did still have a Lisbon flavour with goals by Stevie Chalmers, Bobby Lennox and Willie Wallace. And then it was the *actual* big one. Rangers . . . Ibrox . . . New Year. Yes, Aberdeen were top of the table and Rangers were a woeful eight points off

Celtic's coat-tails in an era when only two were offered for a win, but this one was still the box-office fixture. In the end, it finished 1-1 but behind the statistics lay a story as tragic as anything ever witnessed in a public arena.

Celtic appeared to have snatched a winner in the eighty ninth minute when Jimmy Johnstone scored, but Colin Stein equalised sixty seconds later and, in the post-match confusion, it was theorised, although later dismissed, that this about-turn in the match's fortune was the major factor that compelled hundreds of Rangers fans who were making their way to the Ibrox exits to try to re-enter the terracing to witness the jubilation. On Stairway 13 chaos reigned as a mass of bodies collided with one another in an horrific accident that still, to this day, haunts the reverie of anyone who was present.

Sixty-six Rangers supporters were crushed to death although, in a sign of the more primitive communications networks of the day, it would be hours before the full news of the accident itself, and the horrendous number of fatalities, would be apparent to supporters of both sides. In the ensuing week, a coming together of officials, players and, more importantly, supporters of all persuasions, united in their grief with people from outside the game.

A memorial service was held the following Saturday at which the Celtic and Rangers players and management, alongside boardroom representatives, backroom staff, civic officials and the general public, expressed their empathy with the victims and their families. The rewarding sight of solidarity between the supporters of the clubs who form the greatest rivalry in Britain, if not the world, would become an occasional feature over the years with mutual appreciations of the talents of those who graced both teams but had come to untimely ends.

Baxter, Johnstone and Burns, to name but three, would be concelebrated, but in the early part of 1971 it wasn't about legends;

it was merely about ordinary people who had left home for a football match . . . never to return.

In many ways, football is a metaphor for life and the comforting reality was that the routine existence of the game continued to distract, divert and ultimately consume our minds with its magnificent trivia.

Harry Hood was now emerging as the pack leader when it came to scoring goals. Harry was an unassuming character who had stepped out from the shadows to prove his worth in a team in which the natural forces were established names like Wallace, Lennox and Chalmers. I don't know if he possessed George Harrison's solo epic *All Things Must Pass,* released in the post-Beatles period, but he would surely have appreciated the irony of the quiet Beatle shaking free from fabdom to overshadow his supposed songwriting superiors Lennon & McCartney with a multi-million selling album and a number one single in the shape of *My Sweet Lord.*

In recent times the Celtic supporters had introduced the incantation *Harry Harry* that had formed the basis of both Radha Krishna Temple's hit *Hare Krishna Mantra* from the late 1960s and so infused the refrain in Harrison's evocative chart-topper. The sight of thousands of Celtic supporters swaying rhythmically to a far eastern beat and paying tribute to Harry Harry Hood was becoming a familiar sight around the country as the Hood popped up with vital strikes in the run-in to the end of the season. Decimalisation in February meant that tanner-ba' and tuppenny-ha'penny players now established a new value but Harry Hood's stock was rising by the week.

Europe, alas, wasn't to be particularly fruitful when, once again, a team from Holland would prove to be Celtic's undoing. Having disposed of the unfortunately named Kokkola and Waterford from the ol' country, the Celts found themselves up against a far greater proposition in Ajax Amsterdam and this wasn't the same band of players who had surrendered meekly to AC Milan in the 1969 final. Johann Cruyff was the talismanic leader of a team destined for greatness in the European game and Jock Stein knew that this was a tie fraught with danger.

And yet, for over an hour, he had seen Celtic muscle their way around the midfield and subdue the voluminous Dutch attacks. All looked set for a decent away result when Cruyff arrived to spear Ajax ahead by virtue of a quick strike that caught out the Celtic defence. Even when playmaker Barry Huulshoff put the home team 2-0 up with a free-kick there was still a feeling that the Celts could pull the tie back in Glasgow. It took the intervention of left-winger Piet Keiser with a net-busting drive that seemed like the last kick of the match to make it 3-0.

The Bhoys' chances now looked flatter than the Netherlands. In the pre-match hype both Keiser and Cruyff were the subject of a kidnap scare by an extremist political group and there was tight security before, during and after the match. Unfortunately Big Jock had not had the opportunity to brief the kidnappers pre-match to ensure the non-participation of the highly skilled and supremely influential Dutch duo!

The result, although not as big a shock as Muhammad Ali losing to Smokin' Joe Frazier at Madison Square Garden the week before in the 'Fight of the Century', still registered as a surprise to the Celtic faithful. Jimmy Johnstone, who regarded the Amsterdam match as an affront to his own personal standards, shone like a beacon in the return leg and scored the only goal in a game that, at least, brought some dressing to the final aggregate tally of 3-1. The European adventure was over for another season and with Aberdeen still at the top of the pile, there was no guarantee that Celtic would be taking an active part in the only European trophy that really mattered.

When the team headed north-east on 17 April for the League match at Pittodrie, Celtic knew that an Aberdeen victory would probably ensure the championship for the Dons. Prior to the game, Jock Stein made an announcement. The Big Man knew all about the drama and inspiration of timing his remarks to his players and this team talk had all the resonance of an Oscar-winning performance. Essentially, he decided to end all the speculation that was linking him with the Manchester United job.

Sir Matt Busby, a close friend of Stein, had retaken the reins at the club around Christmas-time but he was only there to steady the ship and Stein was the man he wanted to take the club forward. This was more than idle gossip now as former Celtic favourite Pat Crerand had been appointed as intermediary to see if Jock fancied upping sticks and heading south. Indeed, the story was that Jock had met with the United officials and apparently shaken hands on the deal.

It was in the bunker of the Pittodrie away dressing room, with the media frenzy at their door and the stadium rocking with both sets of supporters racked up to anticipatory bursting point, that Jock Stein told the Celtic players that he would be their manager for the following season and beyond. Such was the joy that Harry Harry had skipped into the Aberdeen box within two minutes of the start of the match and poked Celtic in front. The Dons pulled back an equaliser towards the end of the first-half but with no more goals to come and Celtic with a slightly easier run-in to the title, it seemed that the momentum had swung back to Glasgow.

Aberdeen duly surrendered in their last League match of the season by going down to Falkirk at Brockville. The Celts stumbled a tad with a 2-2 draw against St Mirren but were able to seal the championship two days later with a 2-0 victory over Ayr United at Hampden. Six-in-a-row and, remarkably, none of the titles had been secured at Celtic Park. Even the Ayr fixture, scheduled as a home game, was moved to Hampden as Celtic's ground was undergoing major reconstruction.

The next big outing would be the Scottish Cup Final and a quick chance for silverware revenge against Rangers. Or so we thought. By any stretch of the imagination, the final game of the

League campaign, against Clyde, would be hard-pushed to produce box-office of the highest order. The Celts were champions, homage had already been paid after that Ayr match at Hampden and the Celtic supporters were preparing for a Cup Final encounter against the old rivals. That, of course, is exactly what fired the Barnumesque tendencies of Jock Stein.

Had he not been an outstanding football manager then there was surely an alternative career for him in the world of show business. It was Elvis Presley's bad luck that Colonel Tom Parker got to him before Jock Stein, otherwise the King's career could have been even more successful than the stratospheric heights already scaled. For Big Jock was a master of manipulation; a man who could exploit gold from copper, and in this, the final League game of the season, he announced it would categorically be the last time that the public would get to see the Lisbon Lions take to the field.

35,000 spectators crammed into the building site that was Celtic Park alongside the multitude of press and broadcasters who wanted to capture a moment as rare as that of The Beatles final live performance atop the Abbey Road studios in 1969. And so it was that Ronnie Simpson led out a Celtic team whose names tripped off the tongue like a Buddhist mantra: Simpson, Craig, Gemmell, Murdoch, McNeill, Clark, Johnstone, Wallace, Chalmers, Auld and Lennox.

Faither Simpson had retired, of course, and was only allowed to take part in the warm-up which was more of a photo-op than the red carpet on Oscars Night. Evan Williams replaced him in goal for the actual game, but everything else that was both magical and mystical about that great side was in place as Celtic romped to a 6-1 victory.

Bobby Lennox picked up a hat-trick, Willie Wallace grabbed a brace and fittingly, the hero of the hour in Lisbon, Stevie Chalmers added the sixth. Bertie Auld orchestrated matters from midfield with imperious supremacy even finding time to sit on the ball much to the annoyance of his manager. But *Ten-Thirty* didn't care. He knew it was his final game in a hooped jersey as he was on his way to Hibernian and the dis-assembly of the Lions had started. He was carried shoulder-high from the park by his team-mates in a fitting crowning gesture.

After that, there was the banality of the Scottish Cup Final against Rangers. Despite the League Cup failure, Celtic were still installed as favourites for the match, after all, Rangers had finished fourth, fifteen points behind Celtic and the Bhoys had a special affiliation with the Scottish Cup.

The final itself had an eerie quality about it with Celtic taking a fortieth minute lead through Bobby Lennox and yet failing to capitalise on other chances that meant that, when there was a mix-up between George Connelly and Evan Williams in the Celtic box, Derek Johnstone *again* took the opportunity to score in a major final. There were three minutes remaining at that point which meant that it was all back to Hampden on the following Wednesday for the replay. This time it would be different.

Lou Macari came in for Willie Wallace whilst the only change in the Rangers line-up was brought about by the withdrawal of right-back Alex Miller due to a broken jaw from the first game. That substitution was predictable, but the choice of replacement was bordering on the sensational. Jim Denny, a signing from Yoker Juniors only three months previously, who had never played a first-team game, was pitched in to deal with the Celtic threat.

By now, of course, following on from the Derek Who? debacle from the League Cup Final, Celtic were still wary of any unknown quantities in the Ibrox line-up. That said, it was Lou Macari who announced his presence first when he nipped in to swipe the ball into the Rangers net from a dummied corner-kick.

Within a minute, Jimmy Johnstone, back to his best and putting his name to a major Cup Final in quite the same way as his hero Stanley Matthews had done in 1953, jinked past Rangers centre-half

Ronnie McKinnon only to be felled in the box. Harry Harry stepped up and, with the supreme coolness of a monk who had meditated to the sound of his name, slipped his kick past the wrong-footed Peter McCloy and Celtic were 2-0 up. Jim Craig, in an effort to clear a parried Williams save, could only boot the ball into his own net in fifty-seven minutes and Rangers appeared to be back in it.

But this time there was to be no DJ surprise and the Celts held out for a dramatic win. League champions and Scottish Cup holders? No' a bad way to start the 1970s.

Change was in the air and Bertie Auld wouldn't be the last of the Lions to leave the Den. Within weeks, John Clark, Celtic's 'quiet Beatle' , had packed his wellies, umbrella and Gannex raincoat and headed down to Greenock as a Morton player. In a short space of time, he would be joined by the man who scored the most important goal in Celtic history, Stevie Chalmers.

Her Majesty's Secretary for Education, one Margaret Hilda Thatcher, announced in June that she was seeking to dismantle the practice of providing free school milk to children. Perhaps it was this news that prompted Big Jock's decision that, next season, he would be giving youth a real chance to start earning their *own* milk money.

1971-72
CupLiftin'

Track List:

Rod Stewart/Maggie May; Isaac Hayes/Shaft; The Doors/Riders On The Storm; New Seekers/I'd Like To Teach The World To Sing; T-Rex/Get It On; Hurricane Smith/Oh Baby What Would You Say; David Bowie/Starman; Elvis Presley/American Trilogy

He was one of the most gifted professionals of his generation, a man whose self-taught talent, exuberant personality and creative genius had won him admirers from outwith his own sphere. Not exactly foreign to controversy, a slip of the tongue and with a penchant for the taste of good times, he hadn't led a life of complete chastity but had the wit and charm to overcome these drawbacks. When he died unexpectedly in July of 1971, many people stopped to wonder if they would ever see his like again. I'm talkin' about Louis Armstrong here folks as the summer month saw Satchmo headed for The Cotton Club in the sky, but the same epitaph could also have applied to Charles Patrick Tully of the Celtic, who took his leave of us just a few short weeks after Louis lay down his trumpet.

The bold Charles Patrick was only forty-seven, a ridiculously young age to become history, but he had already franked his name on the Celtic conscience in a 1950s career that was perhaps short on trophies but heavy on tales of the trickery that he could perform both on and off the ball. He had played alongside Jock Stein as well as Sean Fallon and Neil Mochan of the backroom bhoys, although it would be hard to imagine Charlie's lifestyle and flamboyance sitting well with the Big Man and *his* disciplined approach to life and the game.

Tully never lived to see the investiture of Jock's changing side. Neither did Jim Morrison, charismatic lead singer with The Doors who had also shuffled off the proverbial that fateful July as he mixed an asthmatic condition with heroin and took a bath in Paris. Jim ended up taking a longer soak than he had envisaged and although his thoughts on the Celtic have never been recorded, you have to imagine that any man who harboured a love of showmanship alongside a healthy dose of paranoia would have been embraced in The Jungle on any match-day. He certainly would have enjoyed the emergence of life-lovin' Lou Macari, who had already been cherry-picked from the reserves as a potential goal-grabber whilst young Danny McGrain was poised to break into the first-team's defence alongside the ever-maturing George Connelly.

All of this was good news in itself, but for months now we'd been hearing about another talent who'd been bandying away with the nicely-dubbed *Quality Street Kids* in the second XI earmarked for future development. To many, the first sight of Kenneth Mathieson Dalglish was in a testimonial match at Rugby Park, Kilmarnock, at the tail-end of the previous season when he ran riot in the Ayrshire night by bagging six goals. By the end of August, Dalglish had stamped his card at Celtic with thrilling performances against opposition as diverse as Dumbarton and Rangers.

The Drybrough Cup was the *glamorous* setting for the future King Kenny to set out his stall. This was a start of the season tourney that appeared to have been dreamt up in the pub one night at closing time and then sketched out on the back of a packet of Capstan-Full Strength.

I've just had a great idea! Why don't we get the two top-scoring sides from the First Division and the two top-scoring sides from the

Second Division and get them to scrap it out before the season starts properly. We'll pick up a trophy from a Charity Shop, get wursels some brewery tae sponsor it and then rake in the receipts!

You could imagine the birth of this less than prestigious tournament being conceived in no other way. For all its faults – nae glamour, nae crowds, nae sense – The Drybrough Cup did let us see Dalglish banging in the first real goals of his Celtic career. The opposition were Dumbarton, who didn't really resemble the stuffy challengers that they had been for the previous season's League Cup semi and in a 5-2 win, Kenny grabbed four of the available Celtic goals.

Testimonials in Kilmarnock, Diddy-Cup triumphs over Second Division opponents were all well and good, but did Dalglish have what it took to play against the Rangers? That question was answered in the first League Cup sectional match when the Bhoys travelled to Ibrox.

This turned out to be the first of three visits to Govan in a matter of weeks; twice on League Cup duty and once in the League. And if that looks at all spurious as if the Scottish *high-heid-yins* had decided that Celtic's dominance over Rangers was such that from now on the Ibrox men would be awarded home advantage until they won the fixture, relax . . . you're more paranoid than Jim Morrison. Work was still being carried out at Celtic Park to improve the accommodation and the ground was unable to host the seventy-plus thousand who would want to sup the derby match atmosphere. Celtic's home bout was switched to Ibrox Park.

As we would see, this did not exactly work in Rangers' favour anyway, but in the seventieth minute of the first match and with Celtic 1-0 up, the Bhoys were awarded a penalty. Billy McNeill, imperious as ever, decided that young Kenny should be the one to take the kick.

The tension was chilling. A second goal to the Celts would surely seal the game. At twenty, Dalglish had barely started shaving. The rumour was that, in his youth, he had favoured the light blues from Govan (which was forgivable. Hell, in my youth I'd bought a Cilla Black LP!). His father was at the match supporting the opposition. And it was Kenny's first-ever derby!

Would he stride furiously towards the ball and lash it hard like a man who had just been handed the gun to shoot his brother and wanted to get it over with or would he bottle it like that homesteader in the movie *Shane* who wasn't *lookin' fer trouble* and couldn't even pick *up* the gun? All eyes were on the cheek-flushed Kenny as he placed the ball down on the spot. Peter McCloy was, as always, in the Rangers goal and he was about twelve-feet tall with hands big enough to measure Dolly Parton for a bra.

The whole of Glasgow ground to a halt like the traffic in *The Day The Earth Stood Still* and everyone was holding their breath whilst twitching inexorably inside. Well, everybody, that is, except young Dalglish who at this, perhaps the most crucial moment in his fledgling career, decided that the world would have to wait . . . as he bent down to tie his bootlace! Tae lace up the leather . . . now! It was the football equivalent of James Dean lighting up a fag.

Celtic were waiting . . . Rangers were waiting . . . Big Jock was waiting . . . cross-legged women in labour were waiting . . . but Kenny Dalglish decided now would be the time to correct his footwear. When he did stand up, he stared rigidly at the target for a second and then started his run-up. Seconds later, the Celtic supporters were jigging around singing hosannas to their new messiah. *GET IT ON!* as T-Rex were urging us to do at the time.

If Dalglish was the real deal then the rest of his team-mates weren't faring too badly either. The next two Rangers games brought a 3-0 return League Cup drubbing and a more robust 3-2 winning League encounter. In both games, Dalglish was on the score-sheet although, in the harder fought title bout, he was equalising to make the score 2-2. Lou Macari put the Celts 1-0 up early doors but Rangers, heartily sick of Celtic coming over to their backyard and stealing their ba', fought back to go 2-1 ahead. Honours seemed even until the final minute when a high ball into the Rangers box was met by the soaring head of Jimmy Johnstone and looped over McCloy to give Celtic the advantage.

Now, all bias aside, it didn't really seem that fair. In the course of the match Rangers' Alfie Conn had been sent off under dubious circumstances, the Light Blues saw what looked like a legitimate goal chalked off and now, to really rub the salt in, wee Jinky, a personage whose height would have made him an usher at Snow White's wedding, leapt above a collection of lofty Rangers rear-guarders and headed the ball into the net. It was almost as if Big Jock had refereed the match!

In the face of so many defeats to their nemesis in such a short period, it was little surprise that Rangers were not going to provide the challenge to Celtic on the domestic front this season. Once again that seemed to be taken up by Aberdeen.

Celtic made their intentions clear on the first day of League business when they reminded Clyde of the last of the Lisbon Lions days and the 6-1 spanking by going three better to a 9-1 scoreline. As opening nights went, it was quite impressive.

Glasgow had been the focus of the world that summer when the Upper Clyde Shipyards' dispute had arisen. UCS's future prospects seemed as optimistic as a Beatles reunion gig when they approached Ted Heath and his Conservative orchestra in a bid for a government bailout package of £6million. The Tories, of course, were not naturally inclined towards supporting businesses that were unable to support themselves and fancied taking on the unions in a show of strength. The unions, for their part, strategized that a full-blown strike would lead to a complete closure of the yards in question and adopted a policy of 'work-in' whereby they would manage the yards themselves and keep everybody at work until orders were filled.

It was a stand-off that would mark out the course of the 1970s and although this particular dispute would only last for around nine months, or the length of a football season, it crystallised what the Heath government would be about . . . a trial of strength. It would be fair to say that with an estimated 6,000 jobs on the line, then the focus of Glaswegians might not have been on the magnificent trivia that was the fitba'. However, as in previous periods of industrial strife and economic hardship, the game provided an outlet for expression and relief.

Celtic were doing their level best to provide a form of entertainment and remained undefeated in the League until October when St Johnstone motored down from Perth and left with a 1-0 victory in their kitbags. In Europe, there had been a slight shock with a 2-1 first-leg away defeat to Danish part-timers BoldKlubben 1903 Copenhagen, but that was soon resolved in the return match when BoldBhoyen 1888 Celtic romped home 5-0.

Lou Macari had attracted the attention with a hat-trick in that one and he and Dalglish were the talk of the Scottish football world. Such was their stock that Big Jock felt comfortable in dispensing with the services of John *Yogi* Hughes and Willie 'Wispy' Wallace, who both left for Crystal Palace in October. The feeling was that the Celts were in fine fettle for the challenges ahead and thus comfortable with the transfer of the experienced Yogi and Wispy.

One of the immediate challenges was the League Cup Final which, for the second year in a row, was an all-Glasgow affair. The difference was that instead of a mouth-watering, bums-on-seats Celtic-Rangers joust, it was the Maryhill side of the equation that would be providing the challenge in the shape of Partick Thistle.

The Jags fancied themselves as the third force in Glaswegian football circles. If you didn't care for the rivalry, twice-a-season rudeness and general one-upmanship that was the twin preserve of Celtic and Rangers, then you could attach your allegiance to the unfancied Maryhill Magyars. Naturally, they seemed to produce a level of support that cut across all levels of the divide and, in particular, were a reasonably popular choice with the erudite communities that belong in University-land. Either by myth or device, the Jags' student fan-base was played to the full by the press and football satirists on the Scottish scene.

They were a first division outfit, just like Celtic, but a team who, at best, would play out their football in the top half of the table without threatening to win the title. To say that they were not the bookies' choice to beat Celtic in the 1971 League Cup Final is to say that Frank Sinatra could sing a bit. It was not Ol' Blue Eyes who anchored the BBC's flagship Saturday afternoon television programme *Grandstand* though, but another Frank, Bough to be exact, and he was a stickler for detail. So when the news was relayed to him live on-air that the Scottish League Champions, European aristocrats and overwhelming League Cup favourites were trailing Partick Thistle by four goals to nil after thirty-five minutes, he elected not to *'start spreading the news . . .'* until it had been checked, re-checked and re-checked again!

Even then he announced it as though he's been asked to confirm that there was life on Mars whilst various BBC sporting correspondents tried desperately to get the raw details to back up what *The Boughster* was saying. And it was true! 4-0 at half-time. 4-1 at full-time.

In an era when using the phrase *a consolation goal* in a Celtic match report was pretty much a patronising sop to the opposition, Kenny D was the Hoop who netted the Celts only response. I mean, this was Partick Thistle. They couldn't win a *Crackerjack!* pencil – and you got one of them just for turning up!

The Jags fans deservedly partied hard until the wee sma' hours, which was no mean feat since half of them had to hand in dissertations to their tutors first thing on Monday morning! Celtic supporters demanded an enquiry along the lines of the Warren

Commission. Okay, Billy McNeill was out injured, but even without the mighty Cesar in the back row, the Celts should have had enough to compensate. Bobby Lennox wasn't in the team, which seemed a bit mad given that the open fields of Hampden were ideally suited to his pace. Tommies Gemmell and Callaghan hadn't performed, Jinky was on the periphery, Macari and Dalglish were too inexperienced, Harry Harry appeared to have all the aggression and impact of a Buddhist monk, the temperature was too cold, the grass wasn't green enough, the ball too round and so on . . .

In the end it just seemed to be a bad day at the office for everyone in a hooped jersey although, naturally, in the scapegoat hunt, goalkeeper Evan Williams took much of the heat. That seemed a bit unfair but the upshot was that he was dropped immediately as Big Jock nipped over to Paisley and bought Dennis Connaghan from St Mirren, who lined up in goal the following week.

If that purchase appeared to be made in haste, Big Jock's next one was the culmination of a great deal of legwork. From Motherwell there arrived one John 'Dixie' Deans, a centre forward who did what it said on the tin – he scored goals. Big Jock had pursued Dixie before but the deal had never been done, although the wily Stein kept his eye on the situation. There were suggestions that Celtic chairman Sir Robert Kelly would never have sanctioned a move for Deans who also appeared to carry a reputation for always being at the centre of controversy during a match . . . any match. Indeed, when Stein went after the 'Well hit man', he was already in the midst of a six-match ban, although his reputation for soccer skulduggery was greatly exaggerated.

Sadly, Sir Robert passed away in September following an illness that had rendered his chairmanship an honorary one in the final year. Would he have scuppered the move? Had he done so, then Celtic would have missed out on a lethal finisher who would prove his value to the cause on numerous occasions over the next few seasons.

Now, it would be fair to say that Dixie could never be referred to as a 'lean machine'. His girth would always ensure that the prefix 'chunky' would be attached to his name in match reports, but he had a deceptive turn of pace, predatory instincts, was as hard as Tarzan's feet and didn't require a compass to find the goalmouth. He would go on to be Celtic's top scorer by the end of the season. This in itself was remarkable, given that he never made his first-team debut until November.

That was Operation Revenge as Celtic went to Firhill to take on upstarts and League Cup holders Partick Thistle where they won 5-1 with Dixie grabbing his first Celtic goal towards the end of the match. That result took them to the top of the table as Aberdeen had gone down 3-2 to Hearts.

The Dons had once again been the thorn in Celtic's side and had even played out a 1-1 draw at Celtic Park in the first week of that November which maintained their one point advantage over the Hoops. Harry Harry had deservedly put the Bhoys one up with half-an-hour to go but a misunderstanding between Dennis Connaghan and Billy McNeill meant that instead of the captain cushioning a header back to his goalkeeper, he actually put it through his own net as *Connza* had come out to deal with the cross ball but hadn't shouted to his skipper. The lack of communication meant that, as the ball rolled into the empty goal, Cesar glared at the newly christened *Dennis The Menace* for making him look like *Walter, Prince of the Softies.*

Whilst not a complete tragedy, it did keep Aberdeen at the top of the pile until the aftermath of the goings-on at Firhill and Tynecastle when the places were reversed. Having assumed the position, Celtic would now be in the driving seat for the rest of the season.

Lou Macari was chipping in with the goals and would go on to bag twenty four for the season, but the talk of the town was the burgeoning partnership between Dixie Deans and Kenny Dalglish.

From the outset, they looked like polar opposites with fresh-faced Kenny D at twenty being matched up with grizzled old gunslinger Dixie who, at only twenty five, still managed to give the impression that he'd been around before Moses had a beard. As a combination they were proving to be lethal and almost seemed to enjoy a partnership bordering on the telepathic.

In fact, in season 1971-72, they could only be rivalled as a dynamic duo by Lord Brett Sinclair and Danny Wilde who were thrilling us as a couple of modern-day adventurers in hit television show *The Persuaders* on a weekly basis. Every Friday night, right after Hughie Green's *The Sky's The Limit* and commercial breaks that included telling us adolescents that you could take Martini Bianco, *anytime, any place, anywhere*, Roger Moore and Tony Curtis would gallop onto our screens as Sinclair and Wilde.

Together, they would sort out an assorted gallery of toughs whilst warding off international incidents, schmoozing the ladies and sipping Creole Screams with one or perhaps two olives in them. The stories would take us to exotic locations and glory in the fabulously wealthy lifestyles of two playboys with so much time on their hands that they could sort out problems both domestic and continental yet still be able to order dinner in three languages.

Naturally, they drove their cars – Sinclair had a mustard-coloured Aston Martin DBS whilst Wilde favoured a blood-red Ferrari – with reckless abandon and complete disregard for their value as long as the girl was saved or the fiendish plot thwarted. It's fair to say that their insurance was of the comprehensive variety as opposed to third party, fire and theft! They sure as hell weren't Randall & Hopkirk, which was beginning to look dated up against this 'Hollywood hits Europe' buddyfest!

Lord Brett was of noble stock, groomed from birth to assume the titles and wealth that comes with the English aristocracy. Danny was a New York street punk who had had to fight for everything that he'd ever had in life and had amassed a personal fortune in the land of the free at the same time. Together they were as unstoppable as the rotation of the planet, the omnipotence of Martini Bianco or the plundering talents of Celtic's Double D's . . . Deans & Dalglish!

On the other side of the city, it would have required more than the *persuading* skills of Messrs Sinclair and Wilde to convince anyone that season 1971-72 would be the campaign when Rangers would halt Celtic's domestic dominance – especially in the League. However, the New Year joust was upon us and the Celts welcomed the boys in blue over to their patch on the back of a 7-0 pummelling of, yes, you've guessed it, Clyde.

Such was the humiliation that the Bully Wee were acceding to that there was a real concern that they were on the verge of changing their nickname to the *Bullied We Are!* In their last three encounters with Celtic, Clyde had shipped twenty two goals for the advance of merely two. They were being whipped more often than the favourite's rump at Epsom. Naturally, coming off of such a thrashing, expectations and confidence were high in the east end of the city when the men from Ibrox arrived. However, Rangers were not in the mood to go quietly into the night, although they did have to endure a moment of déjà vu when Jimmy Johnstone, for the second consecutive derby match, got his head onto a cross and put the Bhoys 1-0 up in the thirty-fifth minute.

Stein, Colin that is, who plied his trade in a blue shirt and had the temerity and, it has to be said, the birthright to share his surname with *The Master,* equalised late on to set up a frantic finish. Well, perhaps frantic if you were playing for Rangers, as the light blues defended as though they'd just heard the bad guys were coming in on the noon train and they hadn't saddled their horses.

It was no surprise that Celtic bagged a winner in the last minute, although the razor-sharp protagonist was defender Jim Brogan and that took some believing. Quietly efficient Brogan had crept in for a headed goal. In a Celts career that, in its entirety, would yield fewer goals than Celtic had bagged against the unfortunate Clyde all season, this one was priceless. It knocked Rangers out quicker than the odour from a Russian athlete's armpit.

The New Seekers were delivering their New Year resolution with a plea for world peace entitled *I'd Like To Teach The World To Sing* but, in Glasgow, there was only one side of the city with their throats open giving it laldy . . . and they were wearing green and white scarves.

Rangers, to their credit and indeed, our advantage, did deliver a kind of first foot gift when they headed north east to Pittodrie and drew with the Dons a couple of weeks after the derby match. That was just as well since Celtic dropped a point away to Morton the week before in a 1-1 draw. Cappielow Park, Greenock, was tighter than Mama Cass in a basque and was never a favourite away day for the Celts but, at least, they made amends seven days later with a 2-0 defeat of Airdrie at home as the Govan Select were splitting the fish with Aberdeen.

Hibernian were flirting with a title challenge in much the same manner as a schoolboy with a teenage crush . . . you know he wants to but he can't pluck up the courage! So, when they rolled into town at the end of January, there was still a hint that if the schoolboy could stop blushing, then a night of hand-holding and snogging might be on the cards. They were, however, to head back across the corridor to Edinburgh after ninety minutes like the famous wheezy boy with a note from matron. Their League aspirations for this season would just have to sit it out on the sidelines.

And yet, after the first forty-five, it looked as though they might even get a look at the girl's ankle as they led 1-0 courtesy of a Davie Hay own-goal but, in the second half, the Hoops rallied and after a Harry Harry equaliser, the Celtic winner was driven home with barely a quarter of an hour left on the clock.

Granted, a 2-1 defeat wasn't exactly football carnage but, in a remarkable way, the outcome was eerily close to recent box-office hit *Dirty Harry* starring Clint Eastwood. Clint plays the eponymous maverick San Fran cop – hell, is there any other kind these days – who edges more to the right-wing than Jimmy Johnstone and has a tendency to dish out his own version of the law. He gets hot on the trail of a badass hippy dude who looks as if he still wets the bed at twenty six and gets high on Irn-Bru yet has his kicks kidnapping and shooting the young 'uns. Eventually, Dirty Harry just stalks said dude until justice can be meted out Eastwood-style.

For Hibs, read bed-wettin', bru-lovin' hippy dude and for Dirty Harry – read Dixie Deans. 'Twas Dixie who bagged the winner in that Celtic victory but it was also the opening salvo in a one-man campaign against the Hibees over the next few seasons. From the Dixmaster, the message was clear: wherever the Hibs dudes went, he'd be there to score vital goals against them . . . and as we shall see, not just in ones or twos either. As their team bus headed back to the capital, the Hibernians had to ask themselves one question – *did they feel lucky?*

Luck wasn't an issue for Celtic as they swept through February in both the League and Scottish Cup without conceding a goal. It set them up nicely for the final title push as well as a quarter-final meeting with Hearts. Clearly, in the quest for seven-in-a-row, a successful Scottish Cup defence and a tilt at the biggest prize of all, the European Cup, March was looking as tasty as an Auld's savoury pie.

Book-ending a crucial League summit away to Aberdeen and that home tie against Hearts there was the not-so-small matter of a two-legged affair with Hungarian champs Ujpest Dosza. Unlike Boldklubben Copenhagen and then Maltese outfit Sliema Wanderers, whose status was such in Europe that we haven't even mentioned that Celtic swatted them aside 7-1 on aggregate, UD were the real deal. A terrific side borne of typical Hungarian talent, Ujpest were expected to give the Celts a harder time than your wife, should you return home with an opened pay packet. So, the fact that a young Hoops line-up laced with emerging full-back Danny McGrain, classy George Connelly and the diaper threats of Luigi Macari and Kenny Dal managed to eke out a 2-1 away victory was a supreme testimony to Big Jock's faith in the club's youth system.

When you consider that the Hungarians gave Celtic a fright in the return leg when the Hoops held on for a nervy 1-1 draw, then the away-day success was doubly impressive. It's debatable whether *The Persuaders* could have handled the escapade behind the so-called Iron Curtain with as much aplomb.

The Aberdeen match was also a 1-1 draw with Granite City Red Sox star Joe Harper once again coming to the Dons aid with a late equaliser. However, the north east challenge had been pretty diluted right enough, given that they'd parted with their influential captain Martin Buchan, a massive gap to fill in the ranks. He'd swapped the red of Aberdeen for the red of Manchester United, but if the Celtic legions had laughed at the thought of one of their own upping sticks for Old Trafford then the egg would be on their face within the year . . . but we'll get to that later.

Hearts were knocked out of the Scottish Cup after a replay and all seemed well in the Celtic world and especially Danny McGrain's orbit. Slowly, but surely, Danny The Beard, as he would become known much later on, had been making his case for a permanent feature in the Celtic line-up and he didn't look out of place with his tough tackling and the exhilarating overlap run that was becoming his trademark. And then came a League tussle with Falkirk at Brockville on the final Saturday of the month.

Danny had contested a high ball with Doug Somner of the home side and an accidental clash of heads had left him groggier than a night out with George Best. He passed out at half-time and woke up in the local hospital to be told he had a fractured skull. In 1972 that was like saying to Marc Bolan . . . *Yeah, your right hand's been crushed . . . gonna be difficult to play the guitar ever again . . . do you fancy just making tea for the rest of the band?* This was to be the first of the health tests for the brave Beard in the years to come and whenever he was knocked down, he would re-emerge to stake his claim as the greatest full-back in the world.

Of course, a fractured skull was merely a sore head compared to Ted Heath's dilemma over issues such as Northern Ireland and the Common Market. The PM had signed the country up for The European Economic Community starting, for us, on 1 January 1973 in a move that suggested he hoped, on the following New Year's Day, the country would be so drunk that it wouldn't take much notice of our new continental status. It had been a tough battle to convince anybody that this was a worthwhile gig, but not half as tough as trying to sort out the myriad problems in Ulster.

After a raft of atrocities in the province that included the horrors of a confrontation between Civil Rights protesters and British paratroopers culminating in the deaths of thirteen people on Bloody Sunday in January and the rampant increase in IRA bombings/killings, Heath decided to impose Direct Rule on Ulster from London. This took the power away from the Unionist-dominated Parliament for a year. It was an effort to kick-start a peace process that unfortunately would take many, many years to establish and see out more than one Prime Minister.

Unpredictable events like these certainly didn't appear to be typical in the football world where, after striding ahead of Aberdeen in the league race, Celtic turned up to play East Fife on 15 April seeking to make a little bit of history for themselves by achieving their seventh consecutive title. *Seven* had been the number on everybody's lips since the big kick-off but, like the fabled love that dare not speak its name, no-one around Celtic Park would mention the word until the title had been won.

Questions banned from Kerrydale Street included: *How many wee pals did Snow White have? What's the number on Jinky's shorts? Would you like a Coke, a Fanta, an Irn-Bru or that other stuff like lemonade that has the word UP written immediately after it?*

Bayview Park, Methil was as good a place as any to make history I suppose. Bizarrely, it was hard to actually *view* a *Bay* from its hilly slopes and it's highly unlikely that David Bowie, self-styling himself as alter-ego Ziggy Stardust in 1972, would have chosen it as a venue to launch a Spiders From Mars tour, but it had a rustic charm all of its own. Bowie was the biggest thing on the menu in early '72 as he tried to out-glam Marc Bolan in the Glam Rock hierarchy and certainly his albums and singles were going stratospheric.

The image was crucial. Platform heels . . . gaudy silver one-piece suits . . . more make-up than a chorus line and a camp majesty that left Danny La Rue gasping for breath. The music was bloody good though and Davy/Ziggy maintained a reputation for being the most outrageous pop personality of the day who would allegedly try *anything* to keep his career in the spotlight. Of course, there's a difference between *trying anything* and descending from a glitter moon-ball with dry ice swirling around you like a night on the Hackney Marshes, stepping out in front of a screaming crowd and proclaiming in a mock-operatic voice . . . *This Is Rock 'N' Roll . . . Good Evening . . . eh . . . Fife!*

Oh no, Bowie's *anything goes,* left-field tendencies certainly wouldn't have lent their bent to staging stadium rock gigs at Bayview Park, Methil. However, just as Woodstock was once a farm, Bayview Park's status would now become iconic as the ground where the Celts made it seven-in-a-row. It wasn't a foregone conclusion, though.

Given that East Fife were to finish third bottom that season, a point ahead of Celtic's punch bag Clyde and two ahead of the relegation surprise package Dunfermline Athletic, you would have thought it the ideal place to clinch a championship flag. However Jock Stein knew that nothing less than a focused Celtic performance would retain the title and geared his charges up for the battle. There were still four league fixtures to go after all and the luxury of two opportunities to win the title at home . . . if required. It wasn't.

Celtic ran out 3-0 winners with Dixie picking out two goals for himself and Harry Harry picking up the other. A packed crowd of 12,086 (look, it's a small ground – we're talking capacity here!) watched as Celtic marched into history. And there was still more excitement to come.

A Cup Final berth had been attained in one of those bizarre quirks of fate that saw the Hoops defeat Kilmarnock twice by the same score-line of 3-1; once in the League and then again in the Cup Semi-Final in consecutive matches. Imagine the odds you'd have got on that at the bookies. That wasn't the big news, though.

The story of spring 1972 was that Celtic were to face Inter-Milan again but, this time, in a two-leg showdown for a place in the European Cup Final. Inter-Milan – the name that launched a thousand memories of primitive, virginal times. Lisbon . . . convoys of Hillman Imps . . . chartered planes full of green-bedecked supporters . . . the hallowed turf of the Estadio Nacional . . . Big Tam Gemmell's wiggly legs . . . Bobby Murdoch's lash at the ball . . . strategically placed, quicksilver Stevie Chalmers' lightning strike that plunged a dagger into the very heart of catenaccio or, to give it its English translation – *we score first and then bore you to death like a Jethro Tull album!*

This was the imagery that sprang to mind when the name Inter Milan was raised in the clubs and bars of Glasgow and beyond. And now they were coming back into our lives like an old friend to talk about past glories and that corporate dental plan that no-one in the Celtic ranks had yet adopted. It had been five years since the last meeting and that was an encounter so brief that Trevor Howard and Celia Johnston could have been in the Lisbon crowd. What had they made of the Beatles split and all that weird John & Yoko stuff? Where were they when they heard about Neil Armstrong on the moon? What were the odds on David Bowie gigging in Methil? So many questions, so little time.

The first meeting was out in Italy and Celtic elected to play a little bit more cagey and hit Inter on the break. Of course, this wasn't the neutral territory of a Lisbon final. Surely Inter would attack and look for a goal to take to Glasgow? Ye think? For the Lions in the Celtic pack, such as Jim I-never-touched-him-ref Craig, big Cesar, stylish Bobby M and a few others, there must have been that moment in the match when they stood back and went: *Hey . . . you're not attacking us! We'd forgotten . . . That's soooooo you!*

Inter stuck to their style-less policy of suffocating the game like the Boston Strangler and probably didn't even notice as, with a full thirty minutes left on the clock, Big Jock replaced Jim Brogan with nineteen-year old Pat McCluskey. It was only Pat's third outing with the top side and to be thrown on at the San Siro in a European Cup semi-final tended to show Inter how low down the pecking order the Italians were in Jock's estimation and how much confidence he had in his side. Not that Pat was a novelty to the Italian crowd for he had an excellent, controlled game. No, the novelty value for the home punters seemed to lie in the fact that the champions of Scotland had one of their own in their ranks.

One Luigi Macari, to be frank, and they feted Lou on his arrival to the country like he was the offspring of Sophia Loren. Without the proper research, it's hard to know if wee Lou's Italian experience ever got beyond Nardini's Café on the Largs seafront, but the land of his ancestry was the mark-up factor in the Italian press. To be fair, it was a better distraction than watching old Inter knock the ball about like hitting the net would damage it. When the Celts left with a 0-0 draw under their belts and a host of 'Arrivederci' chants to wee Lou, it seemed like a good result and a job half-done.

On the night of the return leg, Glasgow was the centre of the known universe. Not only were Celtic entertaining Inter-Milan in a winner-takes-all tie in the east end, Rangers had German opposition in the shape of Bayern Munich over at Ibrox with a berth in the European Cup Winners Cup Final up for grabs. An estimated 150,000 spectators were present at the matches which meant that the police were on overtime-central. Not that anyone was interested in causing trouble. There were more important issues at stake.

The Rangers game kicked off earlier than the Celtic tie and the Ibrox men were already in the Cup Winners Cup Final as the Hoops were trying to break down Inter-Milan. *Stalemate [Stail-met]:* a chess position which can only end in a draw. So much for the dictionary. What it doesn't tell you is that Inter Milan were the high priests of Stalemate. Like a Boa Constrictor, one with great-looking teeth of course, they suffocated the life out of the game beyond ninety minutes and right through extra-time as well and it was time for Celtic Park's first- ever penalty shoot-out.

Ladies and Gentlemen . . . Celtic FC Enterprises in conjunction with Stifle-Match Internazionale proudly present a battle of wits from only twelve yards starring a cast of characters, two goalkeepers and a guaranteed fall-guy!

To Glasgow, the penalty shoot-out was as much a novelty as Luigi Macari was to the Milan press corps. We were in uncharted waters here. The principle was simple, of course. Five men from either side would be invited to pile pot-shots at the 'keeper from the penalty spot and whomsoever is left standing at the finish is the winner. Not quite the same kind of thinking that gave us the Drybrough Cup but not too wide of the mark either. Now, if there's one thing the Celts had it was people who were used to shooting at goal so there was a certain amount of expectation in the home crowd.

Inter, on the other hand, seemed to be unaccustomed to the whole idea of even being in the penalty box, facing down an opposition goalkeeper and being asked to score. There was a school of thought that their players would place the ball down, run up to it and then try to pass it back to their own goalkeeper! Jesus – it's what they'd been doing for the last 210 minutes of the tie!

That is apart from Sandro Mazzola. The Inter defender had a bit of previous with Celtic given that he'd despatched the penalty way back in Lisbon '67 that had put the Italians 1-0 up and then scurried back to the Inter trench to soak up the Celtic onslaught. *Been there, done that* he must have thought as he duly fired off the first penalty of the shoot-out past Evan the Williams in the Celtic goal.

When Dixie Deans strode forward for the first Celtic bite at the European cherry he didn't seem unduly nervous. The Dixmaster was a proven goal-scorer and had enjoyed the season of his life plus, as the story later went, he'd been blasting penalties past 'keepers in training all week . . . just in case. With that kind of build-up, naturally, you know how this is going to turn out.

Dixie rubbed his hands on his shirt, placed the ball, took a few steps back and then commenced his run-up. At the last second, he seemed to change his mind slightly. And *slightly* can make all the difference. That slight turn into Dealey Plaza, Dallas on 22 November 1963 that meant that JFK would not be seeking re-election. That slight movement on the ship's wheel that punctures the Titanic fatally, side-on with an iceberg. And that slight change of mind that sees the ball clear the bar from Dixie's spot-kick and head towards the crowd. The chunky (see, even I'm using the word!) striker looked like he'd just been told that his wife was actually his sister, such was the look of shock on his face.

But still, if you're gonna miss a penalty, make it an early one.

There's more to come . . . somebody else is bound to miss. Tragically not. Suddenly, the Italians were hitting the net like a British tennis player at Wimbledon, although such a sea-change in their ethos must surely have led to counselling therapy since they were back to their *nae fitba', nae goals* routine in the final a few weeks later when Ajax beat them 2-0.

All the other Celts put their respective spot-kicks away as well, leaving the Dixmaster as the odd man out when the melody stopped in the European Cup musical chairs. Poor Dixie was inconsolable and even Big Jock's edict that *players don't lose matches, teams do* did little to ease the next twenty-four hours for the wee man. Thankfully, he would get the chance to redress the balance within weeks when Hibernian offered themselves up as the Scottish Cup sacrifice at Hampden.

Before that, there was an opportunity for the Celtic support to show their appreciation of the Deans contribution to the hinterland of seven-in-a-row. They did so immediately when the champions emerged from the Celtic Park tunnel the following Saturday for a League match against Dixie's former employers Motherwell. In amongst the chants and songs about Stein's heroes, the name being lustily vocalised was that of Dixie Deans. There was even time for some Vaudeville when, in an almost routine 5-2 victory, the Celts were awarded a couple of penalties and the cry from The Jungle was for Dixie to take the spot-kicks. *The Dixmaster*, however, was having none of that. Teenage boys would embrace a spot before Dixie overcame *his* aversion!

Hibernian hadn't won the Scottish Cup for seventy years. Edward VII had been on the throne. Jimmy McGrory wasn't even born and The Rolling Stones had just started touring after the release of their first album. Okay, that last bit's not quite true although it seemed so long since Mick and the boys started jammin' the blues that you felt as if they'd been around forever. The point was that there was a particular feeling amongst the sentimentalists that this was to be the Hibees year.

In fairness, they had a decent side with the likes of Jimmy O'Rourke and Alan Gordon up front, ever-reliable Jim Herriot in goal, obviously before he became a best-selling author and vet, a defensive line that sounded like a Dulux shade-chart in Black, Blackley and Brownlie and, of course, the Edinburgh legend on a par with the One O'clock Gun, Pat Stanton as their stylish midfield captain.

Stein was a huge admirer of Stanton although it wasn't an exclusive club and he was wary of the capabilities of the Hibernian outfit. This point was highlighted to him when they put paid to a derby showdown by disposing of Rangers by two goals to nil in a replayed semi-final. In short, they were nae mugs and so it's quite astonishing that Celtic racked up the highest score in a Scottish Cup Final for eighty-four years when they ran out 6-1 winners.

That last final was when Renton beat Cambuslang by the same score in 1888 – a momentous year if ever there was one. And the heavy-duty scoreline is only part of the story. Next up on the wow!-ometer is that there occurred the first hat-trick in a Scottish Cup Final since Celtic's Jimmy Quinn in 1904. The Mighty Quinn was joined in the locker of fame by the Dixmaster himself.

Alan Gordon had scrambled an equaliser to Billy McNeill's Celtic opener so the match stood at 1-1 when Dixie Deans then took hold of the Cup Final grabbing the second, third and fourth goals with wee Lou Macca picking up the rest of the tab. Dixie's second goal and the Bhoys' decisive third was a work of art in itself.

Lou Macca lofted a speculative lob towards the Hibs eighteen-yard line that John Brownlie of Edinburgh legal firm Black, Brownlie & Blackley attempted to head back to Jim Herriot in the Hibees' goal. Dixie, assessing the situation adroitly, fastened on to the pass- back and advanced beyond the stricken Herriot before he could say *All Creatures Great And Small*, took on the retreating Brownlie only to find t'veterinary Herriot tackling him at the goal-line. Slipping the 'keeper *again,* he smashed the ball past the astonished Hibee on the line to score one of the best goals in Scottish Cup history.

At one point Hibs seemed to have sent out the British Expeditionary Force to counter the chunky one but Dixie took on all comers before slamming the ball into the net. He then did a somersault on the Hampden turf in acknowledgement of this *what-about-that-then?* moment.

Well, 1972 was an Olympic year after all, although it's highly unlikely that The Dixmaster's unorthodox head-over-heels had the British selectors on the phone after the match. To be 3-1 down and to such an outrageous finish seemed to deflate the Hibs lads. Even the superlative Stanton appeared to capitulate. Alan Gordon's scrappy Edinburgh counter seemed a long, long time ago; lost in a moment when the Hibernian fans, those sentimentalists who favoured the underdogs and the red tops were willing on a Scottish Cup Final headache for the champions.

Elvis might have been crooning about being in *Dixieland* for American Trilogy, but the Celtic Supporters had arrived there before him! 6-1 winners . . . seven-in-a-row League Champions . . . beaten semi-finalists in Europe's premier competition . . . it had been a vintage season for the Celts and the post-match celebrations at Hampden couldn't have been topped had David Bowie descended on his moon-ball in full Ziggy Stardust regalia and invited the crowd to sing *Suffragette City* alongside those Spiders From Mars.

1972-1973
ConnellyPassin'

Track List:
Mott The Hoople/All The Young Dudes; Gilbert O'Sullivan/ Clair; Slade/Gudbye T'Jane; Harley Quinne/New Orleans; Jimmy Osmond/Long Haired Lover From Liverpool; Sweet/Blockbuster; T-Rex/20th Century B(h)oy; Medicine Head/One & One Is One; Strawbs/Part Of The Union; Wizzard/See My Baby Jive; Barry Blue/ Dancin' On A Saturday Night

Jock Stein . . . expert tactician; supreme motivator; tireless grafter; omnipotent force at Celtic Park. In his spare time he was an avowed teetotaller and possessed a set of singing pipes that, whilst not quite being of the same class as Perry Como, did allow him to hold a tune in a pleasant manner. The Big Man was wont to while away trips abroad with Celtic and those endless hours traversing the Scottish border in search of a game to watch by rendering his songbook favourites in lusty fashion. When you rode shotgun with Big Jock, you didn't have to rely on the eight-track cartridge for musical accompaniment.

This much we do know but was he a movie fan? Could he unwind at the flicks and did he keep his eye on the listings and the latest releases? If he did then he would certainly have grabbed a seat for *The Godfather* which premiered in June 1972 and started the rounds throughout the football close season.

We can only speculate as to whether he did but it is tempting to think of Big Jock reclining in the dark anonymity of a theatre,

Butterkist in his lap, Kia-Ora close to hand, enduring the double Gloucester cheese of the Pearl & Dean adverts and then enjoying the main feature as Marlon Brando garbles his way towards a second career Oscar. As he watched silently he may have reflected that he and Don Corleone had much in common.

Both were larger than life figures, beyond rebuke, commanding respect who presided over powerful dynasties that were founded upon hard graft, discipline and above all, loyalty. Okay, Jock never arranged for opposition strikers or rival managers to be silently eliminated with *offers they couldn't refuse,* but he did have a cast of boys with whom the Corleone family could identify.

In David Hay, he had the *Quiet Assassin,* so dubbed by then Scotland manager Tommy Docherty. Hay was a stylish operator who could perform in defence, midfield or attack. His presence was less than vociferous and even in day-to-day conversation he used words as sparingly as a Benedictine Monk, but he was as ruthless and as hard on the pitch as Don Corleone's *consigliere* Tom Hagen when it came to implementing the family policy. He knew his value but will forever be haunted by the thought that he could be unappreciated by the man to whom he owes his career.

Kenny Dalglish was the cherubic, anointed Michael Corleone, torn between the desire to do his own thing but retaining a familial loyalty to his father and Don, Big Jock. Just like Michael, he will one day inherit the kingdom but he must have a sabbatical away from the family in order to grow.

Vulnerable George Connelly is the troubled Fredo. He will do anything that Don Jock asks him to do, including an early display of keepy-uppy for the Celtic supporters during a half-time break in a 1960s European tie, but he has a shyness and a humility that does not lend itself well to the business dealings of the family.

And finally, there is Lou Macari, the football embodiment of Santino 'Sonny' Corleone. A hot-blooded firebrand whose opinions of his self-worth are as Latin as Urbi et Orbi but whose desire to drag the family into the modern world and the treasures that it has to offer leads him into direct conflict with the man whose sandals he is not fit to tie.

The conflicting dilemmas of this cast of characters will determine the shifting sands of the fortunes of both Celtic Football Club as much as the Corleone family in the ensuing years. Of course, one of the legendary passages in *The Godfather* is constructed around the shooting of Brando's character Vito Corleone. As the stricken patriarch lies comatose in a New York hospital, the family members jockey for position, misjudge situations and generally give the impression that, without their Don, they are as useful as a chocolate-firing machine gun.

When Vito finally recovers, he must decide who is to lead the family that he has built onto future successes. Such was the dilemma for Jock Stein as he was admitted to hospital over the festive period of 1972 with a heart complaint. In Glaswegian terms, this was the equivalent of Don Corleone's enforced infirmary stay and, just like *The Godfather*, rumours abounded about the state of Big Jock's health.

Amidst the winter snow, there was a feeling of misdirection out at Celtic Park, almost as if the aeroplane was forced onto auto-pilot in an effort to stay on course. Bizarrely, at the same time as Jock was poorly, the Celtic squad were decimated by a flu epidemic that meant the cancellation of a couple of fixtures, away to Kilmarnock and at home to Morton. The Scottish League's decision to postpone these games was an indication that the flu bug was not illusory.

In light of several Celtic players dropping faster than Ted Heath's job approval ratings, the high heid yins in the administration of Scottish football had taken on the role of a wife who initially suspects man-flu in her loved one but is eventually won round by a persuasive bout of vomiting and the sacrifice of going without something he loves . . . in Celtic's case, the football. To be truthful, it wasn't just the health of the squad that was in question by the Christmas of 1972; there were debates about the health of their football as well.

It had all seemed so easy the season before when the Celts had racked up seven-in-a-row by finishing ten points clear of Aberdeen and a whopping sixteen beyond Rangers. The West End of the city was to supply the critical challenge to Celtic's supremacy in season 1972-73, but that seemed to be a possibility as remote as linking the recent Watergate scandal to President Richard Nixon when the two sides met in the first League encounter in September.

In an embarrassingly one-sided affair Celtic cruised to a 3-1 victory that even had the Hoops acolytes sarcastically applauding John Greig's eighty-ninth minute consolation for Rangers. The Ibrox management duo of Willie Waddell and Jock Wallace appeared to have a similar task to Nixon in that they would be spending the season trying to put out fires. Perhaps Tricky Dicky could have lent them one of his extinguishers as he was fast becoming the honorary fire-chief of Washington DC.

What had started off as a minor burglary in the offices of the Democrat Party at the Watergate building was now brewing nicely into the biggest political scandal in American political history. Nixon denied any involvement and indeed, would win a landslide victory in the 1972 US election but, within days of re-taking office, the tentacles would begin to extend in such a fashion as to eventually paint him as a deviously corrupt public figure whose level of paranoia exceeded anything available on a Celtic bus heading up the M8 on match-day.

Thanks to Nixon's machinations, the American public would never again believe anything that came from the mouth of a President and we would all have to put up with the suffix *-gate* being attached to any scandal or intrigue for the next thirty years: Irangate . . . Dianagate . . . Camillagate . . . Iraqgate . . . Cowangate (that last one's time is yet to come and we'll be first off the mark with the headline as well!).

Anyway, that 3-1 humiliation seemed to anoint Celtic's firm grasp of their championship and send out a clear signal to their greatest rivals. Or so we thought. Out of nowhere, there then seemed to be a worrying level of inconsistency within the set-up that made for some very *un*Celtic-like performances over the next few months.

The League Cup was to raise its grisly head again and although Celtic negotiated the *borefest* that was their sectional grouping with Arbroath, Stirling Albion and East Fife with little trouble, Dundee knocked them off their stride with a 1-0 victory at Dens Park in the first-leg of the Quarter-Final. That score was remarkable in that the Blue Bonnets had already defeated the Celts by 2-0 only five weeks before in a League encounter. It's not often that Big Jock's sides lost twice to one team in a relatively short space of time.

Perhaps The Master was feeling the strain. He'd already shown a side of his character that few outwith the dressing room inner sanctum got to see when, on the first day of the season and in one of those anodyne League Cup tests away to Stirling Albion, his patience snapped.

The Albion played at Annfield but any comparison with Liverpool would have to end right there although the Central Belt club could, at least, argue that they knew how to spell the name of their ground properly. It was one of those tight little grounds in which a fart from the away end would immediately be heard amongst the home support and where conversation was limited because every word would be picked up around the terracing.

It certainly wasn't the type of arena that was best suited to the shocking indiscretions of a section of the Celtic support giving vent to ballads of a political nature that stated nothing for either their team or their club's good name. In short, Big Jock had endured enough of their folly and decided to take matters into his own hands. Making his way around the track at half-time he suddenly defied all known managerial protocol by vaulting a fence and wading into an area of the away support in order to administer one of his famous tongue-lashings.

A loose lion from nearby Blair Drummond Safari Park could scarcely have induced more panic amongst the rowdy spectators than the sight of Jock Stein clambering his mighty way into the Celtic section of the crowd. Photographs exist of bemused individuals staring forlornly at their leader, perhaps wondering if now would be a suitable occasion to shake his hand, thank him for the Everest successes and ask for his autograph or just accept a powerful dressing-down by one of the most revered names in association football.

Huge steps have been taken in subsequent years to eradicate elements of sectarianism on either side of the Glasgow fence, but maybe the opening salvo was fired that day when Jock Stein laid down the law in his brusque Burnbank fashion. Certainly, it was not the most predictable opening to a Cup campaign that only reached a comparable level of excitement when those Dundee quarters rolled around.

In the second leg Celtic ran out 3-2 winners, which levelled the aggregate score, and therefore a third game took place at the fag end of November when the Bhoys finally turned on the style with a 4-1 crushing. By that time, though, they had taken their leave of the European Cup at the hands of the previous season's vanquished Hungarians, Ujpest Dosza.

Nowadays, the Champions League throws up the same combination of clashes with the tedious inevitability of yet another Phil Collins album, but back in the glorious 1970s, i.e. when *only* a nation's champions were allowed access to the tournament, it was fairly unusual for two sides to joust with each other in consecutive seasons.

First time around in March, the Ujpest experience had been a relatively new and exciting one for the Celtic traveller. The Hoops had only played a seriously competitive game in Budapest once before and that was against MTK Budapest in the semi-final second leg of the European Cup-Winners Cup from season 1963-64. *Kelly's Kids* had arrived in fine fettle on the back of a 3-0 trouncing of the Hungarians from the first match and were rightfully expectant of making it to the final. Unfortunately, their naivety beamed out like a headlight on a Lada and a classy Budapest side whipped the Bhoys 4-0.

But all that was *Before Stein* and, just as Chairman Mao had declared all things null and void and that there should be a Year Zero again, the Celtic Supporters had come to view Jock's arrival in 1965 with the same relevance as the New Testament.

The exhilaration of that 2-1 away victory in March had not only entered the chronicles as one of Celtic's most impressive results abroad, there was the considerably enjoyable and unbelievable experience of a party with Richard Burton and Elizabeth Taylor, who happened to be in Hungary shooting a movie. Hollywood's most glittering couple were staying at the same hotel as some of the Celtic support which meant that, either the Bhoys had won a watch with Thomas Cook, or times were a little bit tougher for the warring Burtons, even if they were slumming it in the penthouse suite.

Whatever the case, it was party-time for the green and white brigade and since Dick and Liz were cognisant with the etiquette of letting their hair down, they joined in with lusty abandon. Liz wound up sporting a hooped tammy on her bonce as though it was part of her headgear from National Velvet whilst Big Dick regaled the chaps with stories from Hollywood.

It's doubtful that the couple ever took up the offers to *pop in whenever they were doon the Gallowgate way,* but there was no doubt that they would be starting the first official Hollywood branch of the Celtic Supporters Club on their return to the States. That was, unless it was their day of the week to get divorced, re-married or even re-divorced – it was difficult to keep track of a couple whose marriage was as on-and-off as an Edinburgh title challenge.

Very rarely do you go back to a holiday destination where you had a fantastic time and met a great couple and find the same enjoyment. Such was the case for the Celtic support that travelled back to Budapest eight months later with their heroes sitting precariously on a 2-1 first leg advantage. The 'Uj' were a fine outfit still smarting from the previous season's ejection from the top table and they led the way in a comprehensive 3-0 victory that saw Celtic's European aspirations melt away like the Burtons' wedding vows.

The Celts did bounce back characteristically the following Saturday with a 5-0 humbling of Motherwell at Fir Park but there was a definite staleness in their approach to other domestic affairs and they appeared to be in the habit of eking out results rather than sweeping all-comers away. The League Cup semi-final with Aberdeen on 27 November was a typical example of the state of play.

It had only been one week since the Dundee replay and that 4-1 Hoops demolition, yet The Dons could later take umbrage at the fact that they had not deprived Celtic of a League Cup Final spot for the first time in eight years.

A wet November night on the slopes of Hampden shouldn't have been much to shout about but twice the Granites led only to be pegged back by Celtic with an immediacy that would have satisfied a S.W.A.T. Rapid Response Unit. It took the unsung Tommy 'Tid' Callaghan to knock in a Celtic winner, supplied from a Harry Harry cross and a sublime Dalglish dummy when the bhoy-King carried a couple of defenders in his back-pocket and big Tid took advantage of the space and time to set up a date with Hibs on 9 December.

Yes, the Celts were back in the final but they were making heavy work out of getting there. Then again, it was Hibernian. That self-same Hibernian who had so spectacularly folded like a crinoline cardigan only seven months before in the 'Dixie' final.

The Edinburgh players would surely have required the services of a team of shock therapists to make them return to the scene of *that* crime whilst their supporters must have approached Hampden in the nervous manner of Richard Nixon going to a press briefing on Watergate. The news that Dixie *Dirty Harry* Deans would not be gunning for them due to injury would have raised the optimism level a touch but Celtic still had the quality of such as Dalglish, Hood and Macari to call upon.

It would be fair to say that Hibernian did suffer a little bit from stage fright as this would be the third time that they had faced Celtic in a major final in as many years and on both previous occasions had struggled to keep the score down to six (1968-69 League Cup, 6-2 and, let's mention it again, 1971-72 Scottish Cup Final, 6-1). In such a vein, to lose by five might generally be seen as a statistical improvement.

Naturally with that kind of report card, you should have put the housekeeping on Celtic to win . . . just as well you didn't then or it would have been buttered toast on the menu and bum-wiping with the daily newspapers for a month as Hibs coasted to a 2-1 victory. Yes, the score does seem like less than a pasting but the Hibees also had a third goal denied as a shot was narrowly cleared off the line and the Celts' solitary register, just like the shock that was Partick Thistle from the previous year, was the epitome of consolation.

Once again, a Celtic side had to stand and applaud the League Cup Winners from a position of defeat and this precipitated a bout of winter blues starting with a scrappy 2-1 away day victory in Arbroath. Then came a sombre 1-1 draw with the self-same Hibernian who, pumped up with their first trophy since Brylcreem was a fashion statement, had the temerity to come to Glasgow and hold the Champions in their own lair.

The Hibees were beginning to swagger around like the guy next door who'd got a Chopper bike for his birthday – lucky sod! Who didn't want one of those beauties? The design of the Chopper was the coolest thing about it. Loosely based on the Harley Davidson motorbike from hippy-cool, road journey classic *Easy Rider*, you could lie back on one of these babies and pretend you were Peter Fonda. The curved shape of the handlebars meant that your arms were constantly in a 10-2 position and the seat, tragically, felt like your ass was splayed on top of a thick cigar.

Riding the thing with a pair of flares on was a bugger as well. Every twenty feet, you would have to stop and retrieve the last six inches of your oil-stained bell-bottoms from within the chain. To add to the illusion of riding a real hog, the manufacturers, Raleigh, fixed a T-shape gear-stick on the mainframe above your knees. It didn't really make hellish much difference to your ability to get about and was laced with danger if you slid into it but, at least, there was the sensation of pulling back on it quickly and imagining that you were about to hit warp factor eight on your bike.

The tabloids ran some sensationalist stories about kids doing wheelies and flipping over backwards towards some horrendous injuries and there was never any danger that you would see a guy in a yellow jersey leading the Tour De France on a Chopper but, hell, astride of one you were the hottest cat in town. It was on every boy's wish list for the festive and soon a female version would be manufactured called the Chipper.

In the supersonic early '70s, it wasn't unusual to see a fearfully young couple *chopping* and *chipping* their way around your housing estate, flags attached to the back of their saddles, flashy red lights stuck between their spokes and giving the impression that they were the Ken and Barbie around your gaff. Winning the League Cup meant that everyone at Easter Road was going to get a Chopper from Santa.

We were living in strange times that Christmas of 1972 with the Celts in less-than-convincing form, the flu epidemic that ripped through anyone who coughed at Celtic Park, Big Jock's cardiac problems and, most bizarre of all, an Osmond at number one singing a song about Liverpool.

Little Jimmy Osmond had a coupon that bore close examination with the back of your hand and, over thirty-five years later, it still does. His recording of *Long-Haired Lover From Liverpool* was the kind of performance that had Liverpudlians claiming that they were actually from Manchester and the sort of disc of which repeat plays would have hampered the Geneva Convention during the war. To be fair to the Nazis, they'd only *bombed* Liverpool, they'd never desecrated the name of the city with this type of tuneless hokum.

In LJO, the Salt Lake City family with the glittering teeth, the even-more glittering jumpsuits and the washed hair of a L'Oreal advert had produced an offspring with as much to offer the music scene as Keith Richard had to offer the priesthood. If only Little Jimmy Osmond was the solitary worry.

Back in Glasgow, Little Lou Macari was also flexing his muscles and had been involved in an ongoing dispute about the size of his wage packet. That Lou had talent was beyond doubt. That it was being fairly recompensed was, in Luigi's eyes, open to debate. For a couple of seasons his star had been on the rise and he had never been slow to point out to Big Jock that he and his goals might just be worth more than he was banking.

It had been a saga as long as *The Godfather* and with the same level of intrigue. In the winter of '72 it came to a head when Lou once again submitted a transfer request. He had done so a couple of seasons before but now he was a hotter property and feted by another Don, Tommy Docherty, who had taken control of the Manchester United family and, just like the Corleone nemesis, Virgil *The Turk* Sollozzo, was ruthless in his approach to being the biggest linguini in the bowl.

In a recent and previous existence, Don Docherty, as Scotland manager, had promoted Lou to the international set-up and was a big fan of the wee man's style. It was no surprise therefore that he fancied adding him to the Old Trafford roster. The only problem was that Jock Corleone had decided that, under an agreement with Don Bill Shankly of the Liverpool family, Luigi should be wearing the red at Anfield rather than on the other side of the motorway. In the way of the Mafiosi it was *nothing personal Luigi, just business, you understand.* So Lou found himself sitting in the stand at Anfield watching a Liverpool match at the behest of Big Jock whilst considering a move to the Merseybeats.

It was then that Pat Crerand made his move. Crerand, a former Celt who had lifted the European Cup as a Manchester United player, was practically in the role of *consigliere* when he sidled up to Lou and asked him if he fancied playing for the Red Devils. An appointment was made to meet up the following day in Glasgow to ink a deal.

This was the moment that Lou Macari amalgamated with Santino 'Sonny' Corleone when the eldest boy of *La Famiglia di Corleone* rode off that fateful day in his car on a mission only to be ambushed at the toll booth by a team of gun-toting henchmen. The only difference was that, when Luigi was ambushed, it was by one man, Pat Crerand, and he was offering lire, not bullets. Before January was out, Luigi became a devil.

Given that all this activity came right after a New Year reversal at Ibrox when Rangers had 'done a Celtic' by bagging a last minute winner through Alfie Conn, inevitably there were uncomfortable mutterings around the bars and clubs close to Celtic Park. Would seven-in-a-row be the crowning legacy of Jock Stein's domestic score-card or was this a team capable of potting the '8' ball. After all, it's quite possible that the public were perhaps a little too 'merry' over 1 January to actually notice that the United Kingdom was now a fully fledged member of the Common Market, but Celtic losing the New Year Derby five days later for the first time in four years was something to snap even Richard Burton out of a hangover.

Jock Stein was still officially recovering from his sudden illness in hospital when the match took place but, naturally, he demanded that he be allowed to listen to the game on the radio. Perish the eminent heart surgeon or Hattie Jacques-type matron who would cross the Big Man when Celtic were playing Rangers although, putting the result into perspective, perhaps Jock would have been better twiddling the dial and listening to *Afternoon Theatre* on the Home Service. It's quite likely that a nurse would have been despatched at the final whistle to re-make his bed as Jock kicked every ball for the full ninety minutes.

Sean 'The Brogue' Fallon had taken temporary charge of the team throughout Jock's convalescence and it was left to his deep burr to impart instructions to the troops from the dressing room to the pitch. He wasn't to have it easy either. After the Ibrox defeat, Dundee at Celtic Park were next on the menu and the way they were playing against us that season did not suggest that they could be taken lightly.

Big Jock had been released from hospital but his presence that day was to be in the Directors' Box as a mere spectator. Still, he received a welcome from the home support the likes of which Lazarus could have been proud. But the match would have done little for the big man's health taking, as it did, for Kenny D to notch an eighty-first minute winner for a 2-1 finish.

King Kenny repeated the feat a week later against Ayr United. In fact he did it twice, as a handsome 3-1 score-line disguised the fact that The Honest Men had made the Hoops fight for the points from as early as the tenth minute when they took the lead.

New goalkeeper, Alastair Hunter, had been signed from Kilmarnock and made his debut against Airdrieonians on the last Saturday of the month. Ally's status as a possible Big Game Hunter had been a defiant display for Killie in the previous season's Scottish Cup Semi-Final when he had kept the score down to 3-1 in Celtic's favour.

Big Jock had remembered that solidity although it has to be said that, as a judge of 'keepers, he had proved himself over the years to be as adept as your pet dog picking out the winners at Aintree! He hadn't even been responsible for bringing arguably Celtic's greatest ever custodian and fireguard of the Lisbon Lions, Ronnie Simpson, to the club. Worse than that, Jock so rated the ageing Simpson that he had actually sold him *to* Celtic when he was in charge of Hibernian.

Had you dived in front of Jock Stein on a pavement in the right manner and retrieved a fiver that he had dropped from his pocket, then there was a fair chance that he'd have signed you on the spot and put you between the sticks the following weekend. It therefore wasn't the biggest surprise in the world when the unfortunate Ally was at fault for the Airdrie winner in the eighty-ninth minute at Broomfield.

A 2-1 defeat to a team who would be relegated at the end of the season . . . Bobby Murdoch missing a penalty . . . Rangers edging out Morton by the same narrow score-line . . . question marks being asked about your position for the Airdrie winner . . . as debuts go, Ally Hunter's was right up there with the Titanic's maiden voyage. Credit to the bold Alastair though, he was to recover from the debris and play his part in the rest of the season.

The good news was that Danny McGrain had been fully rehabilitated after his fractured skull and, with the departure of Jim Craig to South Africa during the previous close season, Daniel Fergus McGrain had stepped up to the plate and was establishing himself as a full-back of great note.

Tigerish in the tackle, superb distribution and awareness aligned with an almost uncontrollable urge to overlap on the right flank and contribute to the Hoops attacking options were the qualities that he was bringing to the cause. And they were needed as Rangers, on the bounce from the New Year win, were putting together a run that had them so close to Celtic that they could smell Big Jock's Old Spice.

Points were being dropped by Celtic against unlikely opposition and in even unlikelier places. Partick Thistle came to Celtic Park and spoiled the celebrations of Celtic's six thousandth League goal by taking the lead and holding out for a 1-1 draw as Bobby Murdoch took home a tea-set for bagging the historic strike. He would rather have had the full two points, frankly. And then there was the sit-com that was East Fife on 17 February.

Happy memories, of course, abounded of Bayview Park, landmark of the seven-in-a-row title clincher just ten months before, but the events of that cold, winter's afternoon would stay in the conscience for a long time. The match in itself was a no-holds barred 2-2 draw with the Dixmaster being the Celts hero for putting the Bhoys in the lead and then salvaging the point late on with an equaliser.

In between that, four penalties were awarded with the Fifers using their solitary spot-kick to bring the score back to one apiece. Within minutes it was Celtic's turn to see the referee blowing for a penalty-box misdemeanour and Bobby Murdoch ambled up to take responsibility. Unfortunately he ambled a bit too much and sent his kick high above the crossbar.

However, the beady-eyed whistler had noticed an early encroachment into the box and thus astonished everybody by ordering the kick to be re-taken. Big Murdoch had seen enough though so he passed up the opportunity for glory by letting Harry Hood take the ball. Harry Harry . . . the cool Krishna King who had popped up in a Scottish Cup Final against Rangers only a year and a half before and in front of over 100,000 people had sent McCloy the Lighthouse the wrong way with a smooth finish.

If you can do it at Hampden Harry, surely you can do it in Methil? Nay and twice nay as East Fife goalkeeper Ernie McGarr made the save. To be frank, he could have thrown his cap at the ball given the snail-like pace of Harry Harry's spot-kick. He may have tried to place it, he may have tried to fool the 'keeper with a daisy-cutter, he might even have tried to pot the ball with a snooker cue but, whatever the reason, it was a miss.

Worse was to follow when the Methil Mightys went 2-1 up and it looked as if the penalty farce would seriously cost the Bhoys. The pantomime season was in full swing when Celtic were awarded a third chance to score from a spot-kick. This time it was ice-in-his-veins-fire-in-his-heart Kenny D who was asked to apply the finish.

The young veteran – the man who stared down The Lighthouse after tying his lace and stuck the ball away with such aplomb – now succumbed to the disease by failing to convert. Three penalties . . . three players whom you would have bet the wife's hairdo money on to score . . . and three misses.

Of course, it wouldn't have been a sit-com without an ironic sting in the tail. And so it was that Dixie Deans, the man with the worst ever penalty-miss story to tell, who hadn't been invited to take a spot-kick that day, rammed home a priceless equaliser for Celtic in injury-time. The saved point would be crucial.

The BBC had already beaten Celtic to the punch-line when they aired Episode One of their new prime-time sitcom *Some Mothers Do 'Ave 'Em* on the Thursday night prior to the Hoops' visit to face Methil's Finest on League business that Saturday. Michael Crawford starred as Frank Spencer, who rapidly established himself as the most incompetent, disaster-prone character on British television. Everything that Frank touches breaks . . . every job that he attempts results in a sacking . . . .and every hobby that he takes up ends as an unparalleled fiasco.

His catchphrase *Ooooh Betty* levelled at his unfortunate wife after yet another catastrophe becomes, overnight, the calling card in every playground around the country as well as the preserve of Saturday Night impressionists like Mike Yarwood who would milk the imitation for as much mileage as possible. Yet, even the hapless Frank would have been hard-pressed to miss three penalties in a football match and it's highly unlikely that when the miscreants returned to the dressing room after the match that Big Jock could see the funny side to it all by uttering *Ooooh Bobby . . . Ooooh Harry . . . Ooooh Kenny* to the lads.

Rangers moved three points ahead of Celtic a couple of days later when they beat Arbroath at Ibrox. Admittedly, the Celts had two games in hand but the concern was that their current form didn't exactly augur well for the capture of those points. Ally Hunter was beginning to find his feet in goal, though, as he proved with a fine penalty save against Motherwell in the Scottish Cup that came at a crucial time in the match when the Hoops were 1-0 up. They ran out 4-0 winners whilst a string of commanding saves at home to Morton provided the springboard for a narrow 1-0 victory.

Billy McNeill was now proving pivotal to Celtic's endeavours, which was a bit like saying that John Lennon had been handy for The Beatles. Of course Cesar was pivotal – his middle name was *pivotal* – but he was one of those players you trusted to be there at the right time, providing the right amount of encouragement and offering a bulwark presence at the back. In fact, he had been all of those things for so long in his career that it could sometimes be easy to forget just how important a position he held.

What was required now more than anything if eight-in-a-row was to be achieved was the steady influence of an experienced hand at the tiller. After all, Jock Stein couldn't pull on a jersey and lead the team on the park. Cesar had been here before many times and as one of the last three Lisbon Lions still at the club, the others being Bobby Lennox and Jimmy Johnstone, he knew that the important thing was to work hard, stay calm and the results would fall as best they could.

Rangers hadn't won the title since the last time Cilla Black had topped the charts in 1964, a fact that gave satisfaction to the Celtic support and relief to music lovers everywhere. 1964 was also the year that *The Likely Lads* started on television. The brainchild of young writers Dick Clement and Ian La Frenais, the sit-com starring James Bolam and Rodney Bewes had been a runaway success in the '60s; palpably more than Rangers had, to be frank, in that era. The fact that in early 1973 the sequel, *Whatever Happened To The Likely Lads*, a brand new ultra-70s catch-up on the show still starring the same two actors, was going out on BBC1, emphasised that it had been a long time since Rangers had tasted League-winning success. When were the men from Ibrox to get *their* sequel?

The feeling was that they were coming closest to it in this particular season. Central to this was a 3-1 dusting up of Dundee at home whilst Celtic were being held to a draw by the United contingent of Jute City at Tannadice. Both teams were level on points, although Celtic had a better goal-average – hardly grounds for a wave of optimism coursing through the east end of the city. It was clear that this particular title chase was going to be a last day of the season affair.

In such a climate, the Scottish Cup looked like a bit of an unwelcome distraction and, certainly for Celtic, a midweek replay against Aberdeen up at Pittodrie, held all the appeal of a night out with the in-laws. Rangers put a warm pineapple on Celtic's gammon steak the night before the replay tie by roughing up Airdrie at Broomfield by six goals to two. The Celts were feeling the pressure that night, but Billy McNeill's headed goal was enough to put them through to the semi-finals.

The following Saturday it was Edinburgh's turn to try and derail Glasgow's championship ambitions with Hearts lining up against Celtic at Tynecastle and Rangers welcoming Hibernian to Ibrox. Celtic definitely had the harder looking fixture, but a rugged 2-0 win had the Bhoys support emulating Slade by roaring *Cum On Feel The Noize!* to their blue counterparts all the way down the M8 corridor.

Rangers defeated Hibs by one goal in a match described euphemistically as *a tight affair* which, depending on what side of the field you were on, meant that they were either plucky winners who played to the end of the ninety . . . or they were just as jammy as an Arctic roll. The cigarette paper that separated the clubs was to remain in place for the weeks leading up to the final two fixtures of a long League campaign.

Notable scalps for Celtic throughout this period included a 3-1 win up in Perth against St Johnstone with old hands Cesar and Jinky leading the way and showing the young 'uns how it was done by weighing in with a couple of goals, and a 5-0 rout of Dumbarton that continued to raise the Celts' goal average to the value of an extra point, if required. And it was beginning to look that way as the tenacious Rangers Coyote clung ferociously onto the Celtic Road Runner's tail until the penultimate Saturday of the League season.

Arbroath brought a few 'smokies' through to Celtic Park and proved that they were a sight more animated than the fish by holding Celtic until half-time on a 0-0 score. Squeaky bums were the interval's unwelcome guest to the Celtic support in The Jungle. They had thought that the hardest test would be at Easter Road on the final day of the season when a handsome win might be the minimal requirement. Nobody assumed that it would be so difficult to grill the *smokies* on their own patch. This honours-even first half was bad for the digestive system!

Rangers appeared to have their Mount Everest that day by heading to Pittodrie but the feeling was that if they could negotiate the Granite City hurdle then there was still the chance to pick off East Fife at Ibrox on the last day of the season and transmit that message of pressure through to Easter Road. They would have greeted the 0-0 half-time score from Celtic Park as an incentive to get the boiler suits on and tear into the Dons. But, early into the second half, Harry Harry put the Celts one up at which point the gates opened sufficiently to usher in a 4-0 victory. If that seemed good enough, then the news from the North-East was even better.

Aberdeen had held Rangers to a 2-2 draw and extracted a mini-revenge for those Rangers victories in the last couple of seasons that had de-railed *their* bid to win a first League title since Bill Haley had *Rocked Around The Clock* in 1955. The situation was now considerably simpler than the novelty of goal averages. If Celtic could snatch a draw or a win at Easter Road then the title was theirs and events at Ibrox would be irrelevant. In saying that, it was, in the modern parlance of the football pundit, *still a big ask.*

If Rangers could have chosen an opponent for their biggest rivals to have to shoot down that season then they would probably have selected Hibs. After all . . . the Hibees were good at home . . . they were set to finish third in the table behind the big two and, crucially, they had already beaten Celtic twice in cup finals.

Yes, yes, that League Cup Final was one of them but didn't I mention that monumental trophy the Drybrough Cup way back at the start of the season as well? No? Well there's a reason for that isn't there? It was a pre-season tourney when everybody was merely limbering up for the real challenges ahead and it was such a Mickey Mouse trophy that there were rumours that Disney's next animated blockbuster was to be called *101 Drybrough Dalmatians!*

However, let's not be pedantic here. On the final day of the League season that was 1972-73, Celtic were going to have to get a result against the Scottish League Cup winners and the Fantasy Island Drybrough Cup holders as well. Such is life.

In fairness it would have been suicide for Celtic to play for the required draw as well as being completely alien to their philosophy, as franked way back in 1888, of being an all-out attacking force of nature. On this glorious day, to be honest, one of the best in that long line of championships that would now number eight, *The Persuaders* came to the fore with Kenny D sandwiching a goal in between two choice finishes from who else . . . the Dixmaster!

When it came to getting results against Hibernian, Celtic would simply roll out the barrel that was Dixie Deans. A handsome 3-0 score-line . . . an eighth championship on the trot and won by the slimmest margin of one point as Rangers had East Fife for breakfast . . . one couldn't help thinking back to that day in Methil and an episode of *Some Manager's Do 'Ave 'Em* when a tale of three missed penalties was rescued by Dixie's last minute equaliser.

Celtic had turned the cigarette paper that had separated them from Rangers for so long into a cigar and they were now puffing on it as champions of Scotland. There was even the chance of a double with the upcoming Scottish Cup Final which was to be held the following week at Hampden against Rangers. What, no Hibs you ask?

Well, certainly it was strange for the Celts to be in a cup final and not looking out at a Hibernian side given that the last three finals they had contested was against the Easter Road team. Rangers had put paid to that with a fourth round win against them after a replay. Celtic themselves required a second bite at the semi-final cherry to get beyond a stubborn Dundee. This was little wonder really given that it was the *seventh* time the sides had got together due to League, League Cup and Scottish Cup commitments.

Both teams knew the other so well that each player could probably tell you the colour of his immediate opponent's eyes. In certain parts of the country, well okay then, the Shetland Isles, meeting up with someone seven times over the course of half a year was grounds for an engagement to be announced. Relax. Celtic weren't that sweet on Dundee, even if former be-hooped hero Tommy Gemmell was now on the Dens Park payroll.

Tam the Swashbuckler had returned to Scotland after a fourteen month hiatus at Nottingham Forest to whom Celtic had sold him.

The Blue Bonnets seemed to be so stuck on Celtic that they held out for that Shetland proposal right up until extra-time at Hampden, at which point they were swatted down like the unfit fiancée-elect of a crofter's daughter by three goals to nil. Rangers had the less awkward task of pushing past Ayr United to set up the fourth derby-day Scottish Cup Final in seven years.

As ever, nothing stirs the passions more than a Scottish Cup Final between Celtic and Rangers and, given the tightness of the championship finish, a belter was expected. There was a lot at stake. For the Bhoys there was the chance to maintain Jock Stein's outstanding record of at least two trophies for every full season he'd been in the Celtic Park dugout. For the men from Govan there was only the avoidance of the abyss that was a trophy-less season in this, their centenary year.

It was of little surprise then that Rangers came out of the traps like the whippets at Shawfield Stadium. Celtic remained calm and attempted to play their usual game based on quick movement and visionary passing. Such a move brought the first goal of the match when Kenny D latched onto a Dixmaster pass and put the ball beyond the Lighthouse in the Rangers goal.

You can say what you like about King Kenny, but nobody ever looked as pleased as he did about sticking the ball in the onion bag. He had the sort of teeth that only The Osmonds appeared to have a franchise on; a smile on his face that Picasso would have struggled to capture. Not that he could know, of course, as old Pablo had pegged out less than a month before the final. But as he stood there, hands clapping above his head and his grin out-powering the National Grid, Kenny D's joy was overwhelming.

Sadly, it was a tad premature as Derek Parlane soon equalised for Rangers and there was more drama when Alfie Conn, yet again, burst beyond a Celtic defence early in the second half to put his team 2-1 ahead. When I say early, I mean *early*.

We're talking from the kick-off here when Conn took off as though he had turned up at a Celtic supporters dance wearing a Rangers top by mistake and before Cesar and Co. could shout *What's It's All About Alfie*, the ball was in the back of the net.

The Celts didn't hang about right enough and were correctly awarded a penalty less than ten minutes later when John Greig outdid the Lighthouse by handling a Dixmaster shot off the goal-line. *Great! A penalty! Naw, haud on it's Celtic we're talkin' about here! Shit! A penalty!* Inter-Milan – East Fife – Airdrieonians anyone? The litany of spot-kick failures came haring back into the Celtic support's thoughts. After all that who the hell would want to take the kick anyway?

George Connelly was the Football Writers' Player of the Year and he had truly emerged as one of Big Jock's leading protégés. Big Geordie had it all. He could tackle, see a pass from Mars and had the talent to become a very big name in world terms let alone just his native Scotland. He was also, of course, Fredo Corleone, and still retained that humility and shyness that in far too short a time would condemn his top-flight football career to a premature end.

Not that the 122,000 plus audience at Hampden would have guessed as the soft-spoken Fifer picked his spot, ran towards the goal backing onto the Rangers end with 50,000 people screaming at him to fail and smashed the ball past you-know-who on the Govan goal-line.

At 2-2 it was now anybody's cup and the play was as passionate and as furious as any Glasgow derby since 1888. Jinky thought he had put the Celts ahead with a run-through on goal from the right and a clinical finish only for referee JRP Gordon to rule it offside. It would surely now take a memorable goal to bring the curtain down on this entertainment. Well . . . quite.

If you mean memorable in the way that Charlie Chaplin slipped on a banana skin or Devon Loch crumpled to a heap allowing ESB to overtake him fifty yards from the Grand National finishing line or even Little Jimmy Osmond's chubby, this-jumpsuit's-too-tight-for-a-boy-my-size number one routine, then you'd be right. Critical to this winning goal was an injury to Jim Brogan that meant he was replaced by Bobby Lennox just as Celtic were being asked to defend a free-kick.

As the ball was floated in, Derek Johnstone did his usual thing against Celtic in a cup final and put a pinpoint header beyond the 'keeper, in this case, Ally Hunter. It looked like a goal but it struck the inside of the right-hand post and trickled back along the goal-line and twenty-two footballers and 122, 000 people held their breath – apart from one man. Tom Forsyth had been lurking at the back post unmarked as this was Jim Brogan's beat and he was off the park. All that was required was that he got something on the ball and forced it over the line. *Anything* on it! Yet, Forsyth did his level best to miss the chance by slipping, stumbling and flopping onto the ball like *he* was Devon Loch. Somehow, the ball squeezed into the corner of the net and Celtic were 3-2 down.

There were still thirty minutes to play right enough but, try as they might, the scoring was over and the Celts were forced to accept that it wasn't to be their day. Thus it was that the Govan contingent were to be found *Dancing On A Saturday Night* whilst we were left with a case of the Barry Blues!

The Celtic Park trophy room had a lopsided look to it with only one prize from the season on display; but, in domestic terms, it was the big one and it meant that Celtic were still the Champions of Scotland and could now use the phrase *eight-in-a-row* freely in public. It would be two years before John Lennon would have his Number 9 dream but for the Celtic support, thoughts were turning towards it in the close season of 1973.

1973-1974

6Baggin'Dixie9Winnin'

Track List:

Suzie Quatro/Can The Can; David Bowie/Life On Mars; Elton John/ Saturday Night's Alright For Fightin'; The Faces/Pool Hall Richard; Paul McCartney & Wings/Live and Let Die; Slade/Merry Christmas Everybody; Paper Lace/Billy Don't Be A Hero; Mud/Tiger Feet; Alvin Stardust/Jealous Mind; Rubettes/Sugar Baby Love; Abba/Waterloo

The Scottish Football League, aka *The High Heid Yins,* have had many detractors throughout the years and the supersonic 1970s were no different. After all, this august body conceived of that pinnacle of pre-season curtain-raising, the Drybrough bloody Cup. Someone, somewhere in the SFL decided that the tournament would be a harbinger of attacking football that would encourage goal-scoring and experimentation.

No-one in the corridors of power could relate to the irony that inviting Celtic to a tourney to promote offensive football was a bit like asking Liberace if he fancied playing the piano. The Celts and the flamboyant Vegas showman did both as an instinct, founded on their natural bent.

However, at the start of season 1973-74, the boffins in the SFL laboratory came up with a new variation on the Frankenstein theme when they decided to cancel the offside rule for the duration of this particular competition. This arbitrary decision was fraught with drawbacks. If there was no offside, what could we all argue about after a match? How was it to be enforced? Has that eighteen-yard line been extended to the touchline because the groundsman's been on the drink? What was the point of going to the match if you didn't get at least half a dozen chances to jump up and down, your cheeks crimson with fury, and bellow at the top of your voice *Offffffsiddddde Reffffffff!!!!????*

Explaining the vagaries of the offside rule to women had been like women explaining the celebration of a half-price shoe sale to men . . . they'll never understand it but they accept that it happens. And now the SFL had taken that talking point away. Apparently, that daft touchline-pointing white line constituted the area in which a player could not be offside. *Whatever?*

Anyway, suffice to say that a free-flowing Celtic outfit that had already slain Dunfermline Athletic and Dundee 6-1 and 4-0 respectively, were made to go to extra-time against Hibernian in the final . . . and lost 1-0.

No amount of PR could put a spin on the referee holding up the Hibs hand at the end of the game and proclaiming: *The winners and* still *the Drybrough Cup Champions of the World – Hibernian FC!* The SFL, of course, could boast about the high attendance figures, especially for the final when close to 50,000 people made their way to the national stadium. It still felt like a bit of a dummy run, though. *Opium for the masses* as Marx would have said before the real battles commenced.

For all the pointed fingers though, the one thing the Scottish Football League had never been accused of before was having a sense of humour. An impish delight in pricking the pomposity of member clubs and their directors never seemed to be on their agenda but one can only speculate on the mood at Shawfield Stadium for the recently promoted Clyde when they were handed the fixtures list for their return to the big time of the First Division.

Oh, how the Bully Wee must have laughed at the realisation that that it fell to them to be present at Celtic Park on the day that the champions celebrated the *eight-in-a-row* high point from the previous season. This is Clyde remember, whose last six fixtures against the Celts had read as follows: played six; lost six; goals for five; goals against thirty four.

When they came up against Celtic, Clyde's defence developed more cracks than Barbara Cartland's make-up and were left as breathless and panting as one of her bodice-ripped young goddesses. To add spice to the get-together, Celtic had been made to wait a week for the party as their first game of the new league season was a tight 3-2 win away to Dunfermline Athletic, who were also given a baptism of fire on *their* return to the First Division.

Not that the Pars had made it easy for the visitors as the Celts' three goals came from Harry Harry, the relatively new addition to the side and another product of the Quality Street Kids, Paul Wilson, and an ignominious winning own-goal from Jim Leishman. It's doubtful if Big Leish, eventually to become Poet Laureate of Lochgelly, composed a suitable post-match verse to commemorate the occasion!

So, Celtic were ready to party when the Bully Wee made the short but often painful visit to the East End the following week. For the event, the Bhoys were given special dispensation to wear the number '8' on their shorts whilst Clyde sportingly formed a guard of honour and applauded the reigning champions out onto the park. In return, the Celts offered their own form of sportsmanship by easing up against traditional victims. This time the score was only 5-0!

It could be argued, though, that there was a certain element of disrespect shown by the hosts towards their guests when the name Danny McGrain appeared on the score sheet. The Celtic full-back scored goals the way that Don McLean had number one hits. It did happen but there were long gaps in-between so to witness a McGrain net-bulger in person was a story to dine out on for years. Halley's Comet was a more frequent event.

From the surprise of that intervention came the predictable

headed goal for Jimmy Johnstone against Rangers and it was to prove the winner in the first derby match of the season. Jinky's bonce had become a lethal weapon when it came to the showdowns with the Govan select. If the wee fella had raided Slade's costume basket and made off with Noddy Holder's trademark mirrored top hat it would still be doubtful if the Rangers back four could have picked him out in the box as he stooped to conquer. So far, so Celtic; but behind the green curtain, all was not as it seemed.

David Hay was not a happy man and the *Quiet Assassin* had dropped the veil of silence when it came to negotiating with Jock Stein about the terms of his contract. Typical of the superb player that he was, Hay could play anywhere on the pitch and his career had seen him fill in as a right-back, midfielder and, on the odd occasion, as a centre-half. There seemed to be little beyond this Superman of his times, but even he was not immune to injury and he had endured a period or two of enforced layoff. It was then that he noticed the flaw in the Celtic Park pay structure. This was a system built upon a basic wage with a healthily generous bonus kick-in for winning matches and trophies. In brief, if you weren't playing for whatever reason – be it injury, stress, bereavement or the mother-in-law's annual visit – then you were not a party to the big mullah.

Big Jock had grown up in the environment of the pits when the bonus was that you came out of a mine alive and returned to work the next day. Beneath the earth, there was a genuine catastrophe waiting to happen with every disruption of the coal-face and whilst the atmosphere at some Celtic-Rangers collisions would often be described as gaseous, no-one ever had to send a canary out before kick-off to make sure the air wasn't poisoned (literally poisoned that is, as opposed to the ribald hullabaloo between rival supporters!).

In short, it would be fair to say that, for all their stresses and trials, Jock Stein considered the lot of the late Twentieth Century Bhoy to be a particularly comfortable one. However, there was a new independence in the wind and the modern player was more aware of his value than ever. It might still be more than thirty years before Ashley Cole, a player not fit to polish David Hay's boots, would almost crash his car at Arsenal's *derisory* offer of a mere £50,000 a week to keep him in moisturiser, but in the 1970s, top footballers were beginning to understand that their career was a short one and that financial remuneration was a *cause celebre.*

Unfortunately, the knock-on effect of a discontented David Hay was that his great friend George Connelly was equally less than enamoured with life in Paradise. Cool George was the Euro-night keepy-uppy King, the man who had faced down 50,000 Rangers supporters and the Lighthouse to draw Celtic back to level terms at Hampden *and* a worthy recipient of the Player of the Year award in Scotland for 1973. Nobody laughed when the expression the *Scottish Beckenbauer* was employed to describe his style, but he was struggling sadly with some demons of his own.

With talent, comes expectation; with expectation, comes pressure; and with pressure, comes even more pressure. Big Geordie was toiling to cope. The Master wasn't entirely unsympathetic to the plight of both players but his loyalty to a different era of footballers who were more compliant to his wishes was going to be a hard obstacle to overcome.

The 1970s were a new age complete with fridge-freezers, G-Plan kitchens, hanging basket chairs, chirping telephones, foppish velvet flares, kipper ties and swirly-patterned shirts. Modern footballers cut the ribbon at new boutiques, met architects to discuss dining room extensions, sported furry dice in their Ford Capris and sometimes gave of themselves over ninety minutes on a Saturday. Jock Stein wasn't about to sport a pair of wide-leg Birmingham Bags for anybody's amusement, was presumably happy with the size of his dining room and probably thought that dice were for snakes 'n' ladders.

In the autumn of 1973 an impasse was reached when Hay refused to sign a new contract and asked for a transfer. Tottenham Hotspur immediately got in touch and tabled a bid of around £225,000 for the *want-away star* as the tabloids were calling him. It appeared that Hay *did* want to stay but Celtic's refusal to meet his financial requests left the player with two choices . . . leave the Celts or withdraw his labour until his future could be sorted out. Labour withdrawal, of course, was the flavour of the day as Ted Heath was finding out.

Like Big Jock, he was presiding over an era when industrial disputes were rife and when every working man and woman seemed to own a copy of The Strawbs springtime hit, *Part Of The Union.* In the cinemas, *The Sting* happened to be doing great box office around the country. The story, set in 1930s America when two shrewd operators attempted to get one over on a fearsome boss-man by reeling him into a set-up, struck a nerve with audiences everywhere.

Doyle Lonnegan was the boss in question. He was a big man in every sense of the word – feared, respected, feted wherever he went, the six-footer plus portrayed by Robert Shaw would generally outsmart his opponents, intimidate officials by his mere presence and reputation and was generally perceived as *the law* in his neck of the woods. Recognise anyone from that? Hell, he even hirpled with a limp. Jock Corleone in New York had been re-incarnated as Doyle Lonnegan of Chicago.

For their part, Henry Shaw Gandorff was a razor sharp operator who had chased the big break all his life with an intelligence and natural ability as a string-puller whilst Johnny Kelly Hooker was an eager-to-learn student who would do anything to support Gandorff. His only worry was that he would betray his teacher to *the feds* at the end of the caper.

Had the scriptwriters of *The Sting* arrived in Glasgow in late 1973 and picked up a newspaper, they may just have observed the eerie parallels between their characters and the performance being played out on Kerrydale Street. David Hay attempted to reel in Big Jock by refusing to attend training or make himself available for selection whilst Geordie also decided that he would walk out in support of his pal and in the hope of negotiating a new deal for himself as well. Doyle Lonnegan could have learned a great deal from Jock Stein who had one of the best poker faces in the business.

A détente of sorts was reached between the warring factions, initially Hay and Stein, as the midfielder returned to the fold, put his talents on display and pledged to work hard until the end of the season when the hard money talk could commence once more. George Connelly also rejoined the Players' Lounge but the reality was that the dispute was just being put on ice . . . and by the following summer that ice had melted.

To be fair to David Hay, no-one could ever accuse him of operating on a half-hearted basis and he returned in time to be a part of one of Celtic's best performances of the season when they defeated Rangers 3-1 in the semi-final of the Scottish League Cup. Harry Harry weighed in with a hat-trick, a rarity in derby showdowns, but the talk afterwards was of the craft, endeavour and guile of Davie Gandorff, sorry, Hay.

Of course, the media had anointed this game *the final before the final* but it was difficult to shake the belief that, whoever won this one, would go on to be the Scottish League Cup winners of 1973-74. Even if that meant breaking with Celtic's recent League Cup Final tradition.

It was also the third time that the teams had met on cup business as they were both drawn together in the opening sectional section, if you follow my drift, in August. On realising that they had both been lumped in together with The Big Two, both Arbroath and Falkirk would have been justified in contacting their MP or taking the Scottish League to the United Nations.

The underdogs acquitted themselves well but the carve-up of the table was never in any doubt and both Celtic and Rangers headed off to the next stage leaving the Bairns and the splendidly nicknamed *Red Lichties* free to live a life of peace, harmony and spiritual fulfilment.

For the record, Celtic doused Rangers 2-1 at Ibrox when Harry Harry's side foot to put the Celts 2-0 up resulted in some unsavoury scenes behind Ally Hunter's goal and the 'keeper was forced to head to the half-way line for his own safety.

Rangers drew revenge in a controversial match at Celtic Park when, having dominated proceedings and being a goal to the good at half-time, the hosts lost their way in the second half and ended up losing 3-1. The controversy was supplied when referee, JRP Gordon, (1973 Scottish Cup Final; disallowed Jimmy Johnstone goal) dismissed, you guessed it, Jinky, from the field of play after a skirmish with Ibrox midfielder Alex MacDonald and the day was lost to the Celts.

Notable scalps thereafter were Motherwell after a three-game epic when a replay was required to sort out the men from the Bhoys following a two-leg tie and then Aberdeen in the quarter-finals were vanquished courtesy of a 3-2 score-line from the first game at Celtic Park and a 0-0 draw up at Pittodrie. Galling for the Dons fans must have been the form of recent Celtic signing from the Granite City, Stevie Murray, who had slotted in so well as a midfielder that the momentous decision was taken to move the stalwart Bobby Murdoch on to another club.

The sublime Bobby M was one of those players, like Lennox, Johnstone, McNeill, that you felt would be at Celtic Park all of their days. No-one was more surprised than new Middlesbrough gaffer Jackie Charlton when Jock Stein offered him as the link-man to a promising youngster named Souness (cue thunder and lightning) in the 'Boro midfield. Charlton only phoned to enquire if The Master knew of anyone in the Scottish game who was available and who might do a job for him. It was a bit like calling up a caterer for your daughter's twenty-first birthday bash and finding Fanny Craddock standing on your doorstep complete with her pots, pans and the faithful Johnny by her side. The gobsmacked Charlton would have hoped that all his meringues would have turned out like Fanny's after concluding *that* little bit of business.

And thus it was that the famous Lions now numbered three. Murray was an exciting find though who had fitted into the Celtic set-up as though he had been found on a doorstep with a hooped jersey on. It wasn't just his feet that were cultured, however, as he was that most paradoxical of footballers – a well-read one.

Just as Stevie had progressed from being Dundee's youngest ever captain, to being the lynchpin of Eddie Turnbull/Jimmy Bonthrone's Aberdeen side, and now commanding a position anywhere on the park for Celtic, he had also been studying for a maths and science degree on an Open University course. To most footballers, mathematics was as useful as an eleventh toe unless it was being used to calculate the winnings from the 2.30 at Kempton Park. *Science* was something a groundsman required to feed the grass on the pitch. But Stevie was an interesting, erudite individual whose ambitions outside of the professional sporting career were not to have a quarter stake in a racehorse or operate behind the bar of his own pub.

That's not to say that these weren't laudable and indeed, very profitable aspirations, but he wanted to explore the potential of his brain when the football boots were finally cast aside. Twice he turned down international honours because of his student requirements which naturally created a fuss on the back pages of the tabloids, but he was clearly a guy who was faithful to a set of priorities. Inevitably, there were untold requests by the sports photographers for that tired old pose wherein Stevie would be togged up in a football kit, with a scroll in his hand, a graduate gown draped around his shoulders and a mortar board hat upon his head. Weren't there better things to snap in the great game?

Such as Celtic's annual march to another League Cup Final. Confidence was certainly high around the East End after the handsome win against Rangers and the bosom return of the Quiet Assassin and Geordie. The Celts were playing well, their League form to date had been impressive and the mood was optimistic for the famed nine-in-a-row. Nothing, of course, could compare to the events of 17 November when Partick Thistle were made welcome at Celtic Park.

The Jags supporters always lived in hope of repeating that glorious opening thirty-five minutes at Hampden from two years previously that had witnessed Frank Bough snapping at his Grandstand reporters for exact details and now there was the added attraction of seeing one of their own, i.e. a student in the shape of Stevie Murray, doing rather well on the football pitch. If they were lucky, there would perhaps be the chance to discuss course work and compare dissertation notes with the matriculated Murray once the class was out at Celtic Park.

They little realised that on this particular day it would be Dixie *The Dixmaster* Deans who would be delivering the lecture and that the lesson would be on the art of goal-scoring. Roger Moore had graduated from being a Persuader to becoming the new James Bond with the 1973 feature *Live And Let Die* but even he would have been hard put to displace Dixie's lethal firepower as he created a new post-war record by claiming an incredible *six* goals in a 7-0 rout.

There was the added talking point of Bobby Lennox bagging the seventh goal in this game that took him level with Stevie Chalmers's 241 not out as Celtic's second greatest goalscorer after Jimmy McGrory. But it was, as the confederate rebels would say, *A great day for Ol' Dixie!*

Apart from the Jags supporters, there could only have been one man feeling the urge to remove Dixie from the firing line and that *was* James Edward McGrory himself who was present at the match and had to watch as the Deans double hat-trick came perilously close to equalling his 1928 scoring feat of eight in one game.

Still, a post-war record, the toast of the Jungle and Dixie left with the match ball signed by all the players to commemorate the occasion. The Thistle players good-naturedly put their signatures on the ball as well even though they hadn't seen it all day. It did seem to be like asking a condemned man to plug in his own electric chair.

Aye, the dark nights were fair drawing in and now the Heath Government, which instigated the three-day week in the wake of an emergency power shortage, decided that floodlights were a luxury and that football matches would just have to start earlier to avoid their use. It was official: the country had gone from being just in a state to being in a State of Emergency.

One of the upshots of this little piece of helpful Whitehall advice was that the League Cup Final, to be contested between Celtic and Dundee, was to kick-off at 1.30pm on the third Saturday in December.

There were very few shopping days left 'til Christmas, nobody had any money and a transport strike meant that there were no buses or trains to get the clients out to Hampden. In the event, a sparse 27,000 punters turned up to the national stadium that both in weather and atmosphere resembled the set of *Ice-Station Zebra*.

No-one would have been lifted for lighting fires on the terraces to keep warm and, to be frank, one look at the pitch suggested that a mission of mercy for everyone involved, not least the players, would be to call the whole thing off and wait until the spring.

That would have been the sane choice but referee Bobby Davidson displayed as firm a grasp of the situation as Ted Heath did of the growing energy crisis by declaring the pitch playable. As officials from both clubs argued against this festive madness, Davidson pronounced, *Humbug!* and told his linesmen, Jacob

Marley and Bob Cratchitt, to get themselves kitted out for the kick-off.

Once the polar bears had been removed from the field of play and the Eskimos stopped ice-fishing, the penguins led the two chittering teams out onto the frosty Hampden turf. To be fair to Mr Davidson, the pitch did thaw to a degree once the match got underway and we know this because a passing sea-lion poked its head out from the watery depths to see what all the fuss was about. It wasn't the conditions that defeated Celtic, though, so it would be churlish to make that claim.

It was a seventy-fifth minute strike from Gordon Wallace that settled the match and saw former Lion and still Danny Kaye look-a-like, Tam Gemmell, lift the League Cup above his head as captain of the Blue Bonnets. Even Frank Bough had wearied now of reading out Celtic's Scottish League Cup Final results.

In the 1970s, some do-gooder who quite possibly now is in charge of the Health and Safety Department, came up with the idea of making short public information films pointing out the untold dangers to children of crossing the road without due care and attention; or talking to strangers with sweeties and a collection of Labrador puppies yelping delightfully from the back seat of their Vauxhall Vivas; or, a particular favourite, the hidden jeopardy of playing near rivers and burns. That one could only have been directed by someone who had earned his or her stripes on the roster of Hammer Horror Productions.

Picture it – mist wisping across a foreboding stretch of water, the sound of children playing close by throwing sticks and stones into the seemingly peaceful reservoir, an echoing voice imploring the children to come closer to the water's edge and – the coup de grace – a shadowy figure dressed in nothing but the hooded, faceless cloak of the Grim Reaper himself watching on as a child strays close to his drowning fate. Suddenly, there's a violent splash . . . children's screams

. . . a cry for help and the Grim Reaper moves in for his prey as his cloak lies floating on top of the watery grave!

Bloody Hell! It made me think twice about getting in a bath never mind hanging about the fringes of a death-trap reservoir. Which, I suppose, was always the intention. The do-gooder guru probably hadn't thought about applying the same video to Celtic's recent League Cup Final record but it would surely have fitted.

Mist rolling across a watery Hampden surface – the sound of Celtic players screaming delightedly and passing the ball to one another – the echoing voice of an unseen predator imploring the Bhoys to attack in a 2-3-5 formation, leaving them perilously exposed at the back. Then the sound of hooped screaming as the Grim Reaper appears from nowhere and hands the Scottish League Cup to Rangers, Partick Thistle, Hibernian or, in this case, Dundee.

Alarmingly, Celtic had now lost six out of the last eight Cup Finals in which they had played and no, I'm not including the Drybrough bloody Cup in that lot. Which is probably just as well since they hadn't fared too well on reaching the last hurdle in that one either. Thankfully, they still had their nine-in-a-row ambitions to draw water from and the omens remained good in that department.

The Bhoys rounded off the year with two six-goal hidings of Falkirk then Dunfermline Athletic. It goes without saying that Dixie was among the goals on those occasions, picking up four against the Bairns and, by his high standards, a paltry two on the occasion of the Pars coming to Glasgow. It wasn't just Noddy Holder who was screaming *Merry Christmas!* to everybody, although he and the Dixmaster did appear to share the same Edwardian taste in side-levers.

Not for the first time in his career, Bobby Lennox was the name on all the tongues into the New Year period. *Lemon,* as he was known, had of course by now surpassed the guy who scored the most important goal in Celtic history, Stevie 'Quicksilver' Chalmers'

241 goals mark for the club. This left him out in front, as the speedy forward tended to be, of all the other great Celtic goal-baggers save the mighty McGrory. Given that he had only turned thirty and looked after himself like a thoroughbred racehorse, he no doubt fancied himself to add a few more to his collection.

Bobby was the *foreigner* in the Lisbon Lions set-up in so far as he was the Celt who had been born furthest away from Celtic Park. That is to say Saltcoats on the Ayrshire coast. It was hardly France but combined with the birthplaces of the rest of the 1967 team, it stretched the radius of the Lisbon circle.

He was a highly skilled player with a penchant for hitting the back of the net. Had he been born with four legs instead of two, then Big Jock would surely have entered Lemon for the St Leger. His pace was explosive; an acknowledged asset that typically left defenders for dead as he closed in on the eighteen-yard box with a trail of fire scorching at his heels.

Sometimes, he could be *too* fast and referees and linesmen could be fooled into thinking that Lemon was offside. He would go on to score just short of 350 goals for the Celts but had he played in an era when technology made match officials a tad more conscientious about raising their flags in haste, then it's possible that he could have homed in closer to the 400-goal mark.

Certainly he was the vital difference between Celtic and Rangers in the New Year fixture down Kerrydale Street when a 1-0 victory gave the Bhoys a League double over the Govan select and rendered redundant Rangers' 1974 NY resolution to fight for the title to the bitter end.

Lemon had also been on target a few days before when Celtic bowed to the season of goodwill by dusting off Clyde by two goals to nil. He and Kenny D shared the spoils in a result that, presumably, had the Bully Wee promoting their defence for the New Year's Honours List. It all seemed to be going right to schedule until February when, in the space of eight days, Celtic's plans for domination suddenly looked as fragile as Ted Heath's three-day-week solution.

First up was the trek into deepest, darkest Lanarkshire. Fir Park wasn't exactly Transylvania but the tenants Motherwell managed to give Celtic a fright of which Dracula would have been proud. And yet, at one point, it had all seemed so easy as Lemon and the increasingly impressive Stevie the Student Prince Murray had the Celts 2-0 ahead and cruising like a Ford Capri. It was then that the 'Well stormed back to castrate the furry dice hanging from the Celtic mirror by scoring three goals and running out overall winners.

Sunday week then saw Celtic entertaining Dundee in their first ever day-of-rest League fixture. Nowadays, Sunday is pretty much like any other day when you can do a full week's shopping, work overtime, grab a pub lunch or stay down the boozer all day and digest the satellite footy but, in 1974 AD, these pleasures were as rare as a microwave in your kitchen.

The move to Sunday football was a necessary, if controversial one. Necessary because Uncle Ted's restructured week ensured that Saturday became a working day and, therefore, affected football attendance; and controversial because, to some, the Sabbath was sacrosanct. Sunday activities such as reading a newspaper, travelling by land, sea or air, working a shift, hell, talking to the wife, was considered to be as craven as going for a pint with the devil. To that mindset, the Sabbath was for sitting on a spiked chair with a hair shirt on and contemplating the sins of the previous six days.

Admittedly, there weren't any protests outside the ground before the match; well, there hardly could be, the religious fundamentalists weren't allowed out of the house on a Sunday, let alone permitted to voice disapproval at the turn of events, but the move was denounced from the pulpit.

Perhaps Cliff Richard released a song about it but, for the

record, Dundee were the first football team to play Celtic in a league match on a Sunday when they showed up on 10 February.

However, as it turned out, it wasn't only the religious mafia who were wont to disapprove of events as Celtic proceeded to go down 2-1 in front of their own highly partisan crowd who loudly voiced their disapproval.

Two defeats on the trot and next up were Hibernian at Easter Road, a difficult fixture at the best of times but fraught with considerably more danger given that the Edinburgh greens were emerging as Celtic's closest challengers in the absence of Rangers who seemed to have suffered a psychological reaction to losing the New Year hoedown.

By this time, the country was in the throes of a General Election campaign. Prior to the Dundee game, Ted Heath decided that it was *put up or shut up* time with the miners and thus set up a platform for the British people to decide who they preferred running the country. 28 February was the selected day and the curfew on television that had resulted in a complete channel shutdown at 10.30pm because of the power crisis, was waived in order to promote the political hustings. When I say complete channel shutdown, I mean a shutdown of the only three channels that we had available at the time – Beebs 1 & 2 and ITV. The good news was that the footy highlights would be on again on a Saturday night whilst the bad news was that *Late Call* was restored to the STV schedules.

Late Call did seem to be in breach of the Trades Description Act in that it never really went out that *late*, i.e., after the half-hour Ten O'clock News which even I and my ten-year-old friends hardly characterised as the dead of night and wasn't really a *call* as such but more of a monologue from some worthy yet long-winded clergyman. From a handsomely buffed leather armchair he (it tended always to be a *he*; in 1970s Scotland, women in the church brewed tea, re-arranged flowers and organised jumble sales but weren't really asked to voice opinion on matters religious) would always try to equate the word of God and the miracles of Jesus with the minutiae of Scottish life.

There were five-minute discourses on loaves and fish, raising the dead and how we should meditate on these events as we did our shopping in Galbraith's on the High Street. After the sermon, the camera would pull back, some creepy music would fill the room and the lights would fade to leave the clergyman resting in a silhouette reminiscent of a Bond villain. Not a particularly easy vision to take to bed with you although still preferable to a Party Political Broadcast, which was now the norm.

Before the leadership of the country could be decided, however, there was the small concern of who ruled the Scottish First Division? In truth, were Celtic to lose at Easter Road they would still be at the top of the pile but only by a single point, whereas victory would place them five ahead of Hibernian with the moniker *champions-elect* dangling from their necks. A four-pointer made this essential viewing for the close-on 50,000 who advanced on Easter Road to watch the reigning champions take on the holders of ehhhh . . . the Drybrough Cup. Titter ye not though, the Hibees were a powerful force to behold and had deservedly carved themselves out as potential title-winners. A win would be vital for either side.

As the team sheets were swapped between dressing rooms, Big Jock would have noticed the strength of the Hibs line-up that included names like Arthur Duncan, Alex Edwards and the sublime Stanton but, although Hibs boss Eddie Turnbull would see Celtic coming out with Cesar at the back, Danny McGrain pushing on from defence and Stevie Student and Kenny D motoring in the midfield, the Hibs gaffer might have been a little bit worried that, to his players, the Celtic line-up actually read . . . *Deans, Deans, Deans, Deans, Deans, Deans & Deans, Deans, Deans, Deans & Deans.*

Once again the Dixmaster was to play his Dirty Harry role against the Edinburgh greens and confirmed his taste for the sight of the Hibernian goal by popping up and putting the Celts ahead 1-0 in the very first minute. It was a superb opening to the game from the Glasgow perspective, the overture to a great ninety minutes. The outcome never seemed certain until Celtic made the score 4-2 in the closing moments.

Kenny D and Paul Wilson grabbed the Celts' second and third goals but, as if to remind Hibs that he was still on their trail, the Dixmaster notched that decisive fourth to seal the points. Dixie's personal vendetta against the men from Easter Road seemed almost selfish but when he faced the Hibs it was, to parody a popular advert of the day, *Deanz Meanz Minez!*

Armed with a five point advantage that provided breathing space, the Hoops were duly installed as out and out title favourites. Not for them the ignominy of trying to rule with a patched-up partnership that was now the preserve of Uncle Ted after Labour emerged from that 28 February showdown with marginally more seats than the Conservatives. Heath despised the Liberals almost as much as he did Labour but he had enjoyed his brush with the Number One job in Number Ten to such an extent that he was now willing to send flowers, chocolates and general fondness towards *Libs* leader Jeremy Thorpe in an effort to stay at the head of the table in a coalition government.

Hey Jer . . . we've soooo much more in common than I ever thought! Waddaya say we run this damned country between us with you in my cabinet as . . . eh . . . eh . . . advisor on really important stuff like . . . eh . . . eh . . . what time we should be taking our tea-breaks and should we choose Blue Ribands over p-p-p-picking up a Penguin? Eh? How about it Thorpey baby?

It was all to no avail and Harold Wilson was summoned by Her Majesty and asked to sort out the mess. He was installed as Prime Minister on 6 March. This was precisely four days before I made my Celtic debut. Sort of.

I don't, of course, mean that Big Jock sidled up to me after training that week and said: *It's Motherwell in the Cup on Sunday and you're in the team.* Hell, no. I was still in Primary Five but 10 March 1974 was the first time that I ever attended a game at Celtic Park. Offer me some latitude here as I give our '70s opus a certain personal note.

I'd been badgering the folks for a long time to let me travel to Glasgow for a game. Up until then, finding out the Celtic score had seen me hiding behind the settee as the less-than high-tech *teleprinter* chattered out the scores on Grandstand and staying there until the conclusion of Beau Brummel lookalike Jon Pertwee's outing as Doctor Who.

Radio Clyde 261 had just been launched in 1973 and its Scoreboard feature on a Saturday was a live feed of the goals *as they happened* but the reception could be as fuzzy as Jon Pertwee's hair and there were often moments of real horror when, through oceans of static and hissing, you could hear an announcer say: A*nd up at Dens Park Dundee it's finished Dundee 1, Celtic crackle crackle crackle* . . . and the Hoops score line would be lost in the radio-wave ether.

Such was my experience of the Celtic ritual. How I longed to stand on the terracing in Paradise and watch the Bhoys in action, *live!* with their magnificent green and white shirts bearing down on the opposition. Fortunately, Celtic's unique Scottish Cup run that season had the Hoops playing all of their cup-ties on a Sunday which was a day on which I could be escorted to a game by one of my Hoops-minded uncles.

Before that day-of-rest League game against Dundee, Celtic had actually opened their Sunday account by beating Clydebank 6-1 in the third round of the Scottish Cup. They followed this up with the self-same score when confronted by Stirling Albion. By the time they were due to face Motherwell in the quarter-final, the Sunday fixture had become established and I was allowed to visit Celtic Park courtesy of Uncle Ted Heath and his decision to introduce the three-day-week. It's ironic that Heath had been removed from power by the time that I made my debut.

To my mortification, the folks had me trussed up in my Sunday-best coat which was a leather-looking but actually plastic affair with an irritating faux-fur collar and was a ribald burgundy colour in hue. I had dreamt of taking my Paradise bow in the gear of the day, such as a denim jacket, platform shoes and a pair of flares with matching tank-top. I didn't expect to look like I was just up from Harrow for the mid-term hols and that I was being allowed by mater and pater to take in a sporting occasion!

I took my position round at the Celtic end amidst the faithful with my red cheeks matching the burgundy of my Sunday-best and drank in my first look at Paradise. I'm fairly certain that the denizens around me half-expected me to be in the dug-out given that I was almost certainly wearing the classic overcoat of a 1970s manager. Hell, even the players must have looked up from the pitch during the warm-up, seen this burgundy nightmare and wondered if I was about to give the team-talk.

Not that I would have been much use at that as I found out later on when I attempted to pass knowing comment to my uncle about the state of the team by announcing that, *Ally Hunter in goal looks particularly off his game. Not surprising really,* he replied sagely, *it's Denis Connaghan.*

There was little doubt about the outcome right enough as Celtic fought back twice to level the game at 2-2 and instigate a replay three days later out at Fir Park. Harry Harry was the Celtic double saviour that Sunday but it was the wheezy waves of Clyde 261 that informed me that the Dixmaster had put his former club to the sword on the Wednesday night as Celtic progressed to the semi-finals by 1-0.

By that point, I could call myself a fully-fledged Celtic supporter as I had now attended a game but I had the *Jealous Mind* that leather-clad Alvin Stardust was crooning about at the thought of all those other lucky sods who considered following the Celtic as a weekly outing. With cup progress secured and the League trophy looking increasingly like it would not be moved from a seemingly permanent resting place on the Celtic Park sideboard, it was time to turn our attention to matters European.

The Hoops' progress had been a mix of classic Celtic punishment of an inferior opponent, Turku of Finland, by a Clyde-like aggregate of 9-1 and then a nervy 1-0 away victory in Denmark when Lemon had picked out the only goal of the 180 minutes that Celtic endured against Danish Champions, Vejle. Basle of Switzerland more than surprised the Scottish Press by beating the Celts 3-2 in the first-leg of the quarter-final tie out in ski-land and they were to prove tenacious fighters when they arrived in Glasgow as well. Big Jock was struggling with his goalkeeping options with Alastair Hunter out injured and Evan Williams coming in from the cold to be reinstated for that first match in Switzerland.

Poor Evan the Goal had a torrid experience, however, and Denis Connaghan was the last line of defence when Part Two rolled around in Glasgow. Naturally, for the European fare, a crowd of more than 70,000 turned up at Celtic Park on the night and were stunned when Geordie Connelly was removed from the action early on with a broken ankle to be replaced by Pat McCluskey. That shock was as nothing compared to the fact that, after fifty six minutes, Celtic found themselves 3-2 ahead yet tied at 5-5 on aggregate.

When Kenny D put Celtic 1-0 up on the night and then the Dixmaster put them ahead on aggregate, all within the first fifteen minutes, it looked as if this was another routine Continental victory, but the *Toblerones* had somehow clawed their way back into the fray by scoring twice before half-time. The under-rated Tommy Tid Callaghan edged that 3-2 goal by the fifty sixth minute but the scoring was over for the regulation ninety. Extra-time was required.

This scenario hadn't really been in the script when Basle were drawn out of the hat against Celtic, given the perception that the Swiss were possibly the weakest side left in the tournament but by now the punters at Celtic Park were as nervous as Rock Hudson on his wedding night. It took a neat looping header from Stevie Murray to defuse the situation as the Student Prince weighed up the complexities of calculus and scientific theory to arc a header over the Basle 'keeper and record an absolute mathematical fact – Celtic were 6-5 ahead on aggregate.

By now the brave Swiss were a busted flush and the Celts held on to the finish. It had been a breathtaking 210 minutes of tit-for-tat football but Celtic had survived their . . . *brush with Basle!* (Forgive me!)

The semi-finals now loomed in the shape of a team from Madrid but not Real of that manor, rather their less illustrious rivals, Athletico. Of the Spaniards, not much was known but infamy had long been attached to coach Juan Carlos Lorenzo, an Argentine national.

JCL had been in charge of his nation's interests back in 1966 when Alf Ramsey, a man so mild-mannered that he would have made Mother Theresa look like a street-fighter, had branded the Argentinians as *animals* following a notorious quarter-final dust-up against his England side. And when he was the coach at Lazio in Rome, Lorenzo had allegedly picked up Arsenal manager Bertie Mee by his suit lapels after a war-like scrap with the Gunners. Bertie, in fairness, would have snuck quite easily into Big Jock's pockets given his limited stature and it seemed highly unlikely that JCL would be attempting to hoist the Empire State that was Stein up by his buttonholes. But, the warning was clear for all to see. Lorenzo gotta have it . . . and he didn't care just how it came about.

What followed then was, without question, one of the most diabolically thuggish ninety minutes of football ever witnessed at

Celtic Park. I say *football* but sightings of the beautiful game were as rare as Elton John's hair as Athletico decided to adopt a policy of wearing knuckle-dusters and pretty much hitting anything that came their way in a green and white shirt.

In particular, Jimmy Johnstone was targeted as the number one threat. This was nothing new and many, many full-backs had tried over the years to subdue the wee man's influence but perhaps they hadn't thought of the Athletico method which was essentially to try to decapitate Jinky whenever he advanced more than five yards with the ball at his feet. The tackles weren't mistimed. In fact, quite the opposite as their accuracy was as coordinated and as lethal as a military ambush. Jimmy Johnstone was more battered than a white pudding supper whilst his body colour changed to black-and-blue.

In the midst of such a battle, the importance of the referee cannot be overstated although it would have taken Clint Eastwood to sort out the brutality of the Spaniards. Frankly, there was less violence in a Spaghetti Western. In the event, the Turkish whistler Degan Babacan did appear to have the courage of his convictions when he dismissed three Athletico butchers, namely Ayala, Quique and the ruthless Diaz.

The last-named was on his second trip to Glasgow as he had formed part of another notorious pack of football gangsters who had graced the turf in 1967 disguised as an Argentinian football team called Racing Club when the Celts, then reigning European Champions, had contested the World Club Championship. The encounter had entailed a three-leg tie from which Celtic had emerged as losers but Diaz and the gauchos had dragged both the game and the integrity of the Inter-Continental Championship into the mud of the pampas and the Bhoys, being only human, had responded in kind to the tag-team wrestling tactics that Racing employed. And now, old Diaz was back in town, meting out his hoodlum tactics on a succession of Celtic players.

Celtic actually had a goal disallowed but a game that was as controversial as Richard Nixon's presidency ended at 0-0 and the Athletico players danced about like Pans People on Top Of The Pops. *Now then, now then . . . howz about that then,* as Jimmy Saville would have intoned on the weekly poptastic rundown.

It seemed only natural that, after such a pummelling and with supreme disenchantment at the Spanish performance being keenly felt by both the crowd and the Celtic players, a post-match incident would take place. And it did.

Eusebio, not the Portugese legend please note, but an inferior Athletico hooligan, decided that he hadn't had his piece of Jinky and decided on a novel take on the traditional end-of-match shirt-swapping ceremony by punching Jinky to the ground. He didn't hang around either to rifle the wee man's pockets but the incident combusted into a free-for-all that wouldn't have looked out of place in a John Ford saloon-bar brawl.

How immensely satisfying it must have been for The Dixmaster and his accomplice Davie, The Quiet Assassin, to meet up with one of the Athletico neds in the Celtic Park tunnel and, allegedly with the aid and approval of a Glasgow beat cop, administer some form of retribution. The following day Athletico Madrid were as popular around the football world as a bout of herpes and the whole episode had acquired the mantle of a Quinn Martin production.

Quinn Martin? American television production company that specialised in one hour cop dramas. They were responsible for *The Streets Of San Francisco*, *Barnaby Jones* and, a personal favourite, *Cannon.* William Conrad played Frank Cannon, an ex-cop turned detective. We can only assume that FC was pushed from the streets by his uniformed superiors on account of his failure to pass a fitness test. His girth was akin to Orson Welles and he frequently employed his weight advantage whenever his gun failed him against the bad guys. Indeed, Frank Cannon and his stomach almost edges into the double act format.

The opening titles were a bit of a melodrama in themselves. Quinn Martin employed a voiceover artist who sounded as if he'd trod the boards for the Californian Shakespeare Company and could make the most trivial announcement resonate like the Rights of Man. When his Brechtian tones would announce episodes such as – *Honeymoon With Death, Nest Of Scorpions* or *Death Is The Punchline* – it was difficult to take the whole thing seriously, that is as seriously as Quinn Martin would like you to.

You could spot something from the QM stable as soon as the booming theme opened the show but, just in case you doubted the veracity of your senses, Mr Brecht would put all your fears to rest by uttering dramatically *a Quinn Martin Production;* immediately after the title. Oh how the boys over at QM would have delighted in the Athletico Madrid saga in their new co-British production – *STEIN!*

A two-parter filled with red-blooded heroes (Celtic), swarthy Latino villains (Athletico), a damsel in distress (the European Cup), a principled leading man dripping with integrity (Big Jock) and that undercurrent of corrupt politics (Lorenzo). *STEIN! . . . A Quinn Martin Production . . . starring Jock Stein. Tonight's Episode – SPANIARD OF EVIL!*

The only obligatory that would sadly be missing from tonight's episode would have been a happy ending. There was talk that Celtic had wrestled with the idea of not playing the second leg at all but, in the end, the decision was taken to carry on with the tie. The Bhoys arrived in General Franco's Madrid about as welcome as the International Brigade from nearly forty years before.

UEFA, the body responsible for the European tourney, had responded to the naked violence of the first leg Spaniards by banning six of their players from the return fixture but, as it turned out, they were all second-picks anyway as Madrid had fielded a side capable only of inflicting mutilation upon the Celtic machine, saving their top players for the home tie. Somehow, the Athletico PR machine had cast the Bhoys as the Quinn Martin villain so the only guarantee was for a torrid time. Jimmy Johnstone and Jock Stein were the victims of death threats – the only difference being in Jinky's case that this time the threats were off the park as opposed to on it!

It's unlikely that Celtic will ever kick-off a football match again with the level of hatred that rained down on them from the terracing. Jock and the backroom bhoys were secreted away in a dug-out allegedly safe from the glint of a sniper's rifle, but the JJ Man was dancing around on the park, no doubt in an effort to present a moving target to any would-be Lee Harvey Osvaldo!

Ironically, Athletico proved that they could play a bit and won the game 2-0 but the Celts had created chances and with the teams still deadlocked at half-time, there was always the thought that good would eventually triumph over evil. Perhaps it's just as well that this night was not graced with a glorious Celtic victory because it seems highly unlikely that the team and, indeed, everyone associated with the club would have been allowed a safe passage out of the stadium, let alone Madrid. It was a sorry end to a tawdry tale and when *Y Vive Espana* was unleashed on an unsuspecting, but tasteless, record-buying public by Swedish artist Sylvia later that year, Celtic supporters could only laugh in hollow fashion at the sentiment.

Having just been dumped from the European Cup on the Wednesday night, the good news was that Celtic had the chance to go to Falkirk on the following Saturday and secure their place back in the tournament next season. Nine-in-a-row and all its attendant glory awaited if the Celts could collect one point from the match at Brockville.

Remarkably, not one of the eight previous title-winning days had taken centre stage at Celtic Park. The Hoops always seemed to be on the road when that title-tipping point or two was on the menu. Even when they could have lifted the championship in Paradise back in 1971, ground reconstruction on Kerrydale Street had seen the Bhoys move their home match against Ayr United to Hampden Park. And now they were at Brockville Park and out to equal a domestic record that hitherto had only been achieved by two other teams – MTK Budapest of Hungary (1917-1925) and CDNA Sofia (1954-1962).

The situation had been presented to them just after round one of that tag-team contest with the butchers of Athletico when, on the following Saturday, Celtic had picked themselves up remarkably to win 2-0 at Tannadice against Dundee United whilst Tommy Gemmell and Dundee were beating Rangers at Ibrox and Arbroath were shocking Hibernian at Gayfield. A 6-1 Bayview Park whipping of East Fife and a dogged 2-0 victory at home to Aberdeen meant that Celtic could clinch the title with three games still to play.

The Bairns were fighting relegation that day and needed the two points possibly more than their visitors and therefore made life tough on the Bhoys by taking an early lead. Kenny D, The King, His Royal Dalglishness levelled the match and the score remained at 1-1. It was enough to retain the crown but, sadly, also enough to condemn Falkirk to the Second Division.

You wouldn't open a bottle of champagne beside another's death-bed but it did seem ridiculous not to celebrate such a notable achievement. The Bairns didn't seem to mind all that much and, to their credit, the Brockvillites stayed on to applaud both teams for their efforts over the course of the season.

At the start of the month, the Celts had partially vanquished the memory of that League Cup Final when they dispatched Dundee from the Scottish Cup at the semi-final stage. Jinky had been the architect of that win, scoring the only goal of the game just before half-time, and his form was such now that a recall to the international set-up was imminent.

This was an important factor for the JJ Man as Scotland had just qualified for their first World Cup since 1958. To add honey to the pot, England had been ousted from the qualifiers by Poland, leaving the Scots as Britain's only ambassadors when the groove got going over the summer in West Germany. Nationwide celebrations were in full swing and the best way to gee the country along was to release a musical treat as recorded by the Scotland World Cup squad. Yes, great idea.

What a tragedy that the best they could come up with was a piece of hopeless hokum called *Easy Easy* with an opening lyric of, *Yabba-Dabba-Doo we support the boys in blue!* It made *Billy Don't Be A Hero* by Paper Lace sound like the inspired work of Bob Dylan. Nonetheless, musical limitations notwithstanding, Scotland were on their way to the biggest tournament in the world and Celtic players would be amongst the squad.

The only outstanding piece of silverware business now was the capture of another domestic double by beating the other Dundee side in the final at Hampden. On paper this looked like mere bagatelle but the *Arabs,* as they were known, had accounted for a highly-rated Hearts outfit in the semi-final to reach Hampden. In young striker Andy Gray, they also possessed a teenage sensation to rival Donny Osmond.

AG had been winning admirers from all quarters and certainly he brought out the best in Denis The Menace when Connza in the Celtic goal had to look lively to deny the pup a Cup Final goal. Had that arrived when the Celts were already 2-0 up, then the outcome of the whole game could have been different.

Celtic had shot out of the traps with all the experience of a side contesting their ninth Scottish Cup Final in ten years . . . all of them under the omnipotent eye of The Master. Within half an hour Harry Harry and Stevie the Student Prince had provided that two-goal advantage and although the Tannadice Arabs would attempt to kick sand in the Celtic faces, the Dixmaster produced his usual magic to round the score up to 3-0 in the final minute.

Celtic then attempted a lap of honour which was in direct defiance of an SFA edict on such open displays of enjoyment. The banning of these runs around the park to salute your supporters stemmed from League Cup Final near-disaster when Celtic had celebrated a victory over Rangers but in an uncomfortable proximity to the opposition supporters. Mayhem ensued and the decision was taken to completely outlaw the practice. Understandable perhaps in the white-hot temperament of a Celtic-Rangers clash but maybe a little harsh when the big two were not in direct opposition on the glamorous occasions.

Without a lap of honour, a Cup Final loses one of the characteristics of its appeal. It was to be hoped that such po-faced ideology would one day be as firmly historic as the Roman Empire. For now, the Celtic supporters merely acknowledged the achievement of their side in being nine-in-a-row champions *and* Scottish Cup winners as well.

In doing so, they would little have realised that they were also saying farewell to another of their bloodied favourites and bowing to the maxim that the *Quality Street Kids* were increasingly like their confectionery counterparts – *made for sharing*.

1974-1975
Glavin'Grabbin'

Track List:
Sparks/This Town Ain't Big Enough For The Both Of Us; David Essex/Gonna Make You A Star; Queen/Killer Queen; Pilot/Magic; Barry White/The First, The Last, My Everything; Status Quo/Down & Down; Tymes/Miss Grace; Steve Harley and Cockney Rebel/ Make Me Smile (Come Up And See Me); Bay City Rollers/Bye Bye Baby

David Hay had enjoyed an excellent World Cup. In fact, he probably relished it more than the rest of the Scotland squad *which had narrowly failed to qualify from the first round of the tournament* (n.b. this expression will appear on numerous occasions when referring to Scotland). West Germany, of Cold War fame, had been the playground for the big showdown of the finest sixteen teams on the planet. Oh, and Zaire too.

The Africans were pretty much unknown throughout the football-speaking world, which meant that Scotland were supposed to horse them in their Group Two opening game. A 2-0 scoreline seemed scant reward for their efforts and when it was followed up by a credible 0-0 draw with the World Cup holders Brazil and then an engrossing 1-1 stalemate with Yugoslavia, Scotland discovered a novel route to being ejected from an international tournament . . . don't lose a game, but don't beat the crappiest team in your group by putting at least six goals past them, and going out on goal difference. *Glorious failure!* was the shout from Scots the world over and the SFA moved quickly to copyright the expression so that they could drum it out over and over again for the next thirty-odd years.

By his own stratospheric standards, Kenny D, the man from whom Scotland *Expects,* endured a difficult time out in Deutschland. For sure, he played in all three games but was substituted in two of them with generally around 15-20 minutes left on the clock. And it wasn't because he was the best at running a bath in the Scottish dressing room either. Somehow, the whole World Cup shebang hadn't got going for the almost-crowned King Kenny and he was to return to a marginally resentful Scottish media. Arguably, this would affect his game in the coming season.

Danny McGrain also enjoyed mixed fortunes in the land of smoked sausage, leather shorts and ear-splitting klaxons. He too played in all of the matches and quite rightly was establishing his worldwide credentials, but was left stunned on his return to Scotland to learn that he had been diagnosed as a diabetic. At the time, this was largely kept under wraps and it sure as hell didn't stop him forging the kind of career that schoolboys and even bigger boys can only dream about. But it did seem more than a little rough for an individual who had fought back from a fractured skull to cement his place on both the Scottish and world soccer scene.

Still, at least these two Celtic stars got the chance to *play* in the World Cup which, tragically, was more than could be said for Jimmy Johnstone. In a scenario that could only have been part of the sitcom that Jinky could sometimes engender, the wee man had been preparing to come on as a substitute in the final game against Yugoslavia but the referee failed to notice his attendance. The final whistle shrilled before the entertainer could make his entrance. Was Jimmy coming out to play? Apparently not. It was as close as he ever got to participation in a World Cup tournament.

There was a school of thought that Jinky shouldn't have been in West Germany as a Scottish representative in the first place. This had nothing to do with his ability on the pitch as his performances in the second half of the entertainment that was nine-in-a-row lit up the Scottish scene. Jinky was a justified pick for the campaign as well as being included in the Home International series with fixtures against Northern Ireland, Wales and England.

This end-of-season fare was an established tradition and with the Scots being Britain's sole World Cup representatives, the heat was naturally on the team to prove that they were good value for their passports.

Typically, they started badly with a 1-0 defeat to Northern Ireland but recovered three days later when a King Kenny strike and a Sandy Jardine penalty were enough to beat Wales 2-0. It was now onwards to the big showdown with England at Hampden; the most important game of the sequence and, quite rightly, the Scotland squad under Willie Ormond spent the days leading up to the clash living like monks in a cocoon of self-discipline, meditation and physical purity. Well, not quite.

Willie Ormond was nicknamed *Donny* as his surname bore a similarity to the Osmond Family. His height and girth were probably closer to wee Jimmy of that *Long-Haired Lover* hell than pre-pubescent pin-up Donny, but then again, everybody in Scotland gets called *Jimmy* anyway so the gag would have been lost. When it came to discipline he was a tad lightweight. You got the impression that making wee Willie a dinner monitor at school would have invited near-anarchy with the Primary sixes and he would have backed down.

After the Welsh match and back in the seaside headquarters that was Largs, he allowed the lads to let off a bit of steam in the hotel bar. In one of the legendary incidents in Scottish football folklore, Jimmy Johnstone somehow parlayed a few refreshments into a trip in a rowing boat on the Clyde. Being Jinky of course, the dilemma was heightened by the fact that the boat had no oars and he couldn't swim. By the time the coastguard was alerted and the lifeboats swung into action for a *Code Redhead*, the media were made aware of the situation.

Largs had a foreboding early history of Vikings sailing over from Scandinavia to rape and pillage but even the sight of a longboat that night with a bloodthirsty horde of Danish savages hell-bent on destruction would not have been sufficient to knock Jimmy Johnstone from the front pages. Naturally, the paragons of virtue and temperance that constituted the sporting branch of the Fourth Estate demanded Jinky's withdrawal from the Scottish pool. *Donny* thought differently and in a rare moment of *Puppy Love* he chose not only to keep Jinky as a member of the Yabba Dabba Doo twenty-two but selected him for the all-important England match at Hampden.

The wee man was to play his part as Joe Jordan and a David Nish own goal brought a seismic 2-0 victory. The most memorable moments of the match are Jinky patting the prone England 'keeper Peter Shilton on the head after the second goal and then producing another hand gesture as the team did a lap of honour at the end of the game. By this point, Jinky was clad in Shilton's yellow jersey that drowned him like the *after* part of one of those before and after slimming adverts on the telly. As the team took their constitutional around the pitch, he looked up to the Press gallery and reminded them, with his fingers, that Scotland had scored two goals!

It left little to the imagination. In this kind of form he would have fancied his chances at getting a run out during the festivities in West Germany, but it wasn't to be. Therefore, in stark contrast to Kenny D, Danny McG and Jimmy the Jink, David Hay's cup ranneth over. The Quiet Assassin had emerged from the background to roar out to all and sundry that he was a player at the height of his powers.

This was never better illustrated than a particular moment in the match against Brazil when he attempted an audacious shot from long distance that almost lobbed South American goalkeeper Leao.

It was one of those snapshots that invoked the tired cliché about it being the sort of thing one would expect from a Brazilian but no less true for the fact that it was a Scottish midfielder who had launched it.

Davie was acknowledged as the outstanding Scottish performer in all three of the matches and it was no surprise that he returned to Blighty with his reputation and, intriguingly, his price tag enhanced. This latter point was rammed home when Chelsea contacted Celtic to see if they would be interested in transferring their newly-minted World Cup star to the west end of London for a fee of £250,000. A cool quarter-mil . . . 250 big 'uns . . . it was difficult to see how the club could turn down this offer.

Big Jock had a taste for the theatrical at times and seemingly enjoyed the cloak and dagger of political machinations for he arranged to inform Davie Hay about this turn of events in his managerial Mercedes which was berthed in the car park outside the home ground.

The simple problem was that the offices at Celtic Park were closed but it's hard to believe that Jock Stein, the man who bestrode the stadium like his personal domain and could have built a swing park complete with roundabouts and a chute for his grand-children on the half-way line during the close season had he so demanded, did not possess a key to unlock a door into his kingdom! It was like telling the President to stay out of the White House because there was spring-cleaning going on.

The Quiet Assassin must have felt like Harry Palmer from *The Ipcress File* when he arrived at the ground to see the Big Man awaiting him wedged behind the steering wheel of his powerful Mercedes Benz. It's possible that, despite the daylight hour, Jock Stein may even have flashed his headlamps to highlight the bizarre rendezvous spot and Hay must have wondered what all the Cold War spy transfer actions were leading up to.

He was soon to find out as Stein informed the now stunned assassin that he was on his way out of Celtic Park. Big Jock might just as well have kept on the radio with perhaps *This Town Ain't Big Enough For The Both Of Us* screaming as a melodramatic soundtrack to the plot. Sure, there were theatres-a-plenty in the West End of London but none that could compare with the Coliseum that was Celtic Park on a big European night and Hay reiterated to the Big Man that he did not really want to leave Paradise. To no avail.

Jock had apparently decided that the winter dispute from the previous season would not be an isolated incident and that, in the voice of Fred Astaire, *there may be trouble ahead . . .* trouble that he could ill-afford. Off-loading the presence of the gifted midfielder, though, would have ramifications for the crack at ten-in-a-row.

Not that that would be the immediate assessment for a Celtic side which returned triumphantly to the domestic fold by picking off the *big one* before the anti-climax of the new season was upon us. Oh yes folks, stand up for the new holders of the Drybrough Cup!

At last, this most seductive of trophies that had eluded our grasp like a night out with Raquel Welch was finally deposited in the Celtic Park boardroom. This magnificent cup that glorified great past winners such as Aberdeen, Hibernian and . . . eh . . . Hibernian again, was finally to have the name *Celtic* etched upon it.

Now, you might have noticed that, over the last few chapters I may just have traduced this worthwhile tourney a little bit. Not much, of course, but perhaps enough to make you think that I would not rate a cup that routinely messed about with its format, the offside rule, the markings on the pitch, the established order of cup football, the half-time pies etc, but all that has changed now that we can say without any prejudice whatsoever that, at the start of season 1974-75, Celtic were the Drybrough Cup champions! Not only that, they sat at the top of the Drybrough pile by picking off Rangers in the final, albeit on penalty-kicks.

Denis Connaghan emerged as the shootout hero when *The Menace* pulled off a couple of saves to deny Derek Parlane and Tommy McLean, leaving Jimmy the Jink as the man to poke the ball past Rangers 'keeper Stewart Kennedy and secure the cup. It would be one of Connza's best results whilst guarding the Celtic net. It's almost tempting to use the word *memorable* as an afterthought for the big goalie but he had already provided that moment in the first round game against Airdrie at Broomfield.

The Diamonds had generally been cast as the *pesky kids* in the *Scooby-Doo* that was Celtic given that they had a nasty habit of nabbing a point or two from the Bhoys over the years. *Like, Zoiks!* as Shaggy would say. They had only just been promoted back to the higher ground of the Scottish First Division and would have fancied a bite at the Celts when they arrived in Lanarkshire for the tie.

Celtic were in no mood for a Scooby snack though and were 4-1 up going into the closing stages of the match when Pat McCluskey defused an Airdrie attack by passing the ball back to Connza in goal. The fair-haired custodian duly picked up the ball, made as if to hurl it out to Danny McGrain to start another thrilling Celtic attack and in a moment of inexplicable decision-making that probably still sees him waking up sweat-ridden in the middle of the night, released the ball powerfully towards the unguarded Celtic goal.

It crossed the line quicker than Red Rum, the score was pegged back to 4-2 and Connza realised that a post-football career as a pitcher for the Brooklyn Dodgers wasn't going to be an option. Singapore betting syndicates would never have wagered on such a moment in a professional match even if it had been done by design and the hapless goalie instantly became the laughing stock of Broomfield. Even Big Jock, sitting on the away bench with his trusty crew, found time to laugh at his goalkeeper's embarrassment although he probably wouldn't have seen the funny side had it been the last minute in a European Cup semi-final with his Celts locked at 1-1 and going all the way to the final on the away goals rule. *Goalkeepers? Ya gotta luv 'em, aintcha?*

The Bhoys were away again in the semi when Dundee was the destination. The Dixmaster equalised in the eighty-ninth minute of a tough tie and then Jim Brogan won the match 2-1 for Celtic in extra-time.

Onwards then to Hampden Park on a wonderfully warm day when no-one's spirits were higher than the Drybrough sponsors themselves who, at the fourth time of asking, eventually had the Celtic-Rangers final of which they had been dreaming. Close to 58,000 people inside the national stadium, the name *Drybrough* emblazoned on their minds and parched lips as they watched their favourites square up to each other in an encounter that was so early that it could be called *pre*-first blood and just when the good people of Drybrough thought it couldn't get any better, the match continued into extra-time.

Celtic had been twice ahead; once in regular time through Stevie the Student Prince and then Paul Wilson in the additional thirty minutes but on both occasions they had been pulled back. It was the match sponsors who roared out their approval when the referee blew for full-time and the commencement of the penalty shootout.

Unaccountably, the normally reliable Lemon had missed Celtic's first spot-kick but Messrs Callaghan, McCluskey and Murray spared his blushes whilst Rangers record was scored two, missed two. The last time a Kennedy and a Johnston(e) had squared up to each other with so much at stake was in 1960 when JFK and Lyndon B had crossed swords for the Democratic Presidential nomination. This time, Kennedy was the loser.

A derby day cup final victory was as good a way to start a season as it was to finish one. Doubtless the congratulatory telegrams would have been arriving into Celtic Park, although it was highly unlikely that Richard Nixon would have taken time out to pop one off to the Bhoys. The Tricky One was about to become a busted flush as the burning timbers of Watergate fell around him necessitating the resignation that he grudgingly offered on 8 August. He became the first American President ever to do so. Disgrace, dishonour and obscurity were to follow. Still, it would have given him plenty of time to cross the water a couple of days later and check out another Celtic League Cup campaign.

The League Cup was probably a little miffed that its lustre as the starting point of a season had maybe been poached by the spectacle of the Drybrough cousin. The Celtic support may have felt that the capture of the latter after a few years of trying might bode well for returning the former to the Kerrydale sideboard. Certainly they started competently, qualifying from a reasonably tough section that included Dundee United, Motherwell and Ayr United.

The *Honest Men* were perceived as the weakest of the teams on offer but notably took the Celtic scalp when the Hoops arrived at Somerset Park by three goals to two. United had a nippy wee pest of a winger called Johnny Doyle who played out of his skin against the Celts and Big Jock would assuredly have marked his card for future reference. Celtic won the rest of their matches though, which was just as well given that only one team qualified from the group into the quarter-final.

Hamilton Accies were then summarily dismissed by an aggregate 6-2 over two legs and thus, having beaten two of the Lanarkshire contenders for the trophy in both the Accies and the 'Well, it could have been of little surprise that fate decreed a semi-final against the third force from the county, Airdrie.

That one took place on 9 October, which also turned out to be *Election Eve* as Harold Wilson had decided that if he had to govern with a minority, he might as well be back in Opposition. He had called for a second General Election within eight months of the last one and the country braced itself for the endless posturing, lying, baby-kissing and downright boredom of another campaign. That level of *ennui* would be as nothing though, compared to the tedium that was Celtic-Airdrie on that windswept October evening.

Less than 20,000 people turned up at Hampden Park and the feeling pervaded that the floating voters who had stayed away had got it right. Stevie the Student Prince notched the only goal in a game so bad that he would probably have rather been back at his digs studying mathematical problems. In truth, so would the crowd.

Whatever the case, the Celts set up their Hampden final date against Hibernian just as Harold Wilson prepared himself to run off with the election by a slimmer than slim three-seat majority. Nobody in the Parliamentary Labour Party would be allowed to die over the lifetime of *this* government!

Another League Cup Final appointment was a healthy return though in a season that had hitherto lacked a bit of spark from a Celtic perspective. As we have seen, The Quiet Assassin had been transferred to London and brokered into that deal was the double loss of George Connelly as well.

Quiet, affable big Geordie had found in David Hay a first-team member of the Celtic squad with whom he could commune and it wouldn't have taken Sigmund Freud to theorise that the splitting of that relationship would adversely affect the man from Fife. From this point on his career would amount to a tragedy of Country & Western proportions. Seriously, only Hank Williams could have built a song around it. Season 1974-75 would be one that had Geordie turning the front door at Celtic Park into a revolving one and the first game that he chose to stay away from was not an inconsequential one.

Rangers were the visitors to the East End in the middle of September when Connelly vanished quicker than the expression *President Nixon.* Hardly an ideal time to miss out on the preparations and, possibly, a factor in Celtic's subsequent 2-1 defeat.

The match had been an ill-tempered affair with Jim Brogan and Derek Parlane being sent-off whilst the Celts led with a vital Kenny D strike. The referee, Mr JRP Gordon, did not appear to have a handle on proceedings and the players were misbehaving in the unruly fashion of a playground conkers fight. It was Rangers who came up with the big *'checkies'* though when they hit back through Ian McDougall and Colin Jackson to nick the points and go top of the table.

It was a bit of a shock that, the Govan Select winning at Celtic Park. They hadn't done it since 1968, but there had been a warning bell only a week before when the Bhoys paid a visit to Shawfield Stadium to whip, sorry, force of habit, to *face* Clyde. You've been reading this narrative long enough to know the script of the Bully Wee gigs. Generally, the Celts toyed with Clyde like a cat with a ball of string and then mauled them as that cat turned into a fully-fledged lion.

To the impartial reader, the 4-2 finishing scoreline then would seem to indicate that it was a typical piece of Hoops supremacy but there was a point in this match, on this day of our Lord in 1974, when Clyde were leading Celtic by two goals to nil! Even Frank Bough would have been shocked when that one started coming off the wires.

The *Eugene* that was Clyde had finally faced up to the beach bhoy bully that was Celtic and sick of having sand kicked in their face, pulled out a neat one-two to slap the Celts on the coupon. It was one of those moments when the Shawfield faithful wanted the game to stop and the world to end. After the legacy of those past thrashings, the Bully Wee were trying to blacken some eyes. Tragically, they were to end up with the shiners as *Eugene* finally fainted at the enormity of what he had done and Celtic picked off four goals in reply. But it had been a shot across the bows and a sign that the Celtic defence could be breached by a hint of ambition.

That was a quality in plentiful supply in the shape of European Cup first round opponents, Olympiakos. If you thought they were from Athens, you'd be right. We can only imagine that it didn't take too long for their founders to come up with the name. It's worth remembering that the Celts had been European Cup semi-finalists only months before and for that achievement had been seeded in the Euro draw. They might have anticipated something a little bit easier than the Champions of Greece although the tabloids were dusting down their *Greek Tragedy* headlines with predictable relish.

Big Jock had been out to Athens on a spying mission and recognised the tough calibre of the opposition but even he might have been surprised to be 1-0 down within thirty-five minutes of the first leg at Celtic Park. The Hoops were fighting manfully to get back into the game and perhaps the tie as well when they managed to conjure up an equaliser within the last ten minutes of the ninety. Even then, the Olympians had to be reduced to ten men to make the way back possible for Celtic.

What had seemed like a good night for the Grecian forward Viera as he had snapped up the Olympiakos goal, turned suddenly dark when he was dismissed from the action by grabbing a piece of Harry Harry's shirt as the Hood skipped by him. The Celts turned the screw with the man advantage and Paul Wilson buttoned onto a Lemon headed knock-back to level the scores. 1-1 and an away goal to balance meant that things were going to be mighty difficult on Mount Olympus. No Hay, no sign of Connelly and Kenny D seemed to be suffering from a bout of the post-World Cup blues as well. The omens weren't good.

Celtic were European aristocrats and their nine consecutive seasons in the hunt for the biggest continental trophy had seen them visit some far out places. With names like Kiev, Amsterdam, Milan, Belgrade and Zurich stamped on their passports, they had pretty much traversed Europe like James Bond. The antipathy in Madrid the season before had probably been the most hostile atmosphere that they'd ever been asked to compete in, but for noise and passion, the fans of Olympiakos would take some beating.

It's difficult to see how the average punter at the Karaiskakix Stadium could actually see the match given the amount of fire-crackers and smoke bombs that seemed to go off routinely before, during and after the ninety minutes of combat. Clearly, on match-day in downtown Athens, the fire brigade were as busy as the *polis.*

When Olympiakos went 1-0 up in only three minutes and then doubled that twenty minutes later, it was the cue for the *Support Your Local Arsonist,* Athens chapter, to make the fourth of July fireworks look like a family barbecue. The players should have been equipped with gas masks as the fart-like odour of cordite wafted around the arena as though every Greek, to a man, had been pre-feasting on baked beans. Little wonder that the Celts could not respond and they departed the European Cup in the first round for the first time since 1967.

In truth, the Bhoys had about as much chance as coming back with a victory as they did of returning the Elgin Marbles. Big Jock's fifty-second birthday was four days away. There was still time for his wife to take that Demis Roussos LP back to Woolworths.

The troubling aspect of the whole Greek experience was that Olympiakos weren't exactly going to be worrying the bookies when the odds were being calculated for potential European champs, yet they had disposed of Celtic with little fuss. The feeling persisted that

HMS European Cup was sailing away from Celtic's port and that it would be a few years before the club would realistically be in a position to contest the tournament all the way to the latter stages.

Domestically, Hibs had made a reasonable fist to the start of the season and having a little previous about them when it came to sorting out Celtic in a League Cup Final, they felt that they had little to fear when the Gunfight at the Hampden Corral came around. There was even time to put one of those psychological markers down when that strange animal that was the fixtures compilation chart had the Easter Road Greens visiting Celtic Park one week before the final when League points were up for grabs.

How then did they view a 5-0 gubbing? A multiple choice question?

a) *Well, to be honest we took a pasting but this in no way has any bearing on next week's League Cup Final.*

b) *We were a bit distracted by all this League Cup Final talk but having studied the opposition we now know how to combat their threat.*

c) *Hellllllp!! We're cackin' it! Could we arrange to kidnap Dixie Deans?*

Ah, the Dixmaster; who else? After the Student Prince and Jinky had put the home side 2-0 up, Dixie plundered his way to a hat-trick. This allowed Hibs to tick answer b) in their multiple choice questions because there was loose talk to the Press before the match that their back four was now confident of snuffing out the Deans factor.

What was that warning that Winston Churchill used to put on those wartime posters? *Loose talk costs lives!* Never in the field of Hampden endeavour then have so many words been eaten by so few people! Once again, the Hibs defence were party to the one-man routing system that was the Dixmaster.

Deans picked up yet another hat-trick as Celtic put six past their Edinburgh cousins in a thrillingly similar outcome to the 1972 Scottish Cup Final. This time it was 6-3 at full-time with the only difference being that Hibs had scored two more goals than a couple of years before and that Dixie now sported a rather woolly Zapata moustache. Harry Harry had also taken to wearing a *'mowser'* above his top lip and thus these two bandidos laid siege to the Hibs goal like it was the Alamo.

Paul Wilson shared one each with Jinky and the Student Prince but it was the Dixmaster's second anti-Hibs hat-trick in a week that was the talk of the town. In particular, goal number three of that treble was a testimony to Dixie's instinct for trying anything to hit the target.

Harry Harry floated a corner into the box and the unmarked Jinky saw the chance to grab his second goal with a quick strike. He blootered the ball with all the power of a nuclear missile but one launched by Stevie Wonder as it veered off-course on its way to football oblivion. That was the cue for the Dixmaster to throw his head at the ball and re-direct it straight into the net!

The Celtic end of Hampden erupted in a mixture of ecstasy and disbelief. Jinky flung his head back as if it was some great joke and Dixie's team-mates ran to congratulate him whilst ensuring that his skull had not been ripped from his meaty shoulders. *Alas poor Dixie, I knew him well . . .* Thankfully the Dixmaster was still alive and grinning like he'd stumbled into Ladies Night at the Turkish Baths.

A hat-trick in a major final? How lucky is that? Well, if you were Hibs striker Joe Harper, it wasn't black cat time. Wee Joe had a similar physique to Dixie and a matching predatory instinct so to bag a triple in a Cup Final and finish up on the losing side has to be considered as a sick joke. Harper had been the only decent Hibs retort to the Celtic dominance but his threesome had counted for nothing in the defeat.

And so, on 26 October 1974, every national bauble on the Scottish scene was standing proudly on the Celtic Park sideboard. The First Division trophy, the Scottish Cup, The Scottish League Cup and yes, very well then, the Drybrough Cup, formed a more successful quartet than The Four Tops and they all belonged to the Hoops. The League Cup was a particularly pleasing addition. The Celts had waited five years to bring it back to Kerrydale Street.

Muhammad Ali would have related to this patience. Stripped of his World Heavyweight title by the U.S. courts one month before Celtic won the European Cup in 1967, he was now preparing to win it back from George Foreman in the 'Rumble In The Jungle' fight in Zaire just four days after Celtic's Hampden victory. At thirty-two, he was considered by many to be *past it* but a clever, Herculean performance in the searing Kinshasa heat re-affirmed his status as *The Greatest* when he punished his opponent in the eighth round. Foreman didn't even have time to say *low-fat grill* as he fell to the canvas.

Ali was the king of the world but, in Scotland, only one man could look at the trophy cabinet in his place of work and think . . . *Hmm, no' bad.* It was as if Big Jock had written to *Jim'll Fix It!*

Now then, now then, we have a letter here from the one and only Mr Jock Stein in Glasgow. Dear Jimmy, can you and yer smashing bunch of guys 'n' gals at the BBC fix it for me and my team to win all the domestic trophies in Bonnie Scotland for 1974 including that soddin' League Cup? Yes Jock; your letter was only the start of it . . . Well, Jimmy Savile had certainly made more outlandish dreams come true on his Saturday night television show.

It was a *time* for dreams and Partick Thistle's Ronnie Glavin had been laying his head down at night wondering if his move to Celtic was ever going to happen. Negotiations between the clubs had been running almost as long as Agatha Christie's *The Mousetrap* so it was with some relief that the figures were finally sorted out and the deal was done in the middle of November. Jock Stein unwrapped the midfielder like an £80,000 birthday present and *R.G.* arrived in time to score a debut goal when his new team mates rolled over Airdrie 6-0 at Celtic Park.

As Ronnie Glavin appeared, Lord Lucan disappeared. Richard John Bingham, the seventh Earl of Lucan and a gambler known at the London gaming tables as *Lucky* Lucan, discovered that he had the same run of fortune as Joe Harper in the League Cup Final. From out of their stylish Belgravia home on the night of 12 November, a bloodied Lady Lucan had stumbled into the nearest pub and screamed to anyone who would listen *He's murdered my nanny!*

Sandra Rivett, the twenty-nine-year-old nanny in question, was discovered strangled at the Lucan residence, but of the peer of the realm nothing was to be found. It was the start of a missing persons enquiry that continued into the twenty-first century with endless theories being applied to old Lucky's whereabouts. Africa, Australia, Italy, the Caribbean and California were all offered as possible locations to which Lucan had fled. His complete anonymity was such that other hideaways under consideration were centre-forward for Clyde, musical director for The Osmonds and Britt Ekland's bedroom. Suicide was naturally mentioned but that was pretty much the same thing as a visit to Miss Ekland's boudoir.

In saying that, the Celtic support had more chance of seeing Lord Lucan up front for their favourites than they did of catching a glimpse of Jimmy Bone in a first-team jersey. R.G. wasn't the only Jag from the famous League Cup class of '71 who was now forming a part of the Hoops squad. Bone had arrived in March of the previous season as one of those intriguing purchases that Big Jock liked to experiment with from time to time.

The Master occasionally tinkered with his squad and throughout the years had shown that he was a dab hand at converting Hillman Imps into Bentleys. Unfortunately, Jimmy Bone's Hillman appeared to have an alternator problem . . . he couldn't alternate between the reserves and the first-team. As a second-string Celt he would bag twenty goals but he never really had Harry Harry, the Dixmaster or Kenny D lying awake all night worrying about their positions in the pack.

It was a surprise to most people then, if not perhaps the likeable Bone himself, when he scored his first top team goal against Dunfermline Athletic at Celtic Park in early December. He was entitled to feel that he'd arrived at long last and that a prolonged run in the first team was imminent but tragically that goal in a gutsy 2-1 victory over the Pars was, as they say, *all she wrote.*

Barry White was at number one that weekend so it's to be hoped that Jimmy didn't race out to Woolworths after the match and snap up the Walrus of Love's chart-topper. The irony might not have been lost on him as he cavorted about his living room to *The First, The Last, My Everything!* By early January, he was off to Arbroath.

If sightings of a Bone goal were unusual, then eyes would have been rubbed harder than a nettle sting when Rod Stewart turned up at Celtic Park the week after the Dunfermline game. Dundee were the visitors but it was *The Mod* who attracted more attention as he took his seat in the south stand just before kick-off. Little is known of Rod's take on the Paradise catering, although rumour abounded that he tried to sniff the coconut from a macaroon bar, but he sure raved about the form of hat-trick hero Kenny D. Then again, everybody did!

The King was re-ascending his throne in this 6-0 reeming of the Blue Bonnets and subsequent goal scoring performances against St. Johnstone and Kilmarnock ensured that, by Christmas, Celtic were at the top of the league. The season of goodwill continued when Clyde barfed up their black bun and ginger wine on New Year's Day, losing 5-1 on a first foot to Kerrydale Street. So, Kenny D stamping his greatness out on the park, the Bully Wee taking a horsing, Celtic leading the pack . . . it all seemed like any other season. And then Rangers hovered into view.

The last time we'd caught up with them, they'd caught up with us courtesy of that pools-bustin' 2-1 win at Celtic Park in September and now it was time to head over to Ibrox to right the wrong. It didn't require the mathematical nous of Stevie the Student Prince to calculate the numbers. The Celts were two points clear of the Govan Select and a win in the foreign field would push that lead to four and provide the perfect fillip for the push to Ten-In-A-Row.

Hell, we'd been singing it out loud and proud now for the last couple of months to the tune of Pilot's *Magic: It's Magicccc . . . you know-oh-oh-oh . . . it's gonna be ten-in-a-row!* What did we know?

We should have been listening to Status Quo's first and only number one because from here on in it was *Down & Down* for Celtic's league aspirations. True, the eventual 3-0 defeat at Ibrox only meant that Rangers led the table on goal difference but the Celts now set off on a run of form that was as patchy as your granny's quilt.

Motherwell had the audacity to *do a Clyde* by taking a two-goal lead in Celtic's very next match. If that wasn't ballsy enough, they did it at Celtic Park and although the two goals were pulled back, the Steelmen ran out 3-2 winners. A decent win over Ayr United by 5-1 was only achieved after being a goal down as well and there was a general feeling that the defence had more holes in it than a packet of Polos.

This was savagely confirmed over a period of three days when Arbroath and Dumbarton were able to share the points with Celtic like it was a Sunday picnic. Admittedly the game away to the Red Lichties might have been played on an oil platform given the hurricane blowing in from the North Sea but conditions were the same for both teams in the 2-2 draw.

Dumbarton also eked out the same score-line *at Celtic Park* seventy-two hours later, but this seemed worse as the Bhoys were coasting at 2-0 when former Lisbon Lion, Wispy Willie Wallace, cajoled his team mates from The Rock to punish his former club. Doubts were now being openly expressed about Billy McNeill's capacity to hold the Celtic back-line together.

Cesar was approaching thirty-five and although he could have pointed to Muhammad Ali as a veteran still on top of his sport, niggling injuries and the loss of a yard or two of pace were conspiring against his majesty. Big Jock *rested* him for a 4-1 defeat of Clydebank in the Scottish Cup and then kept him out of a fairly crucial away League fixture to Hibs. His replacement for both matches was the soft-spoken Highlander, Roddie MacDonald.

The Easter Road line-up contained another notable change. The Master had been shuffling his goalkeepers around all season like your wife trying to choose a new frock. Ally Hunter and Dennis Connaghan, the Broomfield pitcher, had been sharing the task with a confidence akin to two soldiers passing a live grenade between them and for the 'Bankies match one Graham Barclay was given the nod.

Naturally, Clydebank scored first which in these shell-shocked times was something that was becoming the norm, but the Bhoys rallied quickly to the cause to put four goals past them. Barclay was only seventeen and probably spent most of the ninety minutes squeezing his spots and wondering about his response should he be offered some champagne after the match.

It was clear that Jock's mistrust of the number one position in his team was preying on the Stein mind. He'd purchased Hunter and Connza on the back of strong performances that he'd witnessed, so maybe it was time to change track on this and pick up a goalie he'd never even seen.

Peter Latchford of West Bromwich Albion was recommended to him, allegedly by *Dossier* Don Revie who was now the England supremo. Sean Fallon was despatched south to check him out in a reserve game on the day that Graham Barclay was trying to keep his hands warm in that Scottish Cup tie. The Master could get him on loan which must have appealed since it would give him time to weigh up his capabilities and Big Latch duly arrived to take his place in goal for a friendly against Ayr United. By the weekend he was the first-choice for the League game against Hibs . . . and Celtic lost 2-1.

It wasn't a great debut for the goalie from the Midlands but it would be unfair to castigate him for the inconsistency of Celtic's performance, which was now becoming a recurring theme. The League title was slipping away and the Bhoys were being rumbled as often as a gang of villains in *The Sweeney*.

To date, the roughest, grittiest and most realistic cop-show on the television, *The Sweeney* had burst onto the weekly scene in January of 1975. Typically ITV in its attitude, the programme had revolutionised the way police were perceived in the whole of Britain, even though it was set in London. John Thaw and Dennis Waterman starred as Regan and Carter of an elite unit of the Metropolitan Police known as the Flying Squad or, to give it the cockney rhyming slang, *The Sweeney Todd*.

Plots tended to consist mostly of bad 'uns trying to offload shooters, dodgy money or just dodgy anything to another even bigger group of bad 'uns. Sometimes it was difficult to tell the difference between the law and the criminals and there seemed to be plenty of scope for angry geezers with silk stockings around their faces to leap out of Transit vans, firing sawn-off shotguns and yelling *Bastaaaaaaard* to anyone who might be in the vicinity.

The cars, clothes and casual sex were the epitome of 1970s living and the temperature of the whole programme was considered to be so hot that it couldn't be screened until the 9pm watershed slot. Whatever, it was unmissable telly and spawned an entire vocabulary across the country where even people in Auchtermuchty were roaming about the streets saying *Gertcha* or *Would you Adam 'n' Eve it* and *You're nicked mate!*

To anyone following the Hoops through the spring of 1975 it appeared that when the Transit van rolled around, it was the Rangers players who would be propelled from it with their masks, shooters and colourful expressions as they staked their most serious claim yet to the First Division title.

Certainly, the reversal at Hibs confirmed that, at best, Celtic were rocky champions and a sequence of results that mixed away defeats to Aberdeen and Airdrie with a dismal 1-0 loss at home to Dundee United, handed the initiative to the Govan Select. On the day the Bhoys were turning on an uncharacteristic surge of power play by horsing Hearts 4-1 at Celtic Park, Rangers ended ten years of League misery by clinching the championship at Easter Road. The Bay City Rollers on *Top Of The Pops* murdering *Bye Bye Baby* seemed pretty appropriate.

As if that wasn't enough, the last two fixtures of the campaign comprised defeats to Dundee and St Johnstone which meant that the Celts ended up in third spot in the overall table behind Hibs. A team of specialists would probably have to be flown down to Kerrydale Street to remove the Championship trophy given that it had been sitting on the same spot on that Celtic sideboard since 1966. And a team of counsellors would also be required to deal with a Celtic support coming to terms with a flag-less season.

At least there was still the Scottish Cup and the possibility of having to get past Rangers to win that one ended when Aberdeen knocked the boys in blue out in the third round. The Celts had greater concerns with the perils of a visit to Easter Road but goals by the Student Prince and the other guy, whatssiname, chunky bloke who occasionally bags one or two against Hibs, oh yeah, Dixie Deans, made for a 2-0 victory.

After Clydebank, Celtic moved slightly further down the coast to beat Dumbarton 2-1 at Boghead and set up another semi-final against the Blue Bonnets. Tam Gemmell, never a guy to miss the chance of a wind-up, contended that his former employers would be a tad deflated having just lost the League to Rangers but RG proved his value to the cause with a second-half goal to ease Celtic onto the Final.

Airdrie were the surprise on the Hampden menu and the Diamonds would certainly fancy their chances. They'd dumped both Celtic and Rangers for a unique double during the League season and beaten Motherwell in a sweet local rivalry semi-final.

Peter Latchford had, by now, bedded in rather well and as he took his place in goal he might not have realised that Big Jock was unconsciously working to a pattern. Celtic had contested the last three Scottish Cup Finals with a different goalkeeper every time. In 1972, it had been Evan The Williams, 1973 was the turn of Ally Hunter and in 1974, Denis the Menace had produced that save from Andy Gray at a vital point in the match. And so, another final, another goalie.

For the big 'keeper who had now assumed the adjective *burly,* it would be an exciting occasion. Only three months before he had been working away in West Brom's reserves and now he was to take part in a major final. Perhaps he'd been writing to Jim'll Fix It as well.

Cesar McNeill could afford to take a more relaxed view of the proceedings. This was his twelfth Scottish Cup Final since 1961. In that time he had won nine championships, six Scottish Cups, six League Cups and was the first British footballer to hold aloft the European Cup. And we'll never tire of saying that! Outrageously for one of the most decorated players of his generation, he had only received twenty nine full Scottish caps. Measured against his stature, that seemed absurd.

At the start of the season he'd become the first Celtic player to be afforded a testimonial match and Liverpool had travelled up to Glasgow to provide the honours for that one. Billy had been everywhere and done everything that a Celtic player could do and now, unbeknown to most of the Paradise set-up, he was to take his final bow as the captain of the club that he had come to personify.

As he led the Bhoys out onto the park, he perhaps reminisced about that moment ten years previously when he rose above a host of Dunfermline Athletic players to connect with a Charlie Gallagher corner for Celtic's winner in the 1965 Scottish Cup Final. Jock Stein had barely arrived through the door at Paradise and this victory was the foundation for all that was to come.

Maybe he thought back to that night when Celtic were locked at one goal apiece with their toughest opponents on the road to Lisbon, Vojvodina Novi Sad of Yugoslavia. The breakthrough, with that same Gallagher/McNeill corner-kick combo, pushed the Celts into the semi-finals of the European Cup in the greatest year of the club's history.

Possibly, he recalled his crucial first goal in the 1969 Scottish Cup Final when Rangers, buoyed by taking all four points against the Hoops in the League that season, fancied that they could win the last piece of silverware and dent Celtic's treble ambitions. Cesar had started the 4-0 rout. Probably, like the true pro he was, Billy McNeill just concentrated on winning another football match for Celtic.

True, there was a brief moment towards the end of the first half when Celtic's season-long defensive frailties were once again re-opened as Airdrie equalised Paul Wilson's opener, but it was a leveller that was to last barely a minute. The prodigious Wilson, preferred to Cup Final king, the Dixmaster, proved the validity of Big Jock's judgement by putting Celtic back into the lead. That one had come from a corner that Big Billy may have fancied was to provide his déjà vu moment as he lurked with intent in the Diamonds' box but it was not to be.

Pat McCluskey put the polish on the show by whipping a penalty into the net shortly after half-time and Billy McNeill had his Hans Christian Andersen finish to the fairytale that was his Celtic career. Once again Hampden was *in the sun* for the Hoops which may have come as a surprise to Peter Latchford. He'd been told it always rained in Glasgow.

The 75,000 plus crowd, as perceptive as Sherlock Holmes on the trail of *Silver Blaze,* suddenly realised that the fuss being made of Billy McNeill was not because he had changed his shampoo and it showed. Word filtered around that *this was it* for Cesar and to a man they applauded and remembered. It hadn't been ten-in-a-row but hey! Let's get on with it.

We'll be back next season after we've all had a nice peaceful summer. Big Jock had lined up a break with family and friends in Menorca . . .

1975-1976

LatchSavin'DannyLappin'

Track List:
Windsor Davies & Don Estelle/Whispering Grass; David Essex/Hold Me Close; Bob Marley & The Wailers/No Woman, No Cry; Sailor/ Glass of Champagne; Queen/Bohemian Rhapsody; Abba/Mamma Mia; Four Seasons/December '63/Tina Charles/I Love To Love; Brotherhood of Man/Save All Your Kisses For Me; Peter Frampton/ Show Me The Way; Manfred Mann/Blinded By The Light

One of the highlights of the summer was the chance to tune in to *Screen Test* on BBC1. Ostensibly, it was a quiz show based on the world of the movies that took over the *Blue Peter* slot during the school holidays. Teenage contestants were shown a clip from a film and then asked questions about it by the ever-grinning presenter Michael Rodd.

The movies tended to be disappointingly out of date and there was *always* a flick from an institution called the Children's Film Foundation. The C.F.F. seemed to specialise in period tales like *Robin Hood* starring a young Keith Chegwin and various Merry Men with Cockney accents. You lived in hope that one day, when the vodka had been drained by the *Screen Test* production team, a three-minute clip of the porn classic, *Deep Throat,* showcasing Linda Lovelace would escape onto the network. We'd all have taken questions on that one!

Nonetheless, for all its shortcomings, *Screen Test* was an

examination of a contestant's ability to observe background and dialogue. Those taking part appeared to have names like Tristram, Julian, Annabelle and Samantha, which wasn't very indicative of the working class experience and they seemed more than happy that the top prize was a collection of Premium Bonds! *Wow! Way to go BBC. Try palming off twenty-first century adolescents with lottery tickets and see who turns up!*

One of the glorious successes of the production, though, was the *Young Film-Makers Competition.* Essentially, this was an inducement for kids to pick up a camera and make their own home movies. Winners hailed from places like Tunbridge Wells, Old Bromley and Much Humping, whereas Drumchapel, Easterhouse or Greenock never figured. Which was a pity because if you were looking for a summer story that had surprise, intrigue, drama and near tragedy then shooting some footage around Celtic Park over *this* close season would have made for a great movie.

Ten-in-a-row was yesterday's dream – as big a fantasy as the lovelies who adorned the Tennent's Lager tins in bikinis. Big Jock, never a man to tread water when there was some swimming to be done, decided that it was time to assess his squad.

He released Jim Brogan on a free transfer on 4 June. The utility player had been at the club so long that he could describe himself in old money as a *left-half* and had picked up his fair share of medals during the glory years of the Stein stewardship. Throughout the previous season, his regular position at full-back had been challenged by Pat McCluskey and Andy Lynch and both players appeared to be ousting Jim from the team on a more frequent basis. Still, it did seem a bit surprising that Jock was willing to dispense with his services completely. A hard-working player who combined aggression with elegance in the manner of 007, he checked into Coventry City at the start of the new season as Brogan, James Brogan.

If news of his departure was enough to lift Roger Moore's eyebrow then the next missive from Celtic Park would be sufficient to rip the toupee from Sean Connery's head. Five days after the release of Jim Brogan it was announced that the Celtic career of James Connolly Johnstone was over! Jimmy the Jink had dribbled the last run for his beloved Hoops.

Arguably, there had been a perceptible decline in the quality of the wee man's performances in season 1974-1975 with the high of the Scottish League Cup Final being his finest moment of the overall campaign. But Jinky was only on the verge of his thirty-first birthday and although at a turning point professionally speaking, he was still able to influence a match when he was in the mood.

His decision to take an early-morning cruise off the coast of Largs prior to the Home International series and a subsequent incident in an Oslo bar as the squad were en route to the World Cup Finals seemed to have put paid to his Scotland career. He played his last game against East Germany in the winter of 1974. The feeling was that the only man who could control Jimmy's colourful excesses was Big Jock. And now Celtic were casting him adrift without the back-up of the Largs coastguard to rescue him this time.

The club had always been built on the reputation of entertainers and in that respect Jimmy Johnstone was to Celtic what Bob Hope was to Paramount Pictures; an all-singin', all-dancin', wise-crackin' talent who held an audience's gaze with consummate ease. He had formed a successful double act with Big Jock over the years with The Master either barking the orders or pulling the strings and Jimmy performing his party-pieces to delighted crowds.

Watching the unlikely pairing of Windsor Davies and Don Estelle on *Top Of The Pops* that week rendering their number one hit *Whispering Grass*, it was difficult not to draw the parallel between

Sergeant Major Stein and the diminutive *Lofty* Johnstone. As Estelle would pour out the enormous gift that was his sweet vaudeville voice, Davies would take it in turns to cajole, mock and then almost cry with pride at the beauty of the wee man's talent.

Sing, Lofty boy, sing . . . Play, Jinky Bhoy, play . . . Any way you looked at it, it was a moment of chrysalis and Johnstone was never the same player again. As one right-winger departed the scene another arrived on the public conscience.

Margaret Thatcher had been running the Conservative Party since February when she ousted Uncle Ted Heath. That there was a woman leading a British political party was in itself historic but the fact that the party in question was an acknowledged bastion of the old-school tie network and the preservation of stuffy male politics was indeed a revelation. We sure as hell were living in changing times.

Of course, the changes taking place at Celtic Park were all at the behest of Jock Stein. Having dispensed with the services of two of his stalwarts, he now indicated that the club were about to move in a different direction. In an Icelandic centre-half he had seen potential for a pivot to replace Cesar in the Celtic back four and freshen up the Hoops. The decision was taken to bring Johannes Edvaldsson on board as a trialist.

The Master would have a more in-depth look at the player when he resumed control at the helm after that family holiday to the island of Menorca. In the movie that is the history of Celtic, Big Jock's departure from the desk at Paradise that day with the name *Johannes Edvaldsson* written down in his diary would then cut dramatically to a scene of carnage.

The A74 dual carriageway connecting Glasgow and Carlisle was a notorious stretch of road that had claimed the lives of many a motorist. On the morning of 3 July 1975 it almost added the name of Jock Stein to its infamous list.

The Big Man was on his way back from that relaxing holiday having flown into Manchester only hours before. He was in the company of his wife Jean and three close friends, at the wheel of his car when a Peugeot, travelling on the wrong side of the road, collided head-on with his Mercedes close to the Borders town, Lockerbie. The considered wisdom is that, had it not been for the robust nature of the powerful big German car, then the events of that morning would have written Big Jock's obituary.

There could be no disguising the seriousness of his injuries though, and just like that earlier heart problem from the winter of 1972, rumours once again circulated that he had died. Certainly, on a personal note, that was the first thing I heard as an uncle of the Celtic persuasion and allegedly *in the know*, 'phoned our house to pass on the news.

The accident had occurred far too late for inclusion in the morning papers, accessing Radio Clyde 261 was still like the French Resistance trying to contact London from a field in war-torn Beauvais, and BBC1, in keeping with the season, were running *Summer Holiday* without recourse to newsflashes. I spent a fruitless morning watching Cliff Bloody Richard and the Shad-bloody-ows crossing Europe in a double-decker when all I wanted was some indication that our leader was well. *We interrupt this programme to tell you that it all works out for Cliff Richard and Una Stubbs on a beach in Greece!* Thank God for that then!

Eventually, genuine bulletins on Big Jock's condition were issued and it was with great relief that we all discovered he had survived the crash along with his passengers, but that it would be some time before he could resume his duties at Celtic Park. In fact, he would be out of commission for the entire season.

Sean Fallon stepped up to the plate and signed Johannes Edvaldsson from Halbek of Denmark, presumably fulfilling Jock's wishes. This seemed an inspired piece of business when he scored the only goal of the game in a pre-season friendly with Derby County at Celtic Park.

The friendly fare is never a reliable guide to the up-and-coming season but Derby under Dave Mackay were the English champions at the time and the Celts gave a good account of themselves. The only problem was that *Johannes Edvaldsson* was as big a mouthful as Marlon Brando's play-piece so the Celtic support re-christened their first-ever Icelandic hero '*Shuggie*'.

It was to be hoped that he would give them plenty of opportunity to chant the name throughout the season. Not only were Celtic having to get used to life under Fallon, there was also a brand new League format to which Scottish clubs had to adapt.

The perennial question for the domestic legislators was how to make the Scottish First Division at least more competitive, if not exciting. While Celtic's nine-in-a-row had been feted throughout the hoop-speaking world, there was a perception that a League so easily won by the same team year-on-year was detrimental to the health of the overall game . . . and that wasn't just coming from Rangers supporters.

The revolutionary idea was to create a League comprising ten teams who would play against each other four times a season. Did you get that? *Four* times a season. Morecambe and Wise didn't face up to each other as often and they were at the height of their powers. It even had a fancy new name as well . . . The Scottish Premier League. *Hey! From the people who brought you the Drybrough Cup!* It looked as if that packet of Capstan Extra-Strength and the bookie's pencil had been fully employed again.

In order to facilitate the new set-up, the top tier reduced from eighteen teams to ten, meaning that the finish of season 1974-75 entailed the biggest cull in the history of sport. *No, No,* argued the powers that be, *nobody is being relegated. They're all just leaving to form their very own Scottish First Division!* Clearly a career in politics awaited the mastermind who promulgated this statute.

In keeping with the new order of events, BBC Scotland decided to get in on the act by re-branding its Saturday night flagship football show. The quaintly-sounding *Sportsreel* with all its connotations of Pathe news broadcasts and Brylcreemed *Hail-fellow-well-met* was redrafted with the racier title *Sportscene.*

Scene was an ultra-mod word. Everybody had a *scene* that they were either into or out of in the 1970s. *It's just not my scene, man,* as hip Dave said to his girl in a popular public information cartoon outlining how cool it was to be a swimmer. Thankfully for Dave's girl, she still had a third wish from her fairy godmother at which point we're introduced to Mike who famously *swims like a fish.* In order for Dave to stop *losing me birds* he is advised to learn to swim. In other words, make it his *scene.* Everybody talked about the *pop scene,* the *Scottish scene,* the *movie scene* so it seemed in keeping with the zeitgeist that the Beeb co-opted the *Sportscene.*

Televised footy in the 1970s was still regarded as a form of light entertainment as opposed to the life-or-death drama that routinely took place on the pitch. *Sportsreel/scene* had an established format from which it rarely, if ever, deviated. Despite the use of the word *sport* the programme was devoted to football 99% of the time.

There would be twenty five minutes given over to a Scottish match, that is to whoever Celtic or Rangers were playing, and then the show would be wound up with a couple of highlights from the offshoot of BBC London's *Match of the Day.* Unlike the wonderful modern world of *Sky Sports,* no trenchant analysis of the game or the individual display of say Kenny D would be offered by a former pro. The presenter would merely point out a couple of crucial moments, replay the goals and then announce the other key scores of the day just in case you'd been on Mars and didn't know how your team had got on. It was slick, polished and invited little reply.

The only alteration to the schedule would be during the Five Nations rugby tournament when the network would cut short the English footy to show us Scotland being horsed by the Welsh or the French all to the dulcet tones of Bill McLaren. *Scotsport* on STV was the only commercial equivalent and it went out on a Sunday afternoon. If the Beeb had the Rangers match, then *Scotsport* would have the Celtic game and vice versa; a cosy arrangement that kept the majority tuning in on a weekly basis.

Scotsport did attempt to embrace other sports by mentioning the US Masters or a bizarrely important basketball match in Stirling but, by and large, they stuck to Scotland's national game. There was the odd Sunday when the programme would be on location at an ice-rink and we knew that we would have to endure half-an-hour of curling before we got to see a ball being kicked. Whoever came up with *that* idea had obviously never watched curling. A topless Pans People team couldn't have sexed it up.

The presenters of both programmes bore the same initials but that's where the similarity ended. In the blue corner, Archie Macpherson for the BBC; over in the red corner, Arthur Montford representing STV.

Archie's stentorian style characterised the headmaster that he had been in a previous life. When he addressed you from the goggle box you had to sit up straight, fold your arms and remove any chewing gum from your mouth. He liked to pontificate majestically about the preceding Scottish match and very much seemed to write his own scripts as well as commentate on the big games.

He would be the originator of phrases such as, *Kenny Dalglish must let fly! Dixie Deans is in splendid isolation* and his favourite expression for a scorcher that either ripped the net off or hit the residents of row Z was *Woof!* If he wasn't in the mood to venture outside of Glasgow, his faithful lieutenant Alastair Alexander would have to cover the match from Pittodrie or Tannadice.

Alexander wore more hair cream than a Spitfire pilot and actually looked as if he'd flown sorties for the RAF during the Battle of Britain. Together, they were a potent no-nonsense team who gave the impression that a sloppy footballer should be sent to Archie's study for a caning or subjected to National Service with utmost haste.

In contrast, Arthur Montford employed a more relaxed manner behind the presenting desk that was at odds with his tendency to lose the plot and scream like he was at a Bay City Rollers concert when the action out on the pitch was almost too orgasmic to describe. His journalistic credentials, honed on Glasgow's vibrant evening newspapers, lent well to the self-editing technique that he would employ to reduce the finest goal in the world to a brief, emphatic summary. *Fine pass Glavin, lovely shimmy Dalglish, bang-bang Deans, 1-0 Celtic.*

Just like Archie, he had a vocabulary of his very own and coined the expression *Stramash* to indicate an unholy mess inside the eighteen-yard box. The Dixmaster, for example, would never be bearing down on goal; he would be *out in front* wherever that was, and defeat was never considered to be trivial but an unmitigated *disaster!*

Arthur wasn't a headmaster, of course. He did seem more like a chemistry teacher, one who had too many unexplained explosions over his Bunsen burner in the lab. And then, there were the jackets. Mention the name *Arthur Montford* to anyone of a certain vintage and they will almost certainly reply . . . *those jaickets* and shake their head.

Arthur wore the kinds of sports coats that even the flamboyant George Melly would have refused to entertain. They had more dodgy checks than the Prague underworld, looked as if they'd been designed for the Alexander Brothers and, when Arthur matched them up with a thrilling lemon or pink tie, would play havoc with the interference on your telly! Let's just say that if you owned one now, you'd be hard-pushed to get rid of it on eBay.

On paper, it looked as if *Sportscene* – with its snappy new title, colourful graphics and heavyweight anchor in Archie Macpherson – would be the authoritative word on the Scottish football jamboree and there wasn't a great deal that Arthur and his *Sunday Post* cosiness could do about it. BBC Scotland even got the chance to trail the late night attractions as they did their own live scoreboard at 4.45 on the Saturday afternoon.

This was presented by Gordon Hewitt who, rather alarmingly for a final scores programme presenter, seemed to have little interest in the game of football at all. He would flash up onto our screens immediately after Grandstand had delivered the classified results and announce the highlights of the Scottish action.

The haphazard live link from London always seemed to catch our Gordon unaware as he sat clad in a blue crushed velvet jacket, neatly pressed shirt, smartly-knotted tie and his disconcertingly tinted spectacles. The wee man always seemed to feign enthusiasm for the comings and goings of the results business and, like all pundits in Scotland, the game was to work out which team he actually favoured, if any. We were convinced that there was a certain glee in his demeanour if the Celts had fared poorly that day . . . although I'd imagine our rival brethren would presume that Gordon's glasses were tinted green. With the first game in the all-new Scottish Premier League there would be a chance to clarify Gordon's persuasion as someone had decided that the campaign would kick-off with a derby match.

Sean Fallon led his troops over to Ibrox to face the new Scottish champions. Just in case we'd forgotten that fact, Rangers very kindly reminded us by unfurling the League flag from the previous season immediately before the game started. Well, it had been more than ten years since they'd won the title and it was a change to see a flag at Ibrox that wasn't at half-mast midway through the season as a mark of respect for the death of yet another championship challenge!

The Govan Select were having a laugh and so it continued as the Celts went down 2-1 on the day. Gordon Hewitt appeared both happy and deflated in equal measure; damn his illusive style!

Captain Kenny Dalglish had put Celtic 1-0 up at half-time almost as an act of celebration for his elevated status but it wasn't enough to see out the match. The toss-up for the Celtic captaincy, the man who followed Cesar, must have been a close call.

Danny McGrain must surely have been a candidate with perhaps Lemon, the senior citizen of the team, equally in with a shout if it all boiled down to experience. Indeed, the last of the Lions had led out the Celtic team when the League Cup action commenced but the official nod was given to Kenny D prior to the start of the Premier League campaign.

To be fair, having recovered from his post-World Cup downer, the King had regained his form in the second half of the thwarted ten-in-a-row season and proved why he was the best player in the country and then some. But there were suggestions at the time that he had advanced to skipper as the result of a transfer request placed with the Celtic board.

Following on from the release of Jimmy the Jink and the horror that was Big Jock's car crash, the news that King Kenny wanted away rolled ashore like an oil slick. What's that they say about *bad things always coming in threes?*

Perhaps, with the intuitive instinct that placed him in the right place at the right time to receive a pass, Kenny D had surmised that the future was not going to be one that restored Celtic as a domestic and European force. The loss of the league title and the exit from the European Cup at the hands of a less-than-creative Greek side the year before had pointed him in one direction.

Eventually, a deal was worked out which may have involved the captaincy or maybe The King just felt that to pursue a move when Celtic were overwhelmed with the unavoidable loss of

Big Jock's leadership was ill-timed and insensitive. Whatever the reason, it was Captain Kenny who shook hands with Rangers counterpart John Greig on the opening day of the Premier League.

The transfer request was in the background but Kenny D had alerted the world to the fact that he had considered a move and there would be one certainty about his season. Every time he kicked a ball in Celtic colours now he would be inviting English scouts to pursue him like the crocodiles who hit the water whenever Tarzan dived in for a swim.

The only positive note about the derby day reversal was that there would be three opportunities in this new league set-up to gain revenge. The League Cup had been the season-opener for 1975. *What? . . . No Drybrough Cup?* Correct.

It transpired that the addition of two extra fixtures to accommodate the fledgling Premier League had been the torpedo that finally holed the good ship *Drybrough.* Celtic and Rangers always viewed the competition the same way that a daughter regarded dancing with her father at a family wedding; you go along with it reluctantly and you want it to be over quickly. All a bit rich really, given that Rangers had never won it and Celtic's record in the final was played four, won one.

In the transport cafe that was Scottish football then, the League Cup was the new starter, the Premier League main course had less portions but you got more chips, the Scottish Cup was a predictable dessert and Drybrough was completely off the menu.

Heading out to Hampden for the Scottish League Cup Final was an established ritual for the Celtic support coming, as it did this year, for the twelfth consecutive time. Had the League legislators not messed about with final dates like, for example, the nonsense that was that joust with Dundee in the Siberian winter of 1973, then booking the last Saturday in October would have been the first thing the Hoops faithful did at the outset of the season.

Thrillingly enough, the 1975 final, with the Celts defending their trophy, was against Rangers. *That* Rangers. The team that had whipped the title from us in what was to be our *Magic, ten-in-a-row* season. The team that had beaten us in our first ever Premier League match. The team that, having tasted the champagne of their first championship pennant in more than a decade, wanted to get drunk on the Scottish League Cup for the first time in five years.

It was the climax to a campaign that never really grabbed the imagination. The sectional opening was interesting enough with the involvement of Aberdeen and Hearts but the quarters and semis were taken up with defeating Stenhousemuir and Partick Thistle.

The 'Muir tie was a two-leg affair played out in front of low gates both home and away. A measly 6,000 people were attracted to the second game which made Celtic Park look like a ghost town. Truly, the curling on *Scotsport* got a bigger audience!

Shuggy Edvaldsson re-established his cult credentials with his goal seeing off the Jags in the semi at Hampden so it was onwards to face the Govan Select at the end of October. By that point, the Celts seemed to have adjusted well to the new League system and had remained unbeaten since the opening day defeat at Ibrox. The main highlight was a 4-0 thumping when the Blue Bonnets had arrived at Celtic Park as Dundee were generally tricky opponents.

The Master was back for that one but only really as an observer. He would try and make his presence felt over the season but the recuperation process was going to be a lengthy one. Thankfully, Celtic performed for him that day like a precocious child in front of daddy; full of invention and vigour and well worth the points. After that, it had been a steady run with the only negative being a one-all draw away to Motherwell but a reality check was in order when Hibs came to town the week before the League Cup final and were 2-0 to the good with less than ten minutes to go.

It was at that point that Sean Fallon pulled a masterstroke

by having a dense fog descend upon the pitch making the game unplayable! Other than divine intervention how else could we account for the sudden change in the weather over Glasgow? A game that had been hard to watch for the Celtic support now literally became impossible to watch as Paradise resembled the pea-soup best of Victorian London.

For all we knew, Jack The Ripper might have been on the pitch by the time referee Bobby Davidson decided to give the whole thing up for the foggy charade that it was and abandoned the game. But it was more than a tad concerning that Hibernian had seemed to be coasting towards their first win at Celtic Park in six years when the mist intervened in our favour. If only we could use that fog trick every time we were behind in a match.

JAWS! had been the movie sensation of the year. The story of the hunting of a great white shark that was terrorising the American coastal town of Amity had been playing to packed theatres everywhere as well as emptying beaches from St Tropez to Saltcoats. Nobody wanted to go in for a dip. Not even cartoon *Mike* who famously *swims like a fish. Being eaten by a shark just isn't my scene, man* as the bird-less Dave may have opined. *JAWS!* also provided the perfect opportunity to daub a nickname onto any footballer who was perhaps renowned for the fearsome nature of his tackling ability.

Such a man was Tom Forsyth of the Rangers; he of the lethal shin-tap over the line for the winner in the 1973 Scottish Cup Final. Forsyth had been one of the main players in the *Stopping The Ten* campaign and his reputation as a no-nonsense defender with a tough edge to his play was one that he seemed to enjoy. Indeed, the nickname *JAWS!* may even have been taken as a compliment by a man who was now establishing himself at Scottish international level as well. He was to be an influential combatant in the League Cup Final.

Harry Harry and Pat McCluskey went into the referee's book

after a couple of clashes with Forsyth whilst he himself received the yellow card for an uncompromising challenge on Danny McGrain. When this was followed up a few minutes later by a robust tackle – hell, a blatant foul – on King Kenny, then the expectation was that *JAWS!* would be taking an earlier swim than anyone else in the Hampden bath-tub. That he didn't was a source of some mystery to the Celtic officials as referee Bill Anderson took no action.

By that point Rangers were leading the match with an Alex MacDonald header and holding the Celtic charge at bay with some comfort. Despite the huffing and puffing of the Celtic wolf, the house of bricks that was the Govan defence would not fall down and another League Cup had been lost. Still, it was early days and the final was part of a derby double header.

In 1974, the Celts had caned Hibs in the League one week before duffing them up Dixie-style at Hampden and now having lost to Rangers in the cup, there was an opportunity for instant revenge with a League encounter at Celtic Park scheduled for the following Saturday at 1pm. This time, the early kick-off could not be blamed on Uncle Ted and his three-day week. In an effort to get ahead of any crowd trouble before and after the game, the police had suggested the lunch-time start. As a concept, it seemed to work and would now become a familiar feature of the coming seasons.

Paul Wilson bagged a goal but the pattern of not being able to put one over on the Govan Select continued in a 1-1 draw. It was beginning to look as if we would need all of these increased fixtures to get a result against them. Shuggy was settling in well though. He'd even managed to claim a hat-trick on a remarkable night down in Ayr when the Honest Men had been ripped apart to the tune of 7-2 by a rampant Celtic.

The Bhoys had never fielded an Icelander until his arrival and there was another first that year when they faced up to Shuggy's countrymen for the first time in the shape of Valur from Reykjavik. The football gods sure had a weird sense of timing.

This, of course, was in the European Cup-Winners Cup which we'd all heard about but had never actually seen since the dawn of the nine-in-a-row sequence. The last time the Celts had lowered their standards to this competition was way back in 1966 when a controversial defeat to Bill Shankly's Liverpool at Anfield had threatened to upset his friendship with Big Jock. Thankfully, his fellow miner with the voice hewn from gravel had the good grace to be the only manager of an English side who would bother to travel to Lisbon one year later so that he could rasp *John, you're immortal* to The Master after the epic European Cup victory. That Liverpool match had been a semi-final which was a hard egg to swallow but at least proved that Celtic had the *cojones* to work the Euro-ticket.

And now we were back and everyone involved in the Cup-Winners gig was assuring us that this was the place to be rather than that high-falutin' European jug with the big ears. We would take some convincing. Anyhow, it gave Shuggy the chance to lead out his new side in Reykjavik when they took on Valur in the first round. Ol' sentimental Sean Fallon made him captain for the match.

The honour was compounded when Celtic were awarded a penalty to take the score to 3-0 and the big Icelander ambled over to take the kick. Back in Iceland . . . say hello to the folks . . . make jokes about the weather and stick a penalty away for a hearty victory. It was all going to plan for Shuggy but then he blasted his shot past the post.

Perhaps the referee was feeling the heat from the big man's blushing cheeks as he ordered the kick to be re-taken. Apparently the Valur goalkeeper had moved as Shuggy started his run-up so it was Take Two for the hometown bhoy. Tragically, the sequel was worse than the original as this time the by-now static goalie made an easy save.

Ah Shuggy . . . you come back here as the bhoy whose made it with your big city ways and your fancy football but you cannot put away a penalty with two attempts! What is the Icelandic for banjos and cow's backsides? At least nobody mentioned the Cod War, to paraphrase Basil Fawlty, who was now appearing to be BBC2's best-kept secret in the sitcom *Fawlty Towers.*

John Cleese and wife/writing partner/fellow cast member Connie Booth had created six half-hour nuggets of comedy gold set in a Torquay hotel. Everybody got it from the irascible Basil with his complete disdain for most of the forms of human life who booked rooms in his hotel. Builders, children, lounge-lizards, old people and, on one legendary occasion, Germans were the source of his fury and every week would bring a fresh episode that, impossibly, was somehow even better than the last one.

You could have sold tickets for the potential stand-off between Big Jock and Basil Fawlty had the hotelier ever graduated to Celtic's favourite seaside retreat, the Seamill Hydro, which was where the bhoys headed in advance of the next game in Europe against Boavista of Portugal.

Big Latch enjoyed his best game to date with a string of excellent saves including a penalty that kept the score at 0-0 in the Portugese sunshine. The return leg at Celtic Park was fairly bright as well, although that had more to do with the Boavista strip. Someone in the Portugese football fashion industry had decided that the boys from Boa would look their best running around a pitch with a blue and white draughts board painted onto their jerseys. From a distance they looked like a crossword puzzle for the colour-blind.

Even at a time when at least 30% of the denizens of Celtic Park were cutting about dressed like the Bay City Rollers in flared trousers ludicrously seamed with tartan, twin-coloured *waister* jumpers with three huge stars at the front and platform shoes that induced vertigo, the Boa's fashion sense was dead on arrival.

Not that Celtic could have opined much on the subject given that, under new European rules, they were having to display numbers on the back of the sacred hoops. Actually, sacrilege just doesn't come close to this edict. It was like painting a baseball cap on the Mona Lisa but rules are rules and there was the Dixmaster scuttling about the park with a large black *9* taking up space on his back.

It may just have confused the opposition as King Kenny had the Celts 1-0 up in thirty-five seconds whilst Shuggy *No, No, Not A Penalty Kick* Edvaldsson made it two by the twenty-minute mark. Boavista pulled one back before half-time which meant that the animal that was the away goals rule was starting to make the Celtic defence nervy. It was a relief when the Dixmaster popped up with five minutes left to make it 3-1.

That finish meant that the Celts were in the quarter-finals and up against Sachsenring Zwickau of East Germany. The name sounded like a cold war villain from a Len Deighton novel but at least you could get it printed onto the match-day programme unlike the club's previous title . . . BSG Aktivist Karl-Marx Zwickau. Who says that politics and sport don't mix when you can put a snappy name to your club like that one? . . . *For we only know that there's going to be a show and the grand old BSG Aktivist Karl-Marx Zwickau will be theeeeeere!* Phew!

Little was known about the club but, then again, the same could be said for the whole of East Germany as well. The Hoops pretty much peppered the goal of Zwickau custodian Jurgen Croy and by half-time had secured the lead courtesy of a great move between Danny McG and King Kenny which ended with the Celtic captain tucking away another spectacular strike. Yet, frustratingly, it could have been 2-0 had Lemon not missed a penalty on the half-hour mark before that sweeping Danny/Kenny combo.

As is the way of these things, the miss was a costly one and returned to haunt the team as late as the ninetieth minute. That was when a long ball that would have cleared the Berlin Wall was punted from the German penalty box out to the half-way line where the only two players in attendance were Celtic's Roy Aitken and Zwickau striker Ludwig Blank.

Roy, soon to be known as The Bear, was, at this point, a mere cub given his schoolboy status and it could have been this tender naivety that stopped him from the cynical challenge that would have halted the German in his tracks. As it was, Blank slipped the cub and tore off down the Celtic half like he'd just cleared Checkpoint Charlie with illegal papers. By now he was, as Archie Macpherson might have said, in *splendid isolation.* Latch in goal tried to narrow the angle but there was little he could do to stop Herr Ludwig from scoring.

All around a stunned Celtic Park there was silence apart from the guys in the press box who suddenly realised that they could now use the headline *Celtic Draw A Blank* with gleeful justification. From a game where the Hoops could have been, should have been, a few goals to the good, they were now being asked to cross over to Zwickau and haul back the away goals advantage. Even James Bond struggled to get a result in East Germany. And no-one ever asked 007 to go on a mission when he was recovering from the flu.

An epidemic had swept through the Celtic ranks immediately after the first-leg; one that was so severe that League games against Ayr United and Rangers had to be postponed. Even the Govan Select were laid low by the bug which meant that the derby match could well have turned into a five-a-side game if it came down to fit players. The fortnight that the Celtic were *on the sick* was the worst possible preparation for a big Euro-tie and by the time they'd made it out onto the pitch in Germany, a makeshift side donned the hoops. How makeshift?

Midfielder Tommy Tid Callaghan playing in defence in place of the injured Andy Lynch and centre-half Roddie *the Highlander* McDonald playing up front as a substitute for the Dixmaster who had to be left at home in Glasgow. Little wonder then that the team looked a little out of sorts; a fact that was confirmed as early as the fifth minute when Herr Blank turned up once again to fire Zwickau into the lead.

There was to be no more scoring although Roddie McDonald induced heart attacks all around the Georgi Dimitroff stadium when he appeared to have grabbed an equaliser in the eighty-seventh minute with a header from a Harry Harry corner. The Spanish referee cut short the Celtic celebrations when he blew his whistle for a mysterious foul on the goalkeeper and awarded a free-kick instead.

In British time, the game had kicked off at 2.00 in the afternoon and was being shown live by the BBC. This was difficult news for me personally, given the whole school scenario, so I did my best to cultivate this flu bug that appeared to be all the rage in the football world. The fact that I was not a member of the first team squad at Celtic Park was a considerable problem to overcome with the folks and so my pleas of a twenty-four-hour high temperature which had mysteriously manifested itself on the day of the match, fell on deaf ears. *No really . . . I picked this up from Kenny Dalglish when he was firing potshots in at me at training!*

Mercifully, the headmaster was a season ticket holder in Paradise and wasn't going to pass up the chance to catch the second leg on the box, so we were all bundled into the school theatre as the grainy, black and white footage was relayed from East Germany. The screen was about fourteen inches in diameter and about 140 of us were all trying to watch it at the same time but even we could see that Roddie the Highlander hadn't touched Jurgen Croy as he rose for that all-important header. It was all a bit deflating but Hey! better than the ninety minutes of arithmetic that was supposed to be our lot that afternoon.

Perhaps if Stevie Murray had been explaining long division to us it might have made for a more stimulating subject but the Student Prince was having enough troubles of his own with a recurring injury problem. Sad to say he retired in September but, like Frank Sinatra, attempted a comeback barely three months later. All to no avail and by the January of 1976, the talented midfielder succumbed to the inevitable and bowed out of Celtic Park. He had cracked a bone in his foot at training and with the savvy that he possessed had reasoned that his top-flight professional football career was over. He was a loss in a season of transition and left the club just before a Scottish Cup tie against Motherwell. Farewell Student Prince.

As one of the perks of being captain of Celtic, King Kenny had been writing a column for weekly football bible, *Shoot!* magazine. Naturally, for an English publication, the main focus of the mag was given over to the game south of the border but they did allow a take on the Scottish product with their faintly patronising *Tartan Talk* section. Even then it was a slot that alternated between the King and John Greig of the Govan Select on a weekly basis.

Shoot! was one of those magazines that rejoiced in the game of football whilst staying well clear of any of the attendant controversies. The murky side to the ninety minutes, such as vicious tackling, diving for penalties and just plain, bloody cheating, was never featured. They did speak to the players who mattered but, unfortunately, had a habit of asking them questions of stunning banality. The best bit was when a footballer would fill in a personal questionnaire about his likes, dislikes, ambitions and so on.

Inevitably, and completely at odds with the revelations in the tabloids, most players in the 1970s seemed to like nothing better than a quiet night out at a local restaurant with their wife for a steak dinner. Their favourite television programme always seemed to be a choice between *Match of the Day* or *The Two Ronnies* and when asked who they would most like to meet in the entire world, it was the Queen, God Bless You Ma'am! Although this was always and I do mean *always* followed up by . . . *as she presents me with the FA Cup at Wembley.*

Her Majesty's only serious rival for the hero worship of the 1970s player was Muhammad Ali, which was as understandable as it was credible. Frank Worthington of Leicester City had the class to list Elvis Presley as his hero but when asked who he would most like to meet, he plumped for a lady by the name of Joyce McKinney. Considering that Joyce's fifteen minutes of tabloid fame had recently consisted of her part in a notorious Mormon sex-in-chains story, it would be fair to say that the editing staff at *Shoot!* allowed a real blooper to pass under the radar. Frankie boy, wot a lad, eh?

The week before the Scottish Cup Third Round clash, King Kenny in his *Tartan Talk* feature suggested that the top clubs should be seeded when it came to the draw. In that way, a Motherwell-Celtic encounter would be more likely to occur in the later rounds. This turned out to be sage advice from the King as Motherwell promptly overturned an early 2-0 deficit to oust the Cup holders by winning 3-2.

The Steelmen had already notched a League triumph against Celtic back in November when they had come over to Kerrydale Street and won 2-0 but they just weren't expected to bump the Hoops from the Cup. A character named Willie Pettigrew was the common denominator as his goal-scoring prowess in both games was the significant factor.

He looked like the lead part in a Peter McDougall play with his long Nazareth hair, woolly moustache and generally dishevelled appearance. At twenty three, he was far too young for the facial hair and it's not very often that you get to call a mowser *unkempt* but there is no other way to describe the top lip appearance.

Given that Oor Willie was the very embodiment of that fabulous Scottish word *glaikit,* he was never going to be much in demand for football modelling contracts but he was on a roll in a season that saw him claim the top scorer spot in the country and gain the first of five Scotland caps.

Surrendered the League Cup, out of the Scottish; the season couldn't have seemed any longer had the home crowd at Celtic Park been asked to read *War & Peace.*

January had been a dubious month for all associated with the Celtic cause, a microcosm of the overall campaign. Once again, Rangers held the upper hand in the New Year derby that finished 1-0 and although that was the only League defeat of the month, there were alarming signs that the Celtic defence was being organised by Manuel, the hapless Spanish waiter from the aforementioned Fawlty Towers. Week upon week, Latch and his back four were to be seen standing with their hands outstretched saying *Que?* to each other as goals were given up with the easy virtue of Jodie Foster in the movie *Taxi Driver.*

Dundee were allowed to pull back two for a 3-3 draw at Celtic Park whilst, up at Muirton, the soon-to-be-relegated St. Johnstone led three times in the match only to be pegged back each time and then surpassed by Shuggy's last gasp winner. The collapse to Motherwell in the cup was the last straw for Sean Fallon and so Alastair Hunter came in from Siberia to replace Latch for the match at home to Dundee United.

Ally took over the same weekend that *Mamma Mia* replaced the epic *Bohemian Rhapsody* at number one which seemed appropriate since he'd been out of favour for as long as Queen had been at the top of charts . . . which seemed like *forever!* Any thoughts that he'd harboured about putting a stop to the goal haemorrhage were scorched as early as the first minute when the Arabs went ahead quicker than you could say *Galileo! Galileo!*

At that point Sean Fallon must have thought that he'd have been better fielding a back four of Benny, Bjorn, Agnetha & Anni-Frid but fortunately King Kenny and Paul Wilson rescued the smorgasbord with two goals to snatch the points.

Despite the evident struggles out on the pitch, and even with that NY defeat to the Govan Select, Celtic were still leading the Scottish Premier League. Gordon Hewitt reminded us gleefully every Saturday that it was by the slenderest of margins – one point. Wee Gordy's demeanour was as hard to read as a Jackie Collins novel and he should have picked up a BAFTA for the level of his performance. You tell me. Was his glee there because the Celts were still at the top or because that one point advantage was negligible and could be overturned by the capricious nature of a ninety minute League outing?

Rumour had it that Big Jock was now taking a more active, if still restricted, interest in the events unfolding in his kingdom. This seemed to bear fruit on 15 March when Johnny Doyle realised a bhoyhood dream by signing on at Paradise for a fee of £90,000. It seems inconceivable that Sean Fallon would have routinely broken the Celtic transfer record unless it was at the behest of Jock Stein. The Celts were at Glasgow Airport on their way out to East Germany for the second leg of the Zwickau tie when Doylie rolled up at the check-in desk to put pen to paper.

The Iron Curtain was replete with transfers taking place at airports but usually involving secret agents and competing powers all played out to a Cold War background. Ayr United were not known to be members of the Warsaw Pact, Jock Stein was not the head of NATO and Glasgow Airport was hardly at the crossroads of international affairs but the whole thing did have a whiff of Harry Palmer about it. I mean, come on, Johnny Doyle moving to Celtic was hardly going to affect the British Government was it?

On 16 March, Harold Wilson resigned as Prime Minister. In a move that genuinely took the political world by surprise, old *white heat* Wilson had finally burned out and decided that he'd had enough of running

the country. Speculation was at boiling point. Had he left because he knew that the country was in an irretrievable mess? Was he going in advance of a huge political scandal that would have brought him down anyway? Did he just blame himself for the inflationary spiral that had seen an Ayr United player valued at £90,000?

Wilson merely said that he'd always intended to retire in March 1976. The press were unconvinced and none too happy about the lack of clarity but the resignation would always remain a mystery. In saying that, there were a lot of mysteries doing the rounds that year.

How had a boring old fart like Tom Good managed to share a marriage, never mind a bed, with the luscious Felicity Kendal in Beeb sitcom *The Good Life*? Who slept in the adjoining room to Lesley Judd when Peter Purves and John Noakes accompanied her on the Blue Peter summer fact-finding trips? What was the real age of that bloke with the moustache in Brotherhood of Man and wasn't anyone concerned that the subject of their Eurovision hit *Save All Your Kisses For Me* was a three-year-old girl? What had happened to Ronnie Glavin?

At £80,000, he had been the most expensive purchase in the Celtic squad up until the Johnny Doyle bank-buster. His transfer to the 'Tic, had only been surpassed by the long, drawn-out tedium that was Queen's video for *Bohemian Rhapsody.* He'd been one of the successes in the 1974-75 season with his debut goal, foraging midfield runs, and the winner against Dundee in the Scottish Cup semi-final and he was a vital cog in the side that had lifted the trophy beyond Airdrie's grasp in Billy McNeill's last hurrah. But this year, Ronnie G's standards had slipped alarmingly with his only goal coming in a League Cup game against Hearts way back in August.

With Stevie the Student Prince retiring and George Connelly effectively off the payroll since September, the way should have been clear for him to rule the midfield berth for the Hoops. The main difficulty appeared to be that Sean Fallon fancied Ronnie more as a defensive midfielder rather than an attacking one. It was a role that he struggled in and combined with niggling injuries, his season had been such a failure that there was talk of him being a part of the deal that brought Doylie to Celtic Park.

Ayr United, naturally, fancied a cash deal more than an added wage on the Somerset Park ledger but it must have been worrying for the G-Man that Celtic were prepared to part with his services. Particularly at a point when they were clinging onto the lead at the summit of the Premier League.

There had been some sumptuous performances – 4-0 versus Hibs in February with the inevitable Dixmaster getting a goal and reprising his *Dirty Harry* role for what would turn out to be the last time; and a similar overwhelming of Motherwell at Celtic Park in March that almost made up for the Cup exit. However, mixed into that were shaky single goal victories over the lesser lights of Dundee and St Johnstone.

The feeling was that the Celts were one defeat away from potential capitulation. One bouncing bomb away from a Dambusters-style soaking. It arrived at Tannadice in April with a 3-2 loss to Dundee United. Kenny D tried to stem the flood with two goals but Celtic never got going in the match and the Ruhr dam that was Celtic's title challenge cracked and then completely collapsed. Where was that fog now when we needed it most?

Rangers assumed bomber command and with dropped points over the next few weeks to Aberdeen (1-1), Hibs (2-0) and the Doyle-less Ayr United (2-1 *at Celtic Park*!) the Celts ensured that they would not be the winners of the very first Scottish Premier League. Oh yeah, and just to add lemon to the pancakes, Rangers won the Scottish Cup as well, which gave them a domestic . . . I can't say it . . . I won't say it . . . it rhymes with *rebel* and involves winning three trophies in one season . . . okay? Now, butt out and leave me with my thoughts!

There seemed to be little to look forward to and then, when the night was at its darkest, a ray of light appeared. In his convalescence, Big Jock had been linked to everything from the Scotland job to a seat on the board at Celtic and possibly replacing Harold Wilson as Prime Minister as well. Jim Callaghan grabbed the latter gig, which was news on the world stage, but the big scoop was that Big Jock was on his way back to Celtic Park. The recovery was complete and he was in the mood to end the enforced sabbatical and have a crack at the new and exciting world of the Premier League.

Comfort it was to see him in the dug-out again when he officiated at a glamour testimonial on 17 May for Bobby *Lemon* Lennox and Jimmy the Jink. Joy it was to see the Celts run over the top of a Manchester United side, managed, of course, by one-time Celt, Tommy Docherty, who had recently contested unsuccessfully an FA Cup Final with Southampton.

King Kenny scored a hat-trick; Lemon got the cheer of the night for getting the opener with a header; the Jink proved why he had been the wing-sensation of the golden era; and there was the bittersweet sight of David Hay organising a Celtic defence for a one-off special. Ah, *The Quiet Assassin,* once of this parish and sorely missed in the way that Big Jock had been.

The Master was back at work . . . he was ready to illuminate Celtic Park again and, in the words of the new Manfred Mann release, we were about to be *Blinded By The Light!*

Stevie the Student Prince

1976-1977

JohnnyDoylein'KennyKingin'

Track List:

Fox/S-S-S-Single Bed; The Wurzels/Combine Harvester; Bryan Ferry/Let's Stick Together; Elton John & Kiki Dee/Don't Go Breaking My Heart; Pussycat/Mississippi; Showaddywaddy/Under The Moon Of Love; David Soul/Don't Give Up On Us; Abba/Knowing Me, Knowing You; Donna Summer/I Feel Love; David Bowie/Heroes

The summer of 1976 was drier than a Vodka Martini (shaken, not stirred). Even Scotland was sweltering under a heatwave that enforced an unprecedented hose-pipe ban in Port Glasgow; a town in which you could have filmed *Singin' In The Rain* on most of the 365 days in the year. The drought was so severe that the legal representatives of the Sahara Desert were looking into the possibility of suing the British Government over copyright. The Wurzels may have had a *Brand New Combine Harvester* but they could do hee-haw with it because the ground was so parched! Drought was also the word coming out of Celtic Park.

It had been two years since the Bhoys had taken the title and, of course, in the season without Big Jock, they couldn't even win a Blue Peter badge. But now The Master was back and hopes were high that he was, once again, about to restore us to our rightful place in the football firmament. Inevitably, there were questions about his health. Had he fully recovered? Were the faculties showcasing that immense football brain still able? Would he still be a visible and viable presence out on the training ground? The latter query was answered immediately when Dave McParland was appointed as the new Number Two in the dug-out.

McParland had been the architect of Frank Bough's *Grandstand* double-take back in 1971 when he steered his Partick Thistle side to that League Cup Final victory over Celtic and now he was to have a strong input in the rehabilitation of Jock's class of '76. Sadly, this appointment was made at the expense of Sean Fallon who was on holiday when he learned he was to become Youth Development Officer. This was clearly a demotion for the man who had stood on the ramparts of Celtic's worst season for a dozen years and must have been bitterly received by him. The YDO seemed to be a bit of a made-up title as well given that it meant the fifty-four-year-old Sligo-man was being asked to *get down with the kids.* The big question though: was it the right decision? Only time would tell.

Certainly, the repercussions of Big Jock's accident were that he was now unable to involve himself completely with the team out on the training ground. The younger McParland would do the running and the coaching, freeing The Master up to organise tactics, signings and team line-ups.

The likeable Fallon wasn't the only member of staff at Celtic Park being told that he was surplus to requirements although he, at least, was shifted to another purpose. Time was being called on the Celtic career of Harry Harry as well. The Hood was released on 29 April after seven years of sterling service and incense-burning, mantra-chanting devotion. No longer could we invoke the mighty Stein to introduce our hero to the action by offering up *Harry Harry* as a Krishna call to arms. Beaded mats and sitars would have to be put away as the only man to bag a hat-trick against Rangers in the 1970s left Paradise.

He was soon to be followed by Dixie Deans. He was soon to be followed by Dixie Deans. Hmm, I've written it twice and it *still* doesn't sit well with me that on Thursday 17 June 1976, The Dixmaster signed for Luton Town. I guess we shouldn't have been surprised at Dixie's destination given that Hatters' chairman Eric Morecambe, had always been an admirer of *short, fat, hairy legs.*

Fair enough, the past season hadn't exactly been vintage for Dixie and he was a player who needed to be involved with the first team all the time to keep his fitness up but, as a striker, his hit rate worked out roughly at a goal for every game and a half in which he played. The pick 'n' mix at Woolworths wasn't as bountiful.

And then there were the memories . . . the Scottish Cup Final of 1972 . . . the hat-trick, that second goal when he beat forty five Hibs defenders, two coppers and the guy selling the Macaroon bars to score! The six goals in one game that lit a bonfire under Partick Thistle in November 1973 ... Guy Fawkes, but Dixie scores! The League winning strikes versus East Fife in '72 and Hibs in '73.

And, of course, the Scottish League Cup Final of 1974 . . . the hat-trick, that third goal when Dixie risked decapitation to divert Jimmy the Jink's Mount Florida-bound strike. Farewell then to the roly-poly, goal-hungry, Hibee-huntin' Dixmaster. He might have been chunky – but, bloody hell, what a striker!

With eighteen goals against them in only thirteen matches (including three hat-tricks) the rumour was that Hibs had organised a whip-round to pay for Dixie's taxi to Luton. You could hardly blame them.

The Easter Road relief, though, was to be short-lived; in fact, barely two months had passed when Jock Stein nipped through to Edinburgh and secured the signing of Pat Stanton. Had he removed the castle brick by brick from the capital, it would have been less surprising. Pat was approaching thirty-two when he signed up at Celtic Park on 1 September. He was at that stage in his career when he was being asked to step out with the Hibs reserves on a more frequent basis.

Whilst not quite having posters of Stanton up on his bedroom wall, Big Jock was still an unashamed admirer of the former Hibs captain. He had, naturally, kept a keen eye on the deteriorating relationship between the Leith Walk legend and the only professional club he'd ever played for but probably felt that the Easter Road side would have preferred to merge with Hearts before selling him on. As it turned out, Hibs were amenable to a swap deal that involved Jackie McNamara leaving Glasgow for Edinburgh.

Jackie, or *Boris* McNamara as he was known around Celtic Park because of his communist affiliations, had been in and around the first team but hadn't really established himself as a first pick. He may well have felt that football was *opium for the masses,* but at Celtic Boris wasn't getting the opportunity to *introduce* much opium and his forty three appearances over three years would be as good as it got for him. It wasn't the McCarthy witch-hunt that put paid to his Hoops career, it was Jock Stein and the swap was on.

The news that McNamara had left Celtic might have come as the last straw for the Chinese leader, Chairman Mao, though, as he died a little over a week later. It's not known if the mighty Mao was actually a follower of Scottish football but it would be great to think that he kept a copy of his Communist manifesto, the *Little Red Book,* under one pillow at night whilst the Evening Times season preview, the *Wee Red Book* was stashed under the other.

From one revered dictator to another though as Big Jock introduced Pat Stanton to the Celtic support when he made his debut against Rangers for the first League fixture of the new season. Pat looked a bit nervy in a first half that had the Celts 2-0 down by the interval but suddenly he sprang into life with an assurance and presence that helped his new club to pull back to 2-2 by the end of the game.

Big Jock had brought him in on the back of some less than inspirational Celtic performances in the League Cup section games against Dumbarton, Arbroath and Dundee United. As ever, the Celts qualified from the group but were hard pushed to draw satisfaction from the quality on offer. The hope was that Pat Stanton would bring stability at the back in a sweeper role behind Roddy McDonald. The soft-spoken Ross-shire centre-half looked as if he'd heard the Highland Clearances were back on, such had been his nerves, but Uncle Pat would now provide a calming influence and spur him on to one of his best-ever seasons in a Celtic strip.

As transfers went, it was a damn fine piece of business. Swapping was all the rage and the BBC got in on the act a month later when they introduced their grand plan for Saturday morning television. Up until then, the goggle box had been a non-event at that time of the day. Badly-dubbed adventure series like *The Flashing Blade* or *Robinson Crusoe* had vied for our attention with DIY programmes, *Teach Yourself Italian* and, if we were lucky, the odd Betty Boop cartoon. Most of us stayed in bed.

But now there was a reason to get up; the *Multi-Coloured Swap Shop* was launched on 2 October. Essentially, it was a live three-hour extravaganza hosted by Noel Edmonds of Radio 1 fame that invited the British public to 'phone in and offer to swap some rubbish that was lying around the house for some rubbish that was lying around someone else's house. Subbuteo teams were always up for grabs alongside Hornby railway sets. Edmonds set the tone with his bouncy, friend-of-the-kids persona whereas John Craven would chip in, trying desperately to shed his image as your serious older brother when he read the headlines on *Newsround.*

The magazine format included interviews with the stars of telly-land and the pop world, cartoon interludes, cookery tips with Delia Smith and at least two visits an hour to an outside location. These Outside Broadcasts were always a big secret. No-one knew where Swap Shop was going to pitch its tent for the morning until presenter Keith Chegwin faced the camera to tell you.

Shrewder TV addicts would perhaps have worked out that the Beeb were accustomed to sending a broadcast unit out to a location in the morning that would be close to a major sporting event in the afternoon. It never occurred to us that it was no coincidence *Cheggers* was in Sefton Park, Liverpool, on the morning of the Grand National or at a Manchester shopping arcade when the Red Devils had a third-round cup tie at home to Arsenal around three o'clock. That was just the way it was.

The *Swaporama* was a huge event though and if you could put up with Chegwin's cheesy patter and appalling jokes then you could get your coupon on the box as you traded your old man's priceless stamp collection for an Action Man figure with gripping hands.

ITV could perhaps claim that they had started the genre with the anarchic chaos that was *Tiswas* but that only went out in one region, the Midlands. *Swap Shop* was a revolution in television and Saturday mornings would never be the same again . . . even if you felt like lamping Noel Edmonds repeatedly with Posh Paws, the stuffed dinosaur that sat on his desk.

Had Big Jock bided his time for a month, he could have nipped down to the Swaporama with Boris under his arm and waited for the Hibs chairman, Tom Hart to show up with Pat Stanton. However, matters were pressing and The Master knew that he had to act fast for his struggling back-line. So much for defence, but the release of Harry Harry and the Dixmaster had left Stein short up front. More and more pressure was being placed on King Kenny to come up with the goods and the strain was showing.

Partick Thistle striker Joe Craig had enjoyed a great season with the Jags when his goals had fired them from the old Scottish First Division into the Premier League. Big Jock liked the cut of his jib and signed him a fortnight after Pat Stanton's arrival. Joe bore a more than passing resemblance to Sylvester Stallone's *Rocky* and was a car mechanic before turning full-time, so there was a fear that Stein had only brought him in to cut down on the service bills for his Merc. It was delightful then to witness the partnership that he formed with King Kenny throughout the new season.

One blond, the other dark; one sensitive and graceful, the other aggressive and direct; one blessed with technique, the other following gut instinct – together they constituted the *Starsky & Hutch* of Scottish football. Oh, yes – Paul Michael Glaser and David Soul were everywhere you looked in 1976. The duo had the hottest cop show on the telly and a bigger following than the Pope.

Starsky & Hutch were the jewel in the BBC1 crown on a Saturday night with their unusual blend of good cop, good cop bonhomie and a wealth of plots involving tarts-with-hearts, rancid drug-pushers and flashy, low-life gangsters. A vital part of the team was loose-as-a-goose huckster Huggy Bear.

Hugs was street-level cool, dressed like a pimp and talked like he had a BA in jive. He was also the word to the wise for S & H with his ear to the ground and his eye on the action. If Huggy Bear told you that Hitler was living in Los Angeles then it was time to get on the blower to Simon Wiesenthal – the guy just knew everything.

And *huggy* was the watchword as every episode involved our two heroes embracing each other in a back-slappin', 1970s manner, brimming with machismo and borne of their tight camaraderie. If Hutch was going out with a hooker, it was down to *Starsk* to tell him; if Starsky was injected with a lethal drug and had only four hours to live, Hutch would frantically search around for the antidote.

A tomato-red Ford Gran Torino with a ludicrous white flash straddling the body was their work car. You didn't need to be Joe Craig to see that it had some serious horsepower under the hood as Starsky would throw it around the streets of LA like he was playing catch-up in the Indy 500. Tyres always screeched, doors were always flung open so violently that you assumed Hutch had farted and Starsky couldn't get out of the car quick enough, and the bonnet was always something that you rolled over rather than walked around.

Every opportunity was given to play up Paul Michael Glaser's zany sense of humour whilst David Soul always seemed to be finger-pickin' his guitar like James Taylor when he needed some space. This was particularly true when his pop career took off with a succession of platinum-selling singles over an eighteen month period. Mind you, the Soul-man Number One, *Don't Give Up On Us,* could have been adopted by the Celts after another you-won't-believe-it's-a-final moment in the League Cup at Hampden.

This time, Aberdeen were the lucky dogs who got to take the bone from Celtic when the pair faced off on the first Saturday in November. Now, admittedly, the Hoops were short on numbers as first-choice signings Pat Stanton and Rocky Joe the mechanic were unavailable for selection due to being cup-tied. This was an Aberdeen side that had walloped Rangers 5-1 in the semi-final but Celtic were still the bookie's favourite. Hard to believe isn't it that given the track record the Bhoys had established throughout the course of the 1970s when it came to League Cup finals, the bookmakers *still* considered them to be odds-on? Jeezo, Mr Ladbroke, six finals, one win . . . don't you read the papers?

Celtic took the lead with a King Kenny penalty in twelve minutes but Drew Jarvie, who looked like Bobby Charlton but played like Charlton Heston, drew the Dons level within a quarter of an hour. The second half was spent with the Bhoys battering at the Aberdeen door in search of a winner whilst Peter Latchford had time to plant some bulbs and design a rockery in the Celtic goalmouth, such was his inactivity. Paul Wilson struck the post and Danny McG almost added to the madness by scoring a goal in the dying minutes but all to no avail.

Extra time was required and naturally, Aberdeen, having chased the Hoops around Hampden for over an hour, scored. Well, of course they did; after all, this was Celtic in the final of the League Cup

. . . a run as long and tragic as *Macbeth* at the Royal Shakespeare Theatre.

Big Jock seemed to be a little more relaxed about this one. He still regarded losing as anathema but he probably realised that, were he able to play his first-choice team complete with Stanton and Craig, then the result would have been different and this boded well for the future. We, on the other hand, had to endure the sight of one Alastair MacLeod cavorting around the old stadium like he was triple-dating Charlie's Angels. White men don't dance, Ally; but the Aberdeen manager practically auditioned for *Saturday Night Fever* with his demented jigging. A smile the width of Huggy Bear's flares didn't help either.

Ally MacLeod or, perhaps more appropriately, Mac*Loud* was, in the parlance, a *character.* The wee man may have been short on tactical nous but he was abundant on his self-worth and had a faculty for public relations that would be the envy of Liberace. In the twenty first century he would have been the soundbite of a million downloads, the glibbest of glib tongues on the after-dinner circuit and his sizeable nose would have protruded from many a copy of *Hello* magazine. Had he lived in the eighteenth century, Ally would have assumed that he was the subject of Handel's *Messiah.* In the first week of November 1976, the only serious contender that he had for Press coverage was the brand new American President, Jimmy Carter, and *he'd* never won the League Cup.

This peanut farmer from the state of Georgia had done mighty well to take the election for the Democrats although there was a view that following on from Watergate and the woeful White House tenure of Gerald Ford, then Bugs Bunny might have whipped the Republicans at the polls. Carter was like *The Waltons* – he had the down-home philosophy of John Walton, the optimism of John-Boy, the stubbornness of Mary-Ellen, the naivety of Elizabeth and, sadly, the ears of Jason. JC was no looker but he possessed a smile that made King Kenny look positively morose when celebrating a goal. And the goals were coming for the Celts.

If one match summed up what Jock Stein's modified Hoops were about that autumn, it would be a meeting at Tynecastle with Hearts. The Jambos led twice with scores of 2-0 and 3-1 and would surely have fancied the points had Lemon not grabbed one back to make it 3-2 at half-time. A resurgent Celtic, differing from the attitude that had prevailed the year before, came out for the second half with the words from Big Jock's ten minute salvo ringing in their ears and drew level on the hour. King Kenny snatched that one from a Danny McG pass and the Celts spent the last thirty minutes assaulting the Hearts goalmouth whilst the Jambos hid behind the sofa awaiting the final whistle. With three minutes left on the clock, Ronnie Glavin secured the winner for the Hoops.

Ah, Ronnie G. He was back in the fold and despite a hairdo that seemed to require more WD40 than shampoo, the G-Man was firing on all cylinders. The influence of Pat Stanton at the back allowed Ronnie G to forage forward and support the attack. Forgotten was the famine of the previous season with his miserly one goal and performances that suggested he was more like Ronnie *Corbett. Glav' gotta have,* and this would be the season of his life. Rocky Joe was also in fine form and although he wouldn't get on the score sheet for the Tynecastle shebang, he more than made up for that in the very next game with the goal that is sweetest to any Hoops follower in any season. He wheeled off a marker to smash the winner in against the Govan Select at Ibrox in a midweek League encounter. Such was his guile that he could have fitted a carburettor up John Greig's nose and still found time to lob Stewart Kennedy in the Rangers goal.

As Rocky Joe stood there with his arms aloft he knew that whatever he did from here-on in, whether it be chasing chickens in Mickey Goldmill's back-yard, fighting Apollo Creed at the Philly Spec or merely adjusting the clutch on an Austin Princess, he would be toasted as one of those Celts who smacked in a winner against the oldest rivals. Astonishingly, it had been almost two and a half years since we'd beaten them at all and over three since an Ibrox victory.

Hearts and Rangers: two matches in November confirming that although the treble was not on courtesy of Dancin' Ally and his syncopated Dons, this was a Celtic side capable of competing for the title and beyond. Tragically, not Europe though.

Celtic hadn't played in the UEFA Cup since 1964 and back then it was known as the Inter-Cities Fairs Cup. Somebody in Europe had thankfully realised that making a major tournament sound as if it was sponsored by British Rail was a mistake on all kinds of levels and so it became the UEFA Cup. Jazzy new name or not, it was still untried territory for the Hoops as they faced the runners-up of the European Leagues. Wisla Krakow from Poland were the opposition which meant disappearing behind the Iron Curtain for the second year in a row.

As a nation, the Poles had finished third in the 1974 World Cup and were clearly no novices but it was still a shock that Krakow could come to Celtic Park and eke out a 2-2 draw in the first leg. Worse than that: it took a King Kenny special in the dying minutes to keep the tie level. Big Jock would have known the game was up by that point although Celtic still had to go out and fight for their reputation. A 2-0 defeat in Krakow meant that the Bhoys were out of Europe by the end of September. Ach, it's only the UEFA, not the European Champions Cup. Why cut about with the ushers when you should be dancing with the bride?

The truth, of course, was that the Hoops just weren't ready for a European campaign and early elimination left us free to concentrate on winning our title back. Certainly, we were getting our teeth into that one although the challengers in the early to mid-part of the season didn't really involve the Govan Select. This was interesting news given that they were the champions but Celtic found themselves contesting a three-cornered fight with Ally Mac*Loud's* Aberdeen and Jim McLean's Dundee United.

It looked as if the master plan of the Scottish football big wigs to open up competition to the Glasgow dominance was going to script as a new challenging force was coming from the North East of the country. It's hard to imagine that Jock Stein would have been a fan of the Dons' manager, what with Ally's preoccupation for raising his profile to Mount Rushmore levels, but Jim McLean was definitely more to the Big Man's tastes.

McLean was a shrewd tactician who had a great eye for a player and the ability to bring out the best in him. He ruled Tannadice like the late Chairman Mao although it's widely believed that the Chinese leader smiled more than his Tayside counterpart. He looked like he'd been ejected from the National Association of Pessimists because he'd been too downbeat and that he'd tried happiness once but it hadn't worked.

Despite the gloomy countenance, however, Jim McLean was becoming an influential figure on the Scottish football scene and he would go on to lead the unlikeliest of country cousins, Dundee United, to unimaginable heights over the next decade. Big Jock would have appreciated that.

In 1976, the Tannadice threat was there for all to see so it was very satisfying that the Celts were able to record a 5-1 League thrashing at Celtic Park in October as well as a vital 2-1 win in Jute City in early January. Things were going rather well and certain players were coming to the fore. Roy Aitken was one of them.

On the night that Rocky Joe's goal had condemned the Govan Select to defeat, Aitken would have been able to celebrate with a pint of Tartan Special as it was his eighteenth birthday. Roy was beginning to look like a veteran and he was only just eligible to vote. Big Jock didn't fancy him much at the back so he'd created a role for him pushing forward from midfield. At school in Ayrshire, Roy Aitken had been a track and field specialist marking him out as an athlete. He'd also played basketball at a level that saw him named in the Great Britain team. Strong as a horse and equally as fast, the sight of Aitken rampaging forward at defenders was something to behold.

We called him *The Bear,* naturally, but his team-mates had another moniker for him . . . *Shirley!* Thankfully, this owed more to his curly barnet than anything that marked him out as the *Duchess of Duke Street,* a popular BBC drama production of the time. The Hoops first-team likened him to Shirley Temple although it was to be hoped that Roy's career trajectory would not mirror the Hollywood child star by being over and done by the time his voice broke.

I guess we saw him more as his namesake, the big football hero of the day, who had now been immortalised in his own comic. *Roy Of The Rovers* had hit the newsstands at the start of the season. Everybody had heard of Roy Race, the captain and star of fictitious Melchester Rovers. He'd been delighting us for years and had been one of the main reasons for buying the comic *Tiger* in the 1970s.

Tiger was packed full of cracking Boys' Own adventure stories with characters like *Hot-Shot Hamish, Nipper Lawrence, Bobby of the Blues,* he-man wrestler *Johnny Cougar* and Grand Prix driver, *Skid Solo.* (*Skid* thankfully related to his driving prowess and not an unfortunate irritable bowel complaint whilst zooming around the dangerous race tracks of Europe!). But Roy Race was the star of the show and the template to which all aspiring young players subscribed. In an era when the excesses of soccer bad boys, Stan Bowles, Rodney Marsh and chairman of the board, George Best, would be front-page material, *Roy of the Rovers* reminded us that not all footballers were scandalous pissheads with a lusty taste for booze, nightclubs and dames.

We'd always thought he was too big for one comic so it was a joy to see him boldly staring out from the front-cover of his own magazine at last. The stories were soap-like in their reality although it was always a bit disconcerting when, during a match, somebody in the crowd would turn to his mate and say something like *Roy's a bit off the boil today. All this talk of him being dropped must be getting to him.* To which Roy, with a bubble above his head, would think, *He's right. I'm letting this dropped business affect my game.*

Melchester Rovers attracted crowds of 40,000 plus. How could Roy pick up what some geezer was saying when he was out on the pitch? Did he have super ears as well as a God-given talent for stripping a full-back? And it happened *all the time!* Such little inaccuracies added to the charm of the stories though and from here on the only way was up for Melchester Rovers . . . and us.

Roy Race had started his career in 1954. Bloody hell! Bobby Lennox wasn't even playing in those days. And he wasn't going to feature much this season either, courtesy of a broken leg sustained that night at Ibrox in the 1-0 victory. Lemon was now thirty three and the media decided that the injury would effectively end his Celtic career, but this would act as a spur for the last of the Lions in the Paradise set-up. We hadn't seen the last of him.

Tommy Burns was also becoming a well-kent face in the Celtic line-up. He'd only featured on a handful of occasions in the luckless Sean Fallon campaign but with a sweet left foot, the ability to spot a pass from a crowded midfield and the advantage of being a dyed-in-the-hoops Celt, we were beginning to see more of him in this season. We liked what we saw although with his flaming red hair clashing with the green of his shirt, he wasn't exactly difficult to pick out on the park.

TB's association with Celtic was to be a lifelong one, broken only by a few spells away from his beloved Paradise, and this would be the year when he would taste his first success. He'd shared the disappointment of the League Cup failure, so there would be a quiet determination to atone for that by lifting at least one other trophy before the curtain dropped on the season. The task of keeping consistency in the League race was made more difficult by the weather conditions across the winter.

The first two weeks of December were a complete wipe-out as most of Scotland returned to the Ice Age and the Celts didn't have a game until the week before Christmas. This gave everybody time to catch up on the festive shopping. I longed to see Farrah Fawcett Majors filling my stocking if you catch my drift, as the poster with her smiley coupon on it was quite the rage for us red-blooded chaps. But I'd rather have been at the footy.

So would Aberdeen, Rangers and Dundee United who all had to sit around writing letters to Santa on 18 December as the Celts took on Ayr United at home in one of the few games to get the go-ahead. A 3-0 win put us at the top of the pile.

Rocky Joe did his best to wipe the smile from Ally Mac*Loud's* face on Boxing Day as he twice pulled the Celts back from behind in a 2-2 draw with the Dons, but the man was haunting us like Baron Samedi and Celtic were his own personal voodoo doll.

There was now another enforced break until 8 January which meant that an away day at Motherwell was postponed and the traditional New Year fare that was the Govan Select match was put over until the eleventh – which almost made it the traditional *Chinese* New Year fixture. The Celts went into it on the back of that Dundee United victory and were desperate to get the game up and running even though there was yet another fraught pitch inspection.

The Celtic Park ground staff put down so much straw that you could have held a barn dance. What a sight Big Jock would have made standing on the centre spot, decked out in a plaid shirt with a bootlace tie, blue jeans and cowboy boots whirling off commands to the players,

> *Grab your partner by the hand; swing him round on my command;*

Lynch square pass to Dan McG who feeds the Bear, then Kenny D.
A quick one-two an' nothing more is all we need to shoot then score;
Let's gather round the straw and hay, and play football the Celtic Way! Yeee-Haaa!

Short of putting a giant sun lamp over the east end of Glasgow, it was difficult to see what more could be done to convince referee Ian Foote that the game was playable. After a consultation that lasted longer than a NATO conference, he gave the nod. Global warming? Bring it on!

To tell the truth, most of the twenty-two players hirpled about like your granny on ice skates as the park did its best to stay harder than pig-iron. Rangers defender Colin Jackson had the sorest moment of all when he got in the way of a Roddy the Highlander header and diverted the ball into the net for the only goal of the game. That indignity was the least of his worries as the smack of the ball in such sub-zero conditions was bound to have left its mark on him. Ouch!

It was pretty clear now that with wins over the Govan Select and Dundee United as well as the credible draw against Aberdeen, this Celtic were in the driving seat. In particular, the Dons seemed to feel the heat as they stumbled through their next three games with draws against Partick Thistle, Rangers and Hibs.

Alarmingly, it was round about this time that a story was circulating about a possible bribery scandal up at Pittodrie. It was a rumour that came to nothing despite a police investigation. After all, what would you bribe an Aberdeen player with? A week in Fraserburgh? A woolly jumper? A phone number for Miss Grampian TV 1977? The whole idea was absurd but it must have helped to subdue the Northern Lights for a while.

Their title challenge seemed to go awry as Celtic piled on the pressure with a succession of fine results. Although they were to enjoy beating the Hoops at Pittodrie on the first Saturday in March, it was felt that, by that time, the result was irrelevant in their quest for the title. In fact, the match itself wasn't even the biggest talking point of the day. That was the substitute who came on for Celtic to make his debut.

His name was Alfie Conn! Yes . . . *the* Alfie Conn! Alfie of the hair, the sideburns, the blistering turn of pace that had taken him beyond two Celtic players to score in the Scottish Cup final of 1973 for Rangers . . . *that* Alfie. The Conn-man had fallen out with the Ibrox hierarchy a few seasons before and headed off for the big smoke of Bill Nicolson's Tottenham Hotspur where he was regarded as the *King of White Hart Lane* by Spurs diehards. Unfortunately, by 1977, new manager Keith Burkinshaw felt that, if Tottenham was a court, then Alfie was more jester than monarch and his was the opinion that mattered.

Big Jock had worked with Alfie briefly when he'd taken charge of the Scotland Under-23 squad on a part-time basis a few years before so there was a bit of previous to their relationship. But, even with the benefit of hindsight, the coming together of Alfie Conn and Celtic would still be a bigger shock than the marriage of Michael Jackson and Lisa-Marie Presley.

Big Jock, of course, was characteristically low-key about the affair. He liked the player and knew what he could do on the park. There was another side to the whole affair though as the Rangers support, in the midst of a poor season, had been making noises to their board about bringing Alfie back to *their* fold. Certainly, the move was being considered when The Master cut in to show the kind of nifty footwork employed by Gene Kelly. In other words, not only had he signed a decent player who could make a difference in Europe the following season, he had also outmanoeuvred Celtic's greatest rivals at the same time. It was, quite simply, vintage Stein. The fact that the movie *The Bad News Bears* was being nominated for a BAFTA award at the same time only seemed to rub in the salt!

If there was ever any doubt about the reaction of the Celtic faithful to the signing then all bets were off when Alfie Conn whipped in a super finish to put his new club 1-0 up at home to Partick Thistle. *He's alright is Alfie!* He was now about to win his first-ever League Championship medal.

If taking a bow at Celtic Park as a former Govanite would require some guts, then it would have taken the cojones of the *Six Million Dollar Man* for Alfie Conn to turn up at Ibrox wearing the Hoops of his new employers. He got the chance to lay that bogey to rest less than three weeks after his signing when it was all over to the West End for the final League derby of the season.

Naturally, Alfie received the kind of reception that Muhammad Ali would have expected at a Ku Klux Klan barbecue but, if anything, he seemed to enjoy the pantomime. If he was on the ball, they booed. If he was running around, looking to take on a pass, they hissed. If he tried some tricks, they would cry, *Oh no you can't!* Frankly, it must have been tempting for Alfie to score an own goal . . . just to confuse everybody, you understand.

He didn't though and the derby was its usual rip-roaring affair with the Hoops taking the lead through Roy the Bear, then being pegged back and overtaken late on.

This, unfortunately, was the cue for a host of Celtic supporters to jump down from the terracing as a hail of bottles appeared over their heads and the game was stopped for a few minutes. Big Latch was also receiving treatment for an injury and Jock Stein emerged from the dugout to check on his goalie whilst also urging the spectators to get back. It wasn't quite the same roasting that he meted out on that famous day at Stirling a few years before but the Big Man's presence was always a formidable sight and the polis would have been grateful for his persuasive tongue.

He also took the chance to spell out the lyrics and the melody to his team whilst out on the pitch and within five minutes his impromptu team-talk had accrued a result. The Rangers supporters were still celebrating the closing moments of the ninety minutes with scarves aloft and the full-throated accompaniment of a victory song when the Bear appeared once more to whack in a volley from close range that damn near ripped through the netting. Behind the Rangers goal, scarves dropped quicker than a brewer's droop as two points became one and the realisation dawned that a League victory over the Celts was not going to be on the Ibrox menu this season.

The only threat left was coming from Dundee United and they duly turned up at Celtic Park one week later to keep up the fight. Mathematically, they were still in with a shout of winning the title. Then again, theoretically, an elephant can hang over the side of a cliff with its tail tied to a daisy – but no-one's ever seen it done. Big Latch was a casualty for this one so Roy Baines took over in the Celtic goal.

Jock Stein had been on the blower to Noel Edmonds again in October and offered a swap deal to Morton for their goalkeeper in exchange for Andy Ritchie. This was a surprise to the Celtic support as the young Hoop had been highly-rated at the club. For all his skill though, the *Talented Mr Ritchie*, had the work ethic of a second year grad student. He was so idle that the makers of the La-Z-Boy chairs were apparently issuing a writ on him and the Ovaltine people wanted to offer him sponsorship. Big Jock viewed laziness as an incurable disease and so it was off to Greenock for Andy as fast as he could go. Miraculously, he got there before the year 1980.

The Dundee United game was a story of two goalkeepers. Roy Baines saved a penalty in the first half that would have put the Arabs in front. That was newsworthy in itself but the fact that the spot-kick was taken by his opposite number in the Tannadice goal put another spin on the story. Hamish McAlpine was the nominated penalty-taker in the Dundee United first team and had already grabbed a brace that season against Hibs and Rangers. He was a Tayside legend renowned for his acrobatics, safe hands and a deadly eye from twelve yards out.

With his blow-back hairstyle, rugged features and a moustache that was thicker than Sherwood Forest, he bore the appearance of a film star – a porn film star! Sadly, the amateur video, *Hamish Does Bainesy,* was, fatally for the genre, a tad premature and the Celtic goalie dived down quicker than Linda Lovelace to thwart his Arab counterpart. There was then a frantic scramble for Hamish to get back home to the safety of the Dundee United box as Celtic launched a quick counter-offensive. He was quick off the dot as well but the inevitable was only delayed until a minute before half-time when Rocky Joe fastened onto an Alfie pass and before you could say *misfiring spark plugs* he cracked in the opening goal.

Having spurned the opportunity to score from the spot, Hamish then had to endure the indignity of giving away one himself a mere five minutes after the re-start. The spot-kick duel was a battle of the blow-dries as Ronnie G tried to control his windswept mane and McAlpine bounced around on his line like an advert for Cossack hairspray. The superior condition of the G-Man's locks won the day and the Celts were 2-0 up and picking up the points.

Over four days, the Bhoys spent more time in Edinburgh than an American tourist. On the Wednesday night they contested a 1-1 draw with Hibs in a match that attracted a touch of controversy. This was a game that had been rearranged after the winter wipe-out over New Year and the Celtic directors had wanted to fulfil the fixture on a more suitable date but the Hibs board were unequivocal and it took the intervention of the Scottish League to sort it out. The patter must have been great that night between the dignitaries of both clubs when they met up before and after the match for polite chat and a few drinks.

It was an issue that would return to the front pages a few weeks later. Right now, though, there wasn't time to brood as the Saturday visit to Tynecastle threw up a 3-0 victory and was then followed up by a tight 1-0 home triumph over Kilmarnock a week later.

It was now Easter and the talk of the telly was Robert Powell's portrayal of the main man in *Jesus Of Nazareth* which was being put out on ITV over consecutive Sundays. Simpler times you see. The 1970s – three channels: *White Christmas, The Wizard of Oz* and *The Great Escape* over the festive; *The Greatest Story Ever Told, King of Kings* and *Jesus of Nazareth* on at Easter. Earning your bread as a programme scheduler in this era was a licence to print money.

Powell, an esteemed Brummy actor who had modified his accent so that Jesus didn't appear to hail from Solihull, was up for an award for his performances. As he moved from a wedding feast in Cana where, remarkably, nobody was teaching the disciples how to do the slosh, to the raising of Lazarus, the Last Supper and Crucifixion, it was clear that he was giving the essential portrayal of the carpenter from Nazareth. No less a miracle, it seemed, was Celtic's transformation from the down and out squad of the previous barren year to champions-elect as they rolled into Lanarkshire three days after Easter Sunday to claim the title against Motherwell.

At least, that was the script. It was all there for us. Wrap up the points; wrap up the Championship. The champers were in the hampers and all that was required was a victory . . . any victory!

Tuning in, as we were, to the scratchy hiss of Radio Clyde 261, it was discernible that the score was 3-0 and that one Celtic player had grabbed two of the goals. Well, that's fine then but unfortunately the bubbly remained trussed up as it turned out the score was 3-0 to Motherwell and the Celt with the brace was Andy Lynch. He had scored two own goals!

Andy had been around the Celtic scene since signing from Hearts in 1973 and his career had gone backwards. That is to say, he was purchased as an outside left, converted to a left-midfielder and when he finally started a decent run in the first-team around 1975, he was in defence as a left-back. He'd made the position his own and would emerge with a credible twenty-five goals over the course of his Celtic tenure. No' bad for a full-back. However, we're not including these veritable howlers on a crisp, spring evening at Fir Park.

Ach well, let's just clinch the pennant when we go to Easter Road. We'd done that before and always got such a warm welcome down Leith way, hadn't we? Hibs were in a huff. Indeed, had Edinburgh University been handing out degrees in huffology then Hibees Chairman, Tom Hart, would have been the Professor of the Faculty.

You took away Pat Stanton!
Yes, but we gave you Boris and sold the Dixmaster.
You didn't want to play us that Wednesday night in March!
Yes, but we turned up and had the good manners to share the points with you.
Eh, we don't like television!
Whit?!

And it was true. The board of directors at Hibernian decided that there would be no TV cameras allowed into Easter Road on the day that Celtic could clinch the title. Archie Macpherson was tearing his hair out. Arthur Montford was taking aff his jaiket whilst checking out the curling fixtures for the weekend in question. The telly folk were making overtures towards the Easter Road admin team. But all to no avail as Tom Hart decided that, unlike his TV namesake Tony, it would be *Vision OFF!* Had there ever been such a cream puff? He'd even banned Celtic's own cine-camera club from recording the moment for posterity. There was more chance of filming inside the Kremlin so there was nothing else for it but for Jock and the Bhoys to get on with the game.

A traditionally tight ninety minutes was settled by Rocky Joe, just after an hour, when he profited from an Alfie cross to score the winner. The Celts were champions and it was all back to Gordon Hewitt again in the BBC studio to describe the action without the use of pictures.

Pat Stanton had always dreamed of picking up a League medal at Easter Road. He just never thought it would be as a Celtic player. Ah, life. C'est La Vie as opposed to C'est La TV.

There was still a Scottish Cup Final to come as well and it was arousing a bit of a stooshie too because of the big bad world of television. For the first time *ever*, the nation's favourite cup competition was to be sponsored.

Scottish & Newcastle Breweries had come up with the cash to be involved in the tournament and whilst the SFA were glad to be pulling in the shekels, the proviso was that the Scottish Cup Final *had* to be televised live. Naturally, there was a bit of a to-do about attaching the healthy name of sport to a product that promoted unhealthy pursuits, but in the 1970s, this was an old argument. It was why Embassy Cigarettes promoted the snooker and the darts, why John Player stuck their name onto Grand Prix motor cars and why, even today in the twenty-first century, it's still possible to blanche at the irony of punters who tip the scales at twenty plus stone wandering around with sweatshirts that say *Russell Athletic* on them.

The good people at S & N must have thought they'd won the proverbial watch as well when both Celtic and Rangers battled their way through to the Hampden showpiece. Celtic had seen off Airdrie and Ayr after shock replays, dispensed with Queen of the South in the quarters, and then harpooned Dundee 2-0 at the penultimate stage. For their part, the Govan Select had dealt with Falkirk, the mighty Elgin City and, to be fair, the mightier Motherwell and Hearts en route to the national stadium.

Oh yes – Celtic v Rangers. The biggest club game in the world. The cans of Tartan Special must have been ordered by the crate when word came through that it was the big two in the final. The derby showdowns for silverware had attracted crowds of more than 100,000 in the last decade with a mammoth 132,000 taking in the 1969 final which Celtic had won 4-0. Even with the cameras beaming out live pictures from the showpiece, there would still be a huge gate wanting to take in the atmosphere on a beautiful, early-summer afternoon, wouldn't there?

The rain was pissing down like the last day at the Battle of Passchendale when a miserly crowd of less than 55,000 found they had a lot of room to get soaked in at the national stadium. Well, I say *soaked.* Such was not the case for our Govan brethren as they occupied the covered enclosure of the old ground as usual. Hampden Park must have been designed by an architect from Tenerife because he elected to shade one end of the stadium from the blistering white heat of the Scottish sun whilst leaving the other end open like a makeshift tanning emporium. Hadn't anyone told him about the weather in the west of Scotland? The climate was pretty much in tune with the game as well.

The G-Man and Rocky Joe had been invited to make their Scotland debuts ten days before the final. Although it was a personal triumph for our lovable mechanic as he came on as a sub against Sweden and scored with his very first touch of the ball, the G-Man had picked up a hefty ankle knock which ruled him out of the big one. Jock Stein elected to play in a slightly more defensive mode hoping to catch Rangers out on the counter-attack. Whoa! Man bites dog! This had been the Govan policy for years in this one so it must have come as a surprise to John Greig and his team-mates to see the Celts sitting off a bit and inviting them on like Mae West in *I'm No Angel.*

We were all a bit confused as well but hadn't Big Jock been delivering all season? Now was not the time to start doubting. And it all appeared to be justified as Celtic won a corner after a quarter of an hour following a panic attack in the Rangers goalmouth. Andy

Lynch sent a header the way of the net when somehow, Govan goalie, Stewart Kennedy, managed to claw the ball away for a corner before wrapping himself around the Hampden goal-post. It wasn't a pretty sight. Well, to be frank, big Stew seldom was, but we'd all seen him collide with posts before back at Wembley in 1975 when the English had humbled us 5-1 and now he was requiring attention. Was he still a bit out of it when the corner was floated over? Who knows? Perhaps he saw Alfie out taking it and wondered why he was defending a set-piece from a Rangers player.

Anyway, confusion reigned once again as Roddy the Highlander bulleted a header towards goal that fell down at Kennedy's feet, only to bundled back to the net by big Shuggy. Derek Johnstone was on the line and the ball appeared to strike his hand before Sandy Jardine controlled it and made his way out of the danger area. Celtic immediately appealed for a penalty and after a moment, referee Bob Valentine agreed with them. Rangers protested. Well, you would, wouldn't you, but this was no funny Valentine. The penalty stood and we all sat at the edge of our seats waiting for the designated Celt to place the ball down.

The G-Man was absent so it would be King Kenny . . . or Rocky Joe . . . or Paul Wilson . . . or, in a moment of delicious irony, Alfie. To be honest, we would have named everybody in the Celtic line-up including Peter Latchford before settling on Andy Lynch as the man to take the spot-kick. Yet, there he was, standing over the ball and preparing to fire the shot that could end in joy or tragedy.

Like most people, we didn't know that Andy had only taken two penalties before, for Hearts, and missed both of them. Yes, indeed, he had scored recently, of course. A pair of beauties – but that was in the infamous Motherwell match and they were own goals! What was going on?

Andy Lynch was probably the coolest man at Hampden, which took some doing with the cold rain running down his neck. He probably didn't even notice as he cantered up and placed the ball to the right and beyond the reach of Kennedy. The Celtic support went mad; the Rangers end buried their heads in their hands. But this was nothing compared to the rancour up in the Scottish & Newcastle corporate lounge.

With the eyes of the world watching Andy Lynch's finest moment in a Celtic shirt, it was apparent that the penalty was being taken in full, unadulterated view of an advertising board displaying the goods of a certain brewery – and it sure as hell wasn't Scottish & Newcastle. I believe they call it *irony.* And that was it.

Nothing like the Faustian jousts of past derby finals although Rocky Joe had two excellent opportunities to put the score beyond doubt in the second half but had uncharacteristically missed them. That year's teen sensation, Chris Robertson, came on as a sub for Rangers and whacked a header off the cross bar in the closing minutes that made the heart stop for a second as well but, all in all, it was a pretty tame affair. Still, after two seasons of comparative failure by Stein standards, it was great to see Big Jock as the manager of a double-winning Celtic side again.

There was also the pervasive feeling that if he could keep this side together with Danny McG pushing down the flanks, King Kenny and Alfie feeding Rocky Joe and perhaps a couple of good seasons out of Pat Stanton, then a tilt at Europe might be on the cards again. There was only one nagging doubt and you didn't have to be a contestant on *Mastermind* to ponder it.

Name: Gerard McDade
Specialist Subject: King Kenny
Question: Why did Kenny Dalglish not take the vital penalty-kick against Rangers in the Cup Final?
PASS!

1977-1978

ShuggyShufflin'BurnsLovin'

Track List:

Rah Band/The Crunch; The Stranglers/No More Heroes; Space/ Magic Fly; Elvis Presley/Way Down; Patsy Gallant/From New York to LA; Sex Pistols/Pretty Vacant; Eddie & The Hot Rods/ Do Anything You Wanna Do; Wings/Mull Of Kintyre; Kate Bush/ Wuthering Heights; Gerry Rafferty/Baker St.; The Bee Gees/Stayin' Alive; The Motors/Airport; The Bee Gees/Night Fever

Of course, it was possible to be English and not to have heard of Kenny Dalglish. You could live in the Home Counties and think that *Ken* Dalglish, as John Motson irritatingly called him, was one of those ubiquitous names that the Jocks shouted out in the same way that Cockneys utilised *Gordon Bennett!* But if there was any doubt, south of Gretna, as to who he was, it was dispelled at Wembley on 4 June 1977 when King Kenny forced the ball over the line to put his country 2-0 up against England.

Scotland were on the way to their first victory at the so-called *home of football* in ten years. Nothing new to Kenny D, though. He'd already humiliated goalie Ray Clemence the year before at Hampden when his snap shot from eight yards out passed through the gaping hole between the England 'keeper's legs and into the *onion basket,* as Nipper Lawrence of *Tiger* comic called it. At that point, King Kenny just knew that he'd be the big man on the Crazy Golf circuit that year.

But this was different . . . this was Wembley . . . this was a global audience. Kenny D's stock was at an all-time high. As was the new Scotland manager, Ally Mac*Loud.* Yup, that's right, the self-styled Muhammad *Ally* was now the Top Jock in the international set-up. *Donny* Ormond realised that a successful Scotland side wouldn't happen until the *Twelfth of Never* so he jumped ship to Hearts. According to Ally, there was only one man for the job and we all agreed with that. The difference being we all thought it was Jock Stein.

Certainly, the SFA thought as much when they offered the position to the Big Man but he turned them down. Ally picked up the reins and the Scotland stagecoach rode off into one of the most exhilarating and calamitous periods in our international history. Central to that was this valedictory win over the English on their own turf.

The Tartan Army liked that turf so much that many of them decided to take a piece of it back home so they invaded the pitch at the final whistle. By the time the stadium had been cleared the playing surface looked like an allotment at harvest time and not for the first time the talk was of cancelling the fixture or at least moving it to a midweek slot. Such was not the concern of the King though, as he rounded off a superb season with the winning goal on the ultimate Scottish showpiece occasion.

That satisfaction was mirrored back at Celtic Park where the Premier League trophy and the Scottish Cup were proudly on display. It was a time for reflection. Big Jock was back to doing what he did best – winning pots.

In Davie McParland, he seemed to have a comparatively youthful and able deputy who could offer a more obvious presence on the training ground whilst the shrewd yet audacious captures of Pat Stanton and what's-it-all-about Alfie ensured that The Master continued to be the foremost expert in his field. He was still only fifty four and appeared to have made a remarkable recovery from the near-death experience in the borders two years previously.

The Celts had turned everything around and in such a short space of time that we dared to dream of a successful European campaign as well as the chance of renewed domestic dominance. In short, the future looked so bright that a pair of Elvis-size shades would have been suitable eyewear. It was hard to imagine the dark clouds that were rolling in towards the East End of Glasgow.

Out in the wider world, there was a terror gripping New York when a combination of the most catastrophic power failure in American electrical history and the appalling murderous campaign of one maniac had reduced the Big Apple to the plot of a John Carpenter film. For more than twenty-four hours, NYC was bathed in darkness at the behest of a freak power cut whilst being caught in the murderous grip of a serial killer known notoriously as *Son Of Sam.*

John Travolta and *Saturday Night Fever* had invited the world to boogie in silk shirts and trousers so tight that there was little room to rumba. So while native New Yorkers were dancing 24/7 they were also keeping their eyes open for sightings of the Sam Jr. The intense heat, the random acts of savagery and the delicious irony of *Stayin' Alive* becoming a leitmotif as well as a tip-top disc-tabulous track meant that this season would always be remembered as the *Summer Of Sam.*

As much as we watched on in long distance horror and fascination, we never imagined that our own close-season would turn into, as John Motson might say, the *Summer of Ken!* Rumours of Kenny D's desire to quit Celtic Park for the playing fields of England were hardly paint-fresh. Indeed, as we have seen, informed opinion – i.e. the line of communication that ran from the Celtic box office right down to the public houses of Glasgow – had it on sound authority that the King postured for a move just before Jock Stein's critical accident in 1975. Out of respect for the uncertainty surrounding the Big Man's health, he had quietly revoked his request but now, two years on and with the Master seemingly restored to the front foot, Kenny decided he had achieved all he could as a player on the Scottish football scene.

I suppose it should have been apparent to us that his thoughts lay elsewhere when he acceded to full-back Andy Lynch's insistence that he be allowed to break the deadlock in the Scottish Cup Final at the end of the previous season. Hindsight is as reliable an art as stockbroking though so we just partied as Lynch whacked the ball beyond Stewart Kennedy rather than debate the reluctance of our skipper to step up to the plate.

It would, of course, be ludicrous to suggest that the King's royal focus was not on securing a League and Cup double as Celtic captain. However, for a player who enjoyed scoring goals with as much relish as Muhammad Ali decking a usurper and who also shared *The Greatest's* nerve for the big occasion, it did seem a trifle odd that he passed up the moment. Then there was the indisputable fact that Kenny D had only re-registered as a player two weeks prior to the cup final. This did little to quell the nerves of those of us who viewed his leaving of Celtic Park as the human equivalent of the ravens taking flight from the Tower of London.

The Hoops were heading out to Singapore and Australia for a pre-season tournament when all the speculation came to an emphatic halt. It was time for Kenny D to ape Abba and tell us exactly what was *The Name Of The Game.* For anyone who thought that the big sporting stories of the summer were the titanic jousts between Bjorn Borg and Jimmy Connors on Wimbledon's Centre Court and Jack Nicklaus and Tom Watson at the Turnberry Open, then all bets were off when Celtic arrived at Glasgow Airport for their Far East flight. Back pages were hastily re-built with the news that Kenny D was not among the travelling squad.

He wasn't at check-in. He wasn't browsing at the magazine

stand for the *Roy of the Rovers Summer Special.* He wasn't even in Boots picking up last-minute travel-sickness tablets and some Handy Andies. There was more chance of John Greig getting on the plane as captain of Celtic than there was of the King.

As press hacks scrambled about for a game of *Where's Kenny?,* the official line was that he'd been allowed leave of absence following a gruelling domestic season and an unnecessarily tiring South American tour with the Scotland squad. The fact that Danny McG had also participated in Ally's Latin American Roadshow in addition to *his* gruelling club season and was now heading for the Far East suggested that United Nations' diplomacy had descended on Celtic Park.

It was a bit like the aftermath of Big Jock's car crash in 1975 again. Trying to get information was useless. The only Press announcement from Kenny D was in the *Shoot!* Summer Special and his *Tartan Talk* section and there was nothing there to indicate that he was soon to change the name of the column to *English/Spanish/Italian Talk.* Besides, that had probably been written weeks before although I, like others, pored over its bland content looking for clues as to the Dalglish thought processes.

The show had to go on, though, and Danny McG was handed the captain's armband for the tour of the southern hemisphere. For the record, a successful Celtic squad returned from the Antipodes with the somewhat overstated *World of Soccer* Cup stowed away in their baggage. To do so, one of the requirements was that they had to overcome a decent Red Star Belgrade side in the final. Having already played out an ill-tempered defeat and draw with the Slavs, the third game was a much better tonic for the Hoops when they won 2-0.

It hadn't been a great visit down under for Pat Stanton. He'd scored an own goal in the first game and been sent off in the second for trading punches with a Red Star forward. Dignified, gentlemanly

Pat being dismissed from the action was as common an occurrence as your grandfather being arrested for breach of the peace.

The other teams taking part in the tourney were Arsenal and an outfit that more or less amounted to the Australian national team. An under-achieving English club, an international team more interested in *tinnies* and *barbies* than footy, the champions of Scotland and the Iron Curtain emissaries . . . Strewth! It sure was a *small* World of Soccer in 1977!

It did seem to us on the ground that Big Jock and his squad were awol when a coup d'état was taking place in the centre of his Government. How could the Big Man know what was happening back in Glasgow when he was stuck out in the metaphoric bush? Would The Master and his disciples be gathered around a camp fire at night, waltzing their Matildas when Skippy hopped into the action? The famous kangaroo would have bounced up and down excitedly like a guy who had backed the Celts for the World of Soccer Cup at 28/1 whilst twittering out the urgent news to Big Jock:

What's that, Skippy? You say Kenny Dalglish has fallen down a mine shaft with a team of football agents and is considering a move to the English First Division or Europe! Ripper!

There were people who considered Aberdeen to be the Far East but, even in the supersonic 1970s, communications were not so unsophisticated that there was no way to relay info to the faithful about the state of play regarding the Celtic career of Kenny Dalglish. By now, the newspapers were awash with the subject. Sightings of the King were as regular as those of Lord Lucan which served only to heighten the fever and with Celtic on the way back from Australia, everything was set for a showdown.

We all hoped that, within hours of disembarking from his plane at Glasgow Airport, the Big Man would have negotiated the baggage carousel and customs control to make a personal call on his disaffected captain.

Pre-season training was up and running and there was a friendly away to Dunfermline Athletic just three days before the start of the defence of the double. Surely Big Jock would just wrap one of his meaty arms around Kenny's shoulder, pat him on the head with the other and convince him that Celtic was still the club to nourish his heightened ambitions. He was still the master poker player, still able to put forward a positive argument like a Government front-bencher, and still the Svengali who had nurtured the King from early promise to international fulfilment.

A cigar in his hand, the rattle-rattle of outrageous jewellery, lurid gold tracksuit on, whatever it took to make the King's dreams come true . . . nae worries – *Jock'll Fix It!* I was on holiday in Ireland when I heard the news that Kenny Dalglish had signed for Liverpool.

Not that my holiday arrangements had any impact on the proceedings. I mean, it's not as if the world's media would have been clambering for *my* thoughts on the transfer but, just like those who can recall their precise geography when JFK was blown away in 1963, I can remember the day, the hour, the minute, hell, even the tee-shirt I was wearing (*New York Yankees*! Go figure . . .) when my cousin announced to me that Dalglish was now a Merseybeat. It was 10 August.

Within a week, Elvis Presley had died and the twin impact of these life-changing events meant that I didn't want to go back to school. I'd always thought that when Elvis died it would be astride a high-powered Harley Davidson, swerving into the path of a truck at ninety miles per hour rather than knocking down the child who had wandered out onto the freeway – spectacular, heroic and above all, pure rock 'n' roll. Disappointingly, it was a little bit more domestic an exit.

Big *E* had sung his last *Glory Glory Hallelujah,* said *thanguvermuch* and headed off to his Graceland bathroom. He may have had an en suite bigger than the size of your average semi but like any other guy, he still wanted something to read when he was occupied. Of course, regular Joes grab the nearest copy of the News Of The World. Elvis, his mind eternally on a higher spiritual plane, carried a book about the Turin Shroud and a few hours later he was discovered by His Latest Flame face down in the luxurious pile of his bathroom carpet, the book sprawling mere feet away, having breathed his last. He didn't even get the chance to wash his hands – uh huh huh!

The King of Celtic Park had abdicated to head south; the King of Rock 'n' Roll had permanently left the building. There hadn't been such a bad week for *royalty* since the French Revolution. The Stranglers were right on the money; there really were *No More Feckin' Heroes!* At least with Elvis, there was the memory of a relatively full career.

Kenny Dalglish was, at twenty-six, still in evolution as the greatest British player of his generation and he would now be fulfilling that potential in a Liverpool jersey. We all awaited the immediate aftermath of this shockwave with a mixture of foreboding and fascination.

Liverpool were League champions, had narrowly missed out on doing *the double* and, more ominously, were the most recent winners of the European Cup. It was hardly surprising that the trophy-thirsty Kenny D should opt for a club that seemed set to rule the English game for years to come. The fact that Celtic hadn't placed him up for auction but had opted to use Big Jock's Merseyside cosiness as a facility to cut the deal didn't really sit well with supporters either.

How would the Big Man handle the loss of our prize asset? What would he do with the money? The dough! The Mullah! The greenbacks! Even that subject became a matter of torrid debate.

Dalglish was the instant replacement on Merseyside for Kevin Keegan. The curly-haired diminutive forward who loved the *great smell of Brut* had packed up his after-shave and moved to Hamburg in a transfer that caused the same apoplexy with Liverpool supporters as King Kenny's defection would to their Celtic counterparts. He would go on to become the most successful act to leave Liverpool for Hamburg since The Beatles. The deal had been completed for £500,000. A neat half-mil!

The fact that the Liverpool board had secured Kenny Dalglish's signature for just £440,000 and would still have enough left over to further strengthen their squad whilst buying a round of drinks for the entire Anfield home gate was something that riled a lot of us with green and white blood. Okay, Keegan perhaps edged it with his three European medals and proven title credentials and the money paid for the King was a British transfer record at the time. But the Reds were still getting one hell of a player without having to 'phone their bank manager.

Then it transpired that the fee was subject to VAT and that 12.5% of that went to the Chancellor, Denis Healey. Not only were we losing our finest player and not receiving the entire transfer fee to spend on the squad, we were financing the Government's coffers to the tune of nearly £50,000! Was there no end to this humiliation? Besides, whilst not being quite Keynesian in my understanding of issues economic, even I knew Value Added Tax was only supposed to be applicable to *luxury* items. Necessities were zero-rated.

So there it was . . . Kenny Dalglish was considered to be a *luxury* in the Celtic line-up! Who came up with *that* tax edict? Ken Dodd?

Once we'd taken our pills, steeled ourselves for the season ahead and I'd been advised about the legalities of not attending school, it was time to put it all in perspective. After all, *one man doth not a team make* as it says somewhere in the Bible. We were still the defending champions.

Still the team to beat with the bulk of the squad that had so thrilled us as they collected the Premier League and Scottish Cup. Did we not still have the internationally-acclaimed and Football Writers' Player of the Year, Danny McG, as our new captain complete with his jazzy new beard? What's-it-all-about Alfie had been the sublime sensation in the Far East and Oz and Pat Stanton was still one of the finest, most composed players in the Scottish game (unless confronted with the red rag of a Red Star centre-forward that is).

By October, when a shaven Danny McG limped off the park with a seemingly innocuous ankle injury to join Alfie and Pat on the long-term injury list, feelings were running high. Those two had pretty much reached the end of their season by picking up bad knocks in *the very first game of the campaign* at home to Dundee United and the word was now official – God had stuck the housekeeping on Rangers doing the treble.

That opening fixture against the Arabs was much more than a dour goalless stalemate. It was Pat Stanton's last meaningful outing in a Celtic jersey. Arguably, he'd had little to do as the men from Tannadice opted to play twenty-five at the back and hit the Celts on the break. They weren't the only team to try this on an away outing to Glasgow but, frankly, I've seen more breaks with a Kit-Kat so it was alarming to watch Pat hobble off less than an hour into the game.

The Conn-man had already beaten him to the treatment table, stretchered off just before half-time. The sight of the St John's Ambulance men congregating around our stricken hero was a sure sign that we were going to have to soldier on without his influence on the park for some considerable time. His appearances throughout the campaign would be fleeting. Ironically, Danny McG was lost to us after an extremely satisfying and, given recent events, surprising 3-1 dismantling of Hibs. The man who would naturally fit into the line-up of all-time greatest Celts would be out of the game for the next eighteen months.

By this point, Celtic's campaign for 1977-78 had become the victim of a *Carry-On* film plot. You could almost hear Sid James cackle when Johnny Doyle miscued a cross at Somerset Park in August, actually hitting the referee with the errant pass and then being sent-off for the alleged misdemeanour in a 2-1 defeat. Kenneth Williams could not have flared his nostrils more indignantly and gasped *Ohhh Matron!* at the sight of one-time Quality Street Kid Vic Davidson bursting past the home defence and scoring the only goal of the game as Motherwell took the points at Celtic Park.

And even a Celtic First XI that included luvvies such as Charles Hawtrey, Leslie Ding-Dong Phillips, Hattie Jacques and Joan Sims could surely not have contrived to throw away a half-time 2-0 lead over Rangers and go on to lose 3-2? *Corrrr Blimey! What a Carve-Up!*

The Rangers game was, as you could imagine, particularly galling given that two goals from Shuggy the Ice-Man had the Celts well in command over a Govan Select who weren't exactly giving the impression that they harboured championship pretensions.

It seemed a masterstroke when Big Jock started with Shuggy up front as a centre-forward and the two goals were testimony to his effectiveness. Yet, at half-time, the manager decided to switch the Icelandic goal machine back to defensive duties instead of letting him try for a hat-trick. Pressure eased on the Ibrox back-line to give the Govanites the confidence to break forward and their winning goal arrived in the final ten minutes of a match that the Bhoys looked to have won by the interval.

The travails continued at Pittodrie the following week when Aberdeen, now managed by Billy 'Cesar' McNeill, came from behind to win 2-1. It was the middle of September and Celtic had played five League matches, drawing one and losing four. For the first time in his career as Celtic manager, Big Jock was hearing the word *relegation* being whispered among the faithful.

A steadfast belief in the tooth fairy seemed more credible than the understanding that the defending Scottish champions were flirting with the nether regions of a ten-man League and if something didn't happen quickly, the Celts would be sinking faster than a double malt in the hands of Oliver Reed. The weekly news bulletins taunting us with Kenny Dalglish's formidable, if predictable, start to his Mersey career didn't help much either.

Nobody Does It Better trilled the theme song of the new James Bond blockbuster *The Spy Who Loved Me*. Didn't we know it as we tuned into *Match of the Day* every bloody week? Even Carly Simon was taking the piss out of us now! It was time to act, time to use the lucre sent to Celtic in return for the artist formerly known as *King*. And so we waited . . . and waited . . . and waited.

We all knew that Dalglish was irreplaceable but £400K would surely allow Big Jock to play the transfer stock market and buy in some Ford Capris to offset the loss of our Rolls-Royce. However, when Jock started splashing the cash, he seemed to be more intent on picking up some unreliable horse-drawn jalopies from the British Leyland stable rather than opting for some brand new marques.

Even before the Dalglish departure, his close-season captures were hardly stirring up the pond. Ian McWilliams and Roy Kay were brought in on free transfers from Queen's Park and the relegated Hearts respectively. At six feet, five inches, Ian became the tallest Celtic player ever. Roy Kay has the distinction of being the Celt with the shortest ever name. Eh, and that pretty much accounts for their inclusion in any rundown of Celtic history.

In fact, Roy's moniker was about as brief as both his and lofty Ian's Celtic careers which were over and out before the close of the season. As was John Dowie, a £25,000 purchase from Fulham who so enthralled Big Jock in the first Rangers game of the season that he was hooked from the pitch and rarely appeared again. He was so anonymous that he could have been a star guest on *The Muppet Show*. Well, did you ever see anyone you'd ever heard of whooping it up with Kermit, Fozzie and the gang? Thought not.

Could we have our Jock Stein back? became the refrain around this time as rumours abounded that the Big Man had actually been replaced by an inferior doppelganger. It was a story that had done the rounds before as a famous Paul McCartney urban myth that enjoyed currency in the late 1960s. Certainly Big Jock's purchases were increasingly being viewed as a mystery tour, more tragic than magic. On it went.

Joe Filippi arrived in November from Ayr United as a replacement for the injured Danny McG and put in some sterling performances punching above his fighting weight but the only arguable success was the acquisition at £60,000 from Dundee United of Tom McAdam.

There was feverish excitement as the Celts were linked with a Tannadice Arab and, it has to be said, the source of the excitement was centred on Paul Sturrock. He did appear to have all the attributes to be a successful Celtic striker – fast, wiry but strong and with an uncanny knack for being in the right place at the right time to score goals. He was also coming up for twenty-one so would be a raw talent that Big Jock could nurture and develop along the lines of, dare we say it, that Dalglish guy. It never happened.

In fairness to Tom McAdam, he would go on to carve out a very worthy Celtic career but it would be as a centre-half and not as the striker that we all thought we had bought. As did Big Jock, for it would be his successor who would reposition Tam from the forward line to defensive duties at a later date.

All of these moves seemed to pale into the shadows, however, compared to the strange tale that occurred in October. Less than twenty four hours before a home game against a St Mirren side managed by the youthful Alex Ferguson, Celtic announced that they had strengthened their squad with the on-loan arrival of Frank Munro from Wolverhampton Wanderers.

Now, let's be honest here. Frank was, at least, a name familiar to Scottish audiences as he had enjoyed a little bit of profile down south at Molineux and had also been capped by Scotland. Yet no-one could have been prepared for the sight of the man soon to be known to the Celtic support as Frank *OH-NO* Munro when he led the

Hoops out onto the pitch. I'll say that again: he *led* the Hoops out onto the pitch.

That's right, Big Jock had handed the armband to a player who had barely met the lads he was now to skipper and would struggle to find London Road with a street map! It was like asking Dopey to lead the dwarves. I mean, *I* was on intimate terms with more Celtic players in 1977 than Frankie and that's because I'd once asked Ronnie Glavin for his autograph! He didn't have a pen and neither did I. Hell, I'd have settled for a handshake.

It seemed to be another sign that Big Jock was taking on the mantle of an eccentric aunt who made random, inexplicable decisions just to see how the family reacted. To be *frank,* and none of us would literally have wanted to be, the game was a disaster for Celtic and a personal Armageddon for Cap'n Munro. In a 2-1 defeat, the *You Tube* moment was our on-loan skipper scoring . . . for St Mirren!

It all seemed so harmless as Munro attempted what we euphemistically call *a strong clearance* from the wing. He evidently did not hear Big Latch shouting, *Frankie, Relax – Don't Do It!* as he swept the ball majestically past our stunned goalkeeper. Future Centenary Hoop, Billy Stark, put the icing on the cake with Saints' second.

Frank Munro arrived at Celtic Park on 14 October. It could, of course, be entirely unrelated that Bing Crosby upped and died on a golf course in Spain on the same day but perhaps the *Old Groaner* knew something that we didn't. Bing's literal sudden-death play-off which he won hands-down, followed on from the even more shocking news that Marc Bolan had been killed in a car crash one month before in London.

It then transpired that both men had a common link. The final guest on Marc Bolan's ITV afternoon music show, *Marc,* was his friend and fellow pop dude, David Bowie. The Thin White Duke, as he now cast himself, immediately took off for his next engagement which was to record a version of *Peace On Earth/Little Drummer B(H)oy* for Bing Crosby's Christmas Special. The fact that both Bolan and Papa Bing were to die so soon after working with Bowie must have dented the Duke's CV a little and made any subsequent collaborations difficult. Was Bowie now officially the kiss of death and, more importantly, had Big Jock secretly signed him up to apply his Black Magic on his ailing Celtic side?

You could almost hear Arthur Montford up in the gantry,

Lovely turn, Glavin. Beautiful ball, Doyle. Wham Bam, thank you Ma'm, Thin White Duke. 1-0 Celtic!

Certainly, there seemed to be some hocus-pocus jinx affecting the Hoops. And now it was getting serious. We'd trousered the King Kenny deal. We'd sat through *Carry On Down The League.* But now we were being forced to state the unthinkable – was Jock's time up? I still dropped to my knees, Mecca-like, when the Great One lit up our television screens to impart his wisdom on all things football but the carpet was beginning to look as threadbare as Bobby Charlton's scalp and there was less belief in my Hosannas.

Could Europe offer us some salvation? Fortunately, and perhaps because we were reeling from the loss of our King, the gods of football had been kind to us in the initial stages of the continent's premier competition. The Celts tuned into Radio Luxembourg with an 11-1 aggregate despatch of the colourfully named Jeunesse d'Esch, who happened to be the top team in the Grand Duchy. Admittedly, the lofty status of being the best football side in Luxembourg did not carry quite the same weight as being the best *It's A Knockout* team in this neglected part of Europe.

Indeed, the only thing missing from Celtic's 6-1 slaying of Jeunesse in the away leg was the sound of *Knockout* commentator, Stuart Hall, collapsing in a heap of hysterics at the antics of the Luxembourg back four as they attempted to shackle a rampant Hoops forward line. Even Eddie Waring would have fancied banging a couple in that night. Still, in these decadent times, a win was a win and we accepted it gratefully.

Now we wanted a *big* draw. A teutonic joust with Borussia Monchengladbach perhaps? The Caballeros of Real Madrid? The Old Lady of Turin in the shape of Juventus? What we got was SWW Innsbruck.

They were the champions of Austria and proved to be no sprig of Edelweiss when the Celts could only scrape a 2-1 win in Glasgow. After twenty-seven minutes in the Tyrol we were 3-0 down and our Sound of Music was Beethoven's 'Death March'. It would be fair to say that the Von Trapp family enjoyed a better last night in Austria and they'd spent it being hunted down by the Nazis.

In a distinguished career that had seen Big Jock respected on the continent like the reigning monarch of a great European household, it was depressing that the foot-soldiers of SWW Innsbruck proved to be the final footnote in a competition wherein he had established his name. Of course, we weren't to know that at the time but there was now open talk of Big Jock being replaced. A leader was required.

Tough, no-nonsense, strong streak of hewn Scottish Calvinism; a man who operated a crack squad of modern, young gunslingers; who viewed their lusty excesses as a needy makeweight for the demands of their front-line jobs; a man who knew what it took to be a *Professional* . . . in short, we needed George Cowley of CI5!

The Professionals was British television's answer to *Starsky & Hutch* and paired the relatively unknown Lewis Collins and Martin Shaw as covert operation geezers, Bodie and Doyle. CI5 was ITV's credible take on the shadowy goings-on and need-to-know chicanery of the British Intelligence Services. They operated out of Whitehall in a building that positively reeked of the old boy network mixed with the intensive care patient that was political security.

Bodie, or as he should have been called, *Body,* given his penchant for ripping off his tight-fitting, black turtleneck sweater at every opportunity to afford us a look at his magnificently-honed *pecs,* was an ex-paratrooper with some previous in the SAS. Well, naturally. The granite chin, the closely cropped pseudo-'Nam haircut, the *Who-Dares-Wins* gung-ho marked him out as a guy who lived by a code. He would have busted his grandmother for not having an abdomen you could bounce a 10p off whilst thinking nothing of disbanding an entire regiment because they'd all gone to the Odeon to see '70s weepy *The Way We Were.*

Ray Doyle provided the slightly pink-liberal to his partner's *junta* tendencies with his flared, brushed denims, cheesecloth shirts and a flowing barnet of poorly-conditioned, chemically-curled hair. He was an ex-cop although you got the feeling that he'd spent his *polis* days stuck in a panda lamenting the passing of Dixon of Dock Green and contemplating a permanent wave. The die was cast: Bodie was tough, uncompromising, even with the ladies, whom he referred to as *birds,* and couldn't countenance a disobeyed order. Doylie regarded his conscience as a *good thing,* dated girls who expected a box of Terry's All Gold and an orchid before puckering up, and was more likely to question the chain of command before reaching for his shoulder holster.

A typical storyline would be built around the questionable protection of a foreign diplomat who was in the UK to promote a controversial arms deal, simultaneously fending off the attentions of an ex-KGB assassin. As a sub-plot, Doyle would be involved with a stunning, borderline Right-Wing blonde or Bodie would be boxing out of his league with a piece of posh, Home Counties totty called Jemima. The boys had toys, of course.

Bodie usually sat behind the vulcanised steering wheel of a top-of-the-range two-litre Ford Capri. This was a machine designed to work out as often as he did and could handle the aggression of those rock-hard *pecs* putting it through the paces of 110 handbrake turns per episode. Doyley cut about in a souped-up Ford Escort which, even in all of its uncomfortable customised glory, still managed to look like your Uncle Frank's car when he went through his mid-life crisis.

George Cowley was at the apex of the team and Gordon Jackson was superb in the role with his Caledonian ferocity, an underlying rage at the faceless Whitehall mandarins, and a sworn devotion to Queen and Country. Tuning in on a Friday night, we would all fantasise that with Cowley in the dug-out, Doyley prompting the midfield with his dog-like tenacity, and Bodie partnering Rocky Joe up front, then the season could once again be revitalised.

At least our old compadre, the League Cup, was offering us something to cheer about, up until the final anyway. The highlight was a 5-1 aggregate stroll over St Mirren; no mean feat in these troubled times, especially as the first-leg involved nipping into Paisley and emerging with a 3-1 advantage. Hearts, now getting used to life in the First Division, provided little resistance in the semis and so, emboldened with our 2-0 victory, it was off to Hampden to face the winners of the other tie.

Forfar Athletic had that whole *Hobson's Choice* thing going on when it came to the draw. Should they be praying for a tie against the confidence-scarred Hearts or a money-spinning gratuity against either Celtic or Rangers? The accountants offended the purists by cheering when the Angus club were paired with the Govan Select and were left to count the roubles as another derby day final was set-up for December.

Or, at least, it should have been but the weather was so atrocious that the whole shebang was delayed until the spring. Fabulous, surely by then, we would, once again be a free-flowing thing of beauty? Hmmm . . . there wasn't much in the League form to suggest that this was just around the corner. In fact, it's worth recalling that the Celts were second from bottom after Cap'n Munro's, shall we say, *interesting* debut.

Come early winter, any victory, moral or otherwise, would be deemed acceptable and we were doing it all the hard way. In the lead-up to the next Rangers game, we twice had to come back from 2-1 down against Ayr United and Motherwell to win 3-2. Triumph built in the teeth of adversity or were we just slower than a day spent shopping with the wife?

The Govan Select were quite rightly licking their chops as they boarded the bus that ferried them across the city. And it seemed justified at half-time, leading as they were by a goal to nil. Big Tam the Tar McAdam threw his cap into the ring as a potential new hero when he netted the equaliser five minutes into the second period. Moments later and the former Arab's newly-toasted status seemed assured when he banged in a second and there was a sudden belief that the tide was turning our way at last. It sure was! The only problem was that it was turning in the same manner as the giant wave that engulfed the good ship *Poseidon*.

As Big Tam and his team-mates celebrated taking the lead, referee Eddie Thomson called back the play indicating that he'd blown his whistle earlier in the move to award Celtic a free-kick. The goal was disallowed on a technicality – the official had neglected to play the advantage rule. This aberration seemed even more mysterious ten minutes later when Rocky Joe, bearing down on goal, was almost stripped of his manhood by Jaws Forsyth in a moment even Ray Charles could have identified as a penalty.

The loose ball broke to Tom McAdam who, quite naturally, had stopped playing. The big chap didn't even bother to boot the ball into the pokie as he knew very well that a penalty kick was about to be awarded. Everybody stopped – the Rangers players – the Celtic players . . . hell, even the grass ceased to grow as we all waited for the whistle to sound. It didn't. In a moment akin to that Sherlock Holmes short story, *Silver Blaze,* when the dog *did nothing in the night,* fast Eddie waved play on indicating that he was now employing the famous advantage rule so ruthlessly misplaced minutes before!

He was indeed fortunate that this game was in November as the summer sun would surely have constituted a hazard when it bounced off his brass neck! November? Conspiracy theories?

Celtic's championship defence in an open-top car driving through Dealey Plaza with Lee Harvey *Thomson* taking aim from the book depository? All that was missing was the grassy knoll! Little did we know that this was only the prelude to an even bigger farce come New Year. And still the artist formerly known as *King* was haunting our reverie.

In the same way that you get chucked by your first love, it's not just the loss of the relationship you mourn. It's the fact that you keep seeing her coupon as she parades around town with her new suitor. Not only was Kenny D pushing Liverpool to newer and greater heights, he'd actually invited everyone in Scotland down to his new gaff at Anfield when the nation was facing the biggest challenge to qualification for the World Cup in 1978.

Wales, ostensibly in recognition of the desire for tickets for the vital heads-down between them and us in October, opted to switch the venue for the match to Liverpool. A win for Scotland would mean automatic qualification for Argentina '78 and everybody wanted to see the game. I say *ostensibly.* Probably the Welsh FA had looked at Wembley being turned into a potato field by the Tartan Army after that infamous Home International in May and decided that it was a case of *not in my back yard, boyo.*

So there it was – not only had you been dumped by the love of your life, she'd also asked you over to her new boyfriend's flat to let you see how wonderfully she'd adjusted to life without you. And just to prove what a complete bitch the whole situation was, once you were at the party in said boyfriend's bigger and better pad, she would fix you a drink and then snog the face off him as you just stood there, red-faced and staring at the avocado dip with a Tudor's Pickled Onion crisp in your lonesome hand.

Anyone who'd ever experienced that scenario could sympathise with the forlorn Hoops as Kenny Dalglish crowned the evening with a superb header to put Scotland 2-0 up and en route for the Pampas. Everybody wanted to be Scottish now! Even Paul McCartney who, along with Wings, released the dirge-like *Mull of Kintyre* in time to become the Christmas number one. By then, the Celts had hauled themselves gingerly up onto their collective feet like a punch-drunk, fairground heavyweight.

The great news over the festive season was that the BBC was running an Elvis movie marathon every day. We could luxuriate as the King sang, fought, raced, romanced and dived through a succession of forgettable travelogues. At last, a legitimate reason to skidge school. In response to all this *Fun In Acapulco,* the 'Tic too seemed to be clawing some performances together.

Okay, there was a 3-3 draw with St Mirren to endure after a sound 3-0 thrashing of Partick Thistle. Yet even this seemed like a moral victory given that we were 3-1 down with ten minutes to play at Love Street. A 1-0 victory at home to Dundee Utd on Christmas Eve courtesy of a Shuggy the Iceman goal took us up to the heady heights of fifth in the table. It sure as hell wasn't vintage Celtic but at least we were leaving the uncertainly of the relegation zone.

Settling down on Christmas Night, stuffed with turkey and being part of the biggest British audience ever to watch a television programme – i.e. the 26 million who laughed at the festive edition of the *Morecambe & Wise Show* – we dared to think that the worst was behind us. Oh, and then Ayr United beat us 2-1 on the last Saturday of the year. Only Lisa Marie Presley was having a worse Yuletide, her first without Daddy!

As if to prove that this wasn't a fluke, Motherwell took the points off us too with a Jimmy O'Rourke goal in our first match of the New Year. *O'Rourke?* Shouldn't a guy with a name like that be playing *for* us rather than scoring against us?

The annoying thing was that we knew Rangers weren't really all that much better than us so we chose to shrug off the first foot 1-0 reversal and focus on the big one the following week against the Govan Select. After all, on the day, it was only one set of eleven players against another, wasn't it? Well, not quite.

On the day in question, Rangers appeared to field a twelfth man. It was JRP Gordon again and he was easy to spot . . . he was the one wearing black! His first name was John and the RP bit apparently stood for *Rangers Preferably.*

Once again, the common theme was that Celtic were 1-0 down but playing with a vim and vigour that suggested an equaliser was just around the corner. When Rocky Joe rose in the box like the rev-counter on a Ferrari to convert a cross into a certain goal, Govanite defender, Colin Jackson, barged into him with all the subtlety of a rhino charging a jeep on safari. Jacko played the percentage card by opting to give away a penalty instead of a definite equaliser.

The Hoops supporters feared a déjà vu moment when old JRP seemed undecided how to call it. The ball had gone behind for a goal-kick, everyone in green and white appealed to the ref, the crowd were whipped up like Saturday night down at the Coliseum when the besieged whistler rushed over to his linesman seeking a second opinion.

However, at some point on his trot over to the assistant, JRP had his Damascene conversion and in a moment of clarity, suddenly realised that he did not require the aid of the flag-man. He did an immediate about-face, at which point he must have noticed that Rangers had very helpfully restarted the game without putting him to the trouble of blowing his whistle and were moving the ball quickly into the Celtic half.

There were only two Hoops in the vicinity and one of them was Latch in goal. The inevitable happened. Celtic's position was overrun quicker than a Verdun trench and Rangers scored. JRP covered himself in even more glory when he allowed the goal to stand. He must have reasoned that if veteran defender and Rangers captain John Greig had converted, then it must be legitimate. I mean, after all, Greigy usually bagged a goal every third season or so, didn't he? Jock Stein would have looked less out of place popping up in the Celtic box and netting for Rangers. The Ibrox skipper could barely celebrate for the nose-bleed he incurred from being so far up the park!

The match was now in more disarray than Jim Callaghan's Labour government with the Celtic players seemingly threatening to walk off the pitch in disgust at the abject judiciary. Even the Govanites were less than convinced by the decision as they stood around in an embarrassed throng as though one of them had farted anonymously. It was left to Big Jock and the combined efforts of the backroom Bhoys to persuade the Hoops that such a gesture would be as futile as the Lib-Lab pact. It was to their credit that the Celts were able to continue although another penalty, this time for handball, was denied and the match finished in a 3-1 defeat.

To be frank, our League aspirations had probably evaporated around October when Celtic couldn't even go out at Halloween *guising* as a football team, but still there was that belief that a victory over Rangers might just raise the bar for the remainder of the season.

What was left of that season? Well, there was still the inevitable League Cup Final to look forward to, which had now been set-up for March. And there was the Scottish Cup. We were, after all, the holders and seemed intent on hanging onto that little item of silverware when Dundee were humped 7-1 at Celtic Park in the third round.

Apologies for the use of the vernacular but really, 7-1, that halcyon scoreline recalling Hampden In The Sun from twenty years before. Worthy a glass of bubbly I'd have thought. Even for a schoolbhoy. Tommy Gemmell was in the managerial hot seat up at Dens and it's debatable that he hadn't endured such a spanking in Glasgow since he'd faced Jimmy the Jink in training.

Of course, we already knew about another Lion who was cutting his teeth in management and seemingly to great effect. Billy McNeill had made a couple of telling purchases since taking over from Ally I-walk-on-water Mac*Loud* at Aberdeen and it was his Dons side who were contesting the title scrap with the Govan Select. We gazed towards Pittodrie with envious, some might say, covetous eyes.

Dundee were in the First Division working hard to come back up to the Elysian Fields of the Premier League, as were Kilmarnock, our next opponents in the Scottish Cup. Excellent! Let's dismiss a couple of lower League teams before facing any of the bigger guns in our march to Hampden. But this was Celtic in the early exchanges of 1978 and there were shocks-a-plenty about.

Leon Spinks, a name so obscure you felt he'd actually made it up, had just wrested the Heavyweight Championship of the world from Muhammad Ali. Out in Switzerland, an attempted kidnapping of Charlie Chaplin took place. This was odd in itself perhaps. But rendered bizarre by the fact that *The Tramp* had died on Christmas Day and was barely cold in his coffin when the abduction took place. It was the ultimate silent movie. Even Top of the Pops was looking decidedly odd with a whirling dervish called Kate Bush ballet dancing her way to the summit of the charts with the exquisite *Wuthering Heights.* With all that going on then, it was hardly a surprise when Killie threw us out of the Scottish Cup.

Hell, they'd had the temerity to come through to Celtic Park on the last weekend in February and force a replay in a 1-1 draw. Even then, it took a Roddie the Highlander header to secure parity for the Celts with minutes remaining on the clock.

The Hoops supporters approached Ayrshire on a dank, cold Monday night with the quiet fear of Tam O'Shanter and that fear was not misplaced as our status as cup-holders went the way of Rabbie Burn's titular anti-hero. Ten months before the rest of the country, Celtic were enduring the winter of discontent. A 2-0 victory over

Rangers at our patch at the end of March might just have gone a long way to warming the cockles had it not been for the League Cup Final the week before.

Not for the first time, Celtic were in the record books. This was their fourteenth consecutive appearance in this particular final; a feat unheard of in a national cup competition. It would have been nice if Roy Castle had taken time out from organising the largest tap-dance in the world for his *Record Breakers* programme on BBC1 to appear at Hampden and acknowledge the fact.

Norris McWhirter, the vaguely creepy anorak and stats giant who looked as if he'd rather be sitting in a bath of cold beans than sharing bench space with a crowd of teenage guests, would also have been a welcome participant. In saying that, McWhirter would have probably had more fun working out if Gordon Smith's winner in the dying moments of extra-time was the lowest recorded header ever to win a trophy.

Big Latch had been in outstanding form throughout the match but with the score locked at 1-1 and penalties only moments away, he went up for a cross ball with Govan midfielder Alex MacDonald. The Ranger could claim to be many things but no-where on his CV would it say that he was tall. Hence, as he got the step ladders out of his pocket to challenge our burly Brummie hero, he must have thought that the very best he could do was make a nuisance of himself.

This he did to startling effect, bouncing into Latch's midriff as though it were a sandbag on an army training camp. He looked as guilty as the proverbial puppy sitting beside a pile of poo when the Celtic custodian was nudged and the ball spun away towards Gordon Smith. The Ibrox forward must have been saying his prayers at the same time because he was on his knees when he headed the ball back across the stricken Latch and into the net.

I say referee, don't you think that the Rangers chappie fouled our goalkeeper? we all cried in Croft Original voices. Apparently not as whistler David Syme pointed to the halfway line in indication of the goal.

Fourteen League Cup Finals in a row – with seven defeats and seven victories the glass was half-full or half-empty depending on your outlook. The really galling thing is that on four of those occasions throughout the Supersonic '70s, the surrender of the League Cup had been conducive to missing out on the Holy Grail of the treble. Bloody hell – I sound like Norris McWhirter here. It must be contagious. Ah, yes, that whole treble thing.

Throughout Big Jock's reign, Celtic had bested Rangers over ten out of the twelve championships available. But the Govan Select did seem to have the greedy knack of gorging themselves whenever a League flag came their way. Okay, they hadn't done it in season 1974-75 but the following season saw them winning everything that was available on the Scottish scene. And now as winter turned to spring . . . as the Bee Gees turned from pop to disco . . . as Jim Callaghan turned from left to right . . . the Govanites turned from famine to feast. They had the League Cup. They were motoring well in a Celtic-free Scottish Cup and the League was all but theirs.

The best we could hope for was the chance to land a bloody nose when they came east at the end of March. The 2-0 victory was a watershed game, marking, as it did, Big Jock's last presidency over a Celtic-Rangers match. It was a sunshine interlude in a season when the brightest thing we had seen at Celtic Park was the introduction of Punk Rock to Paradise.

One day, a young dude appeared in the Jungle complete with ripped leathers, leopard-skin brothel creepers, Johnny Rotten tee-shirt, fluorescent green and white hair (do you see what he did there?), and more chains than Tescos about his personage. Perhaps he was hoping to persuade the match day disc jockey to spin *Pretty Vacant* as he had taken the trouble to bring the Sex Pistols' single with him. Well, he was never going to play Sid Vicious & Co's take on *God Save The Queen*, was he? Even if Big Jock had stuck a safety pin through his nose the feeling was that he still wouldn't have been *au fait* with the current climate and his sorry season petered out with an away defeat to Fergie's St Mirren at Love St on the final day of the campaign.

The result left Celtic with *Close Encounters of the* Fifth *Kind* as the Bhoys finished in this unprecedented position of mid-table mediocrity. To add insult to injury, on 10 May, Kenny Dalglish accepted his Mersey coronation exactly eight months to the day that he had signed for the Reds when he scored the winner in a lacklustre European Cup Final against FC Brugges at Wembley. He was now, officially . . . *Kenny Dee of Dee Kop!*

The last time Mr Dalglish, as we now had to call him, bagged one at the English national stadium was the year before when Scotland had beaten Hadrian's XI 2-1, precipitating the biggest dig since the excavation of Tutankhamen's burial spot. On that day, he was the outstanding talent of his generation and the captain of the top team in the country who had just won the League and Cup double. Back then he was *ours.* Now he was *theirs* and had a European Cup medal to prove it. Elvis had truly left the building . . . and he wasn't coming back.

God was able to collect on his Govan treble bet and we were left to ponder that a prodigal son was the only guy who could set our people free. Thankfully, out at Celtic Park . . . a calf was being fattened.

1978-1979

TenMenin'HailHailin'

Track List:

Clout/Substitute; Frankie Valli/Grease; John Travolta & Olivia Newton John/Summer Nights; 10cc/Dreadlock Holiday; Dan Hartmann/Instant Replay; The Undertones/Teenage Kicks; Boomtown Rats/Rat Trap; Blondie/Hangin' On The Telephone; Village People/YMCA; Ian Dury & The Blockheads/Hit Me With Your Rhythm Stick; Gloria Gaynor/I Will Survive; Roxy Music/ Dance Away; The Bee Gees/Tragedy; Elvis Costello/Oliver's Army; Patrick Hernandez/Born To Be Alive

Big Jock knew the system. In his time as Celtic manager he had been as miraculous as the Messiah, as tough as John Wayne, as despotic as Doyle Lonnegan and, at times, as soft-hearted as Mary Poppins. In May of 1978, he harked back to another role – Don Corleone. The Big Man decided, as you always thought he would, that he was the best judge of when to leave the Celtic family and, like the head of the Cosa Nostra, he would determine who was to be his successor.

The satellite-saturated system that is football in the twenty first century determines that success must be instant and it must be consistent. Hence, the big players, like Real Madrid for example, take the view that the career of a losing manager should be as brief as that of an X-Factor winner. In the 1970s, things were a little bit different . . . but only just. Jock Stein's curriculum vitae may have boasted more treasure than Aladdin's cave but one bad season seemed to indicate to the Celtic board that the genie had left the Big Man's lamp.

From the outside looking in, his partnership with the club had always appeared to be as solid as Holmes and Watson; as cosy as Terry and June. Appearances can be deceptive of course and he had endured his share of storms with the Celtic board throughout the years. More so since the passing of his supreme ally, Sir Robert Kelly, in 1971 but his riposte was always to win trophies. A campaign as disastrous as the Dardanelles had left him vulnerable and, in the *Happy Ever After* that was their relationship, Big Jock had decided that he was tired of playing *Terry* to Celtic's *June.*

But he wasn't going to sit around and be dictated to. As a master poker player, he surveyed his hand and made his move for an honourable withdrawal. Approaching the board in the spring of 1978, he suggested that Billy McNeill be enticed back to manage the club. Furthermore, he himself would pave the way for that return by approaching 'Cesar'.

On paper, this looked a better banker than rainfall in Greenock but all was not as it would seem. Cesar was enjoying the working atmosphere at Aberdeen. He was building a decent side that had run Rangers close to the title, narrowly losing the Scottish Cup Final to them as well. Crucially, the wife and weans were settled nicely by the Stonehaven seaside and the working relationship with *his* chairman, the affable Dick Donald, made Big Jock's employee arrangements look like the fractious last days of Lennon & McCartney.

In the parlance, taking on the job at Celtic Park was a *big ask.* Ironically, Cesar was in Glasgow, picking up an award for Manager of the Year, when Jock Stein played his hand. To be honest, this tactic showed more cheek than a troupe of Can-Can dancers. Aberdeen had ridden into town as happy as *Oor Wullie* in a sweet shop only to find out that *Fat Bob* and *Soapy 'Celtic' Soutar* were about to nick their joob-joobs!

Big Jock still lived for a whiff of political intrigue and invited his former captain out to the car for a hush-hush tête-à-tête along the lines of Deep Throat and Bob Woodward in that movie about Watergate. He still considered Billy McNeill to be one of *All The President's Men* and that an entreaty to come home would not be turned down. The short answer is that the lure of Celtic proved too strong, although you wouldn't have fancied being in Billy's cowboy boots when he had to tell the missus and the kids that it was time to hitch up the wagon and head way back west.

By 28 May, it was a done deal and Cesar was paraded as the new Emperor in Paradise. Big Jock's timing was still a thing of beauty as well. Could it be mere coincidence that he slipped out of the bunker when practically all the Press Corps were away on active service in the Argentine preparing for the World Cup? It didn't seem likely. The Big Man would probably have enjoyed the sight of newspaper editors scrambling about for cub reporters and agony aunts to get over to Celtic Park. Jock Stein was singing *My Way* and this was his final curtain.

Out in the Pampas, Muhammad Ally would also be crooning Sinatra but his karaoke choice wouldn't have been *It Was A Very Good Year.* Scotland had been riding on the crest of a wave since securing qualification for Argentina '78 but they were about to find out they had no surfboard.

That Anfield victory over Wales had occurred in October so there was a hell of a long time to build up the nation for the first game against Peru in June. To sweeten the pot, for the second World Cup in succession, England had failed to qualify. Whilst the Scots had been planning a mass invasion of the Argentine, the English were thumbing through the Hoseasons brochures. Scotland were the new rock 'n' roll and everyone wanted a piece of the action.

Comedian Andy Cameron released the single *Ally's Tartan Army* onto a tone deaf public. The title alone should tell you all you need to know about the quality of the vinyl. Nowadays, they would only release this tosh if it displayed a parental control sticker to warn you about explicit lyrics. There's no actual cursing but any piece of music proclaiming that Scotland would *win the World Cup* should never be heard by impressionable children. Apparently, they still play it over the tannoy at Barlinnie Prison when the inmates get a bit rowdy. That usually does the trick.

The winner of the *he-above-all-people-should-know-better* award went to Rod Stewart for the shameless profiteering of his collaboration with the Scotland squad on *Ole Ola.* It's a fair bet that, no matter how inebriated his audiences get around the world at any of Rod the Mod's gigs no-one's ever been so pissed as to call out for a rendition of this beauty, even though it charted at number four. Any songwriter who attempts to rhyme the word *Ola* with a strangled *Over Thar* on numerous occasions deserves to be locked in a room with the greatest hits of Tony Blackburn.

The Scotland squad, too, got in on the act with a succession of sponsor deals, the most famous of which had midfielder Asa Hartford leering from the open door of a Chrysler Alpine with his full home kit on encouraging us to get down to a certain car dealership. Top of the pile, quite literally, was Muhammad Ally's alternative career as a carpet salesman. Every time you turned on the box or opened a newspaper, there was the cheerful Scotland manager hawking the beauty of pure wool-blended Axeminsters. Before the campaign was over, the wee man would yearn to be Ally *Baba* as a *flying* carpet would be needed to spirit him away from the baying Scottish public.

But there was no hint of all that was to come as 20,000 punters turned up at Hampden Park to see the squad off to South America. 20,000 punters to see Scotland catch a bus! Most football teams get the old, open-topped Routemaster out after they've won something because it gives them the chance to parade the trophy. Only in Scotland would a bus drive around a stadium and a team have nothing to show for it. It could not have been more comical had Reg Varney been at the wheel.

When Teofillo Cubillas sliced a free-kick beyond Alan Rough in Scotland's first match of the campaign to put Peru 3-1 up, it was clear that Ally's team were like his carpets – lacking in substance and prone to a beating. Crucially, the Scots had been 1-0 ahead and even at 1-1 were awarded a penalty to regain the lead but Don Masson failed to convert. The resulting scoreline was considered to be one of the worst results in Scottish history . . . but only for the time being.

Four days later, Iran fielded a Shah's Select and held Scotland to a 1-1 draw. By now, the Tartan Army had more deserters than the Foreign Legion. Between both matches, West Brom winger Willie Johnston was sent home for failing a drugs test. It certainly wasn't Valium as presumably Ally was cornering the market with that substance. What had gone wrong?

Ally was the master motivator as far as the nation was concerned but he perhaps hadn't translated this to his players. The public were hungry for the kind of brash bravado exemplified by the Scotland manager. If you were one of the millions who were queuing up to get into Grease at the cinema, then you could identify with that musical sequence for *Summer Nights* that has John Travolta boasting about his vacation-time conquest of Olivia Newton John.

Ally was JT in his leather bomber jacket and greasy, cocks crow quiff and we were his worshipful T-Birds. With every step of his outrageous claims over Scotland's World Cup aspirations, we would be following him up and up through the sports benches begging him to *tell me more, tell me more . . . like do we have a chance?*

The belief of the Tartan Army was sadly at odds with the performances of a team that hung cool like the T-Birds but played like the Pink Ladies. Ally could hardly have fared worse had he stuck Rizzo, Frenchy and the virginal Sandra Dee up front in his Scottish attack.

Typical of the Scots psyche was the ability to suggest that all was not lost. So, when it came to playing against the former finalists, Holland, in the last group game when only a three-goal victory would suffice, they rose to the challenge. After the greatest Scottish international goal ever scored, when he emulated the Dixmaster's 1972 Cup Final trick of dribbling past eighteen players and a programme-seller before poking the ball away, Archie Gemmill's seminal strike meant that one more goal for an unlikely 4-1 win would see Ally's Tartan Army through to the next stages.

The Sandra Dee that was Scotland had gone from being a pig-tailed, fresh-faced schoolgirl into a hot-to-trot, leather-clad minx who was now teasing the nation with the possibility of taking our World Cup relationship to the next level. Naturally, this burgeoning excitement was to last mere minutes until Dutch striker Johnny Rip let rep, or something like that, from about ninety-five yards out to bring the score back to 3-2 and suggest that Scotland's chances were as likely as mine with Olivia Newton John.

The Scots had been looking to go all the way but had to be content with a *hickey from Kenickie!* While all this was going on, Billy McNeill was acquainting himself with the manager's chair at Celtic Park.

The first thing he did was get on the blower to Lemon Lennox and call his veteran mate back from a year stuck in the tumbleweed of Soccer USA-style with Houston Hurricanes. Well, perhaps, not quite the first thing. Cesar's initial task was to pose at his desk, telephone in hand, attired in a Pringle sweater and shirt combo and have his photograph taken, just in case anyone wondered who he was and what he was doing!

Cast away in the States, Lemon may have thought his Celtic career was over but Cesar thought otherwise. Perhaps the experienced Lion would get confused over the coming season by regarding Aberdeen as the Granite City Red Sox, Morton as the Rainytown Ramblers and

Rangers as the Union City Blues but he still had the touch and pace required to aid his fellow Lisbonite in his time of need. And much would be required.

Across the River Styx, the Govan Select held all the cards and if it was going to be strange for the faithful to look over from the Jungle into the dugout and see Billy McNeill there, it would be the same for the Rangers support as they beheld former captain John Greig as *their* new manager. Cesar and the Greigster had enjoyed parallel careers out on the pitch, jousting for titles and symbolising what it was to be a figurehead at their clubs and now they were to lock horns as managerial rivals.

The first derby match, scheduled for the second Saturday in September, was as eagerly anticipated as the upcoming Superman movie and with the same attendant hoop-la. Could Celtic nip into a phone box and change from being last season's Clark Kent into this year's Man of Steel or would the Lex Luthor that was the Govan Select *kryptonite* our ambitions.

If the summer of '78 was the story of two managers then equally it was also the seeming absurdity of three Popes. The reign of Paul VI came to a dignified end on 6 August when he succumbed to a heart attack. Speculation immediately focused on who would be his successor. The only certainty was that he would be Italian. There hadn't been a non-Italian Pope since 1542 . . . and they say the Scottish Cup draw is rigged!

Even in 1978, the rituals governing the selection of a new Pontiff were as old as the Good Samaritan's credit card. A conclave of Cardinals was convened and they were shut away from the outside world until they had voted for *the man!* No need to call Big Jock and tell him to set up a clandestine meeting with a future Pope in the front seat of his Merc then.

This was a democracy and so it was that after nearly three weeks since the leaving of Paul VI, John Paul I arrived. And, yup, you guessed it . . . he liked the pasta. New Pope, new name – the Catholic world rejoiced and all over the globe, but particularly Coatbridge, a host of *John Pauls* were being christened. What would the new Pontiff be like? What was his take on all things ecumenical? How did he feel about the ongoing issues dividing the church and, more importantly, who were his favourite team?

He was probably an AC Milan supporter or perhaps he liked the flair of Juventus or the tedious predictability of the Inter Milan catenaccio system. We were never to find out. Hardly had the white smoke been blown away from St Peter's Square when John Paul I passed away, also from a heart attack. To paraphrase Oscar Wilde: losing one Pope was unfortunate but to lose two seemed careless.

The reign of John Paul I had lasted little over a month and now the Cardinals were being asked to cash in more of their frequent flyer miles and hightail it back to Rome. Once again the world looked on, albeit this time with a little more disbelief. You don't audition for a Pontiff. The Cardinals just have to go on gut instinct, ignore the callous barbs about polo mints lasting longer than Popes and get on with the job of finding another successor. Two days into the conclave, the white smoke once again billowed out from the chimney and the Vatican chefs started working on their spaghetti dishes.

Except that this time the Pope would not be looking to dine out on bolognese or carbonara – he was more likely to enjoy a plate of goulash; Polish goulash. Cardinal Wojtyla, a native of Wadowice in Poland, ripped up 336 years of Catholic Papal tradition by becoming a non-Italian Pope and, just to keep the good parents of Coatbridge happy, he retained the name John Paul, this time as JPII.

New Popes? New managers? What a swell party this promised to be. The Pope was in Rome but Cesar was in Glasgow. Big Billy was preparing his charges for the first game of the season which was to kick off against Morton in Greenock. This was a tricky one.

The team from Cappielow had only just been promoted and

were hungry to make their mark. Well, one of their squad was anyway. Andy Ritchie, he of the slumbering gait and the dastardly dead-ball skills, *always* looked hungry and this initial meeting against his former club, who had left him stranded on the Greenock coastline like a beached whale, afforded him the opportunity to repay the Bhoys in full.

Delicious it must have been, therefore, for Ritchie to plant one in the seventy fifth minute, but it was a bitter fruit as the Celts were already two goals to the good by that point. Still, it did make for a nervy last fifteen minutes when Cesar's troops were required to show that they had lost that frustrating habit of conceding vital points from the previous season.

The Bhoys done well, as many an untutored commentator would have observed with their 2-1 victory at a difficult away ground. And they would continue to do well for the whole of the month and even into September when that first derby encounter reared its head.

It was hard to believe that the same players from Jock's last fatal campaign were now suddenly in control of matches that saw them roar over the two Dundee sides in the League Cup and enjoy four-goal winning margins over Hearts and Motherwell in the Premier Division. Ah, but they were yet to face the champions, weren't they? Their mettle was yet to be tested against the Govan Select who had won that thing again . . . rhymes with rebel etc.

The fact that Rangers, under John Greig, had started poorly with a shock defeat to St Mirren and then a couple of draws with Hibs and Partick Thistle meant that Celtic were automatically installed as favourites. The Bhoys were at home, Rangers had yet to score in the League whereas Celtic had accrued maximum points and potted eleven goals for the loss of only two in their title bid. Even at that, it was probably still a surprise to everyone at Celtic Park – including John Greig – who was still trying to decide which side of the dugout to sit in, when Tam the Tar McAdam paved the way to goal in only the second minute.

Gorgeous George McCluskey had us 2-0 up twenty minutes later and the score stayed that way till half-time. The dressing room patter at the break must have been classic.

Cesar reminding his legion that they were similarly well-placed with a two-goal cushion interval lead in the corresponding fixture from the previous year and lost 3-2 whilst Greigy would have been tearing up his first scorer slip for the fourth league match in a row. His Govan Select had now played 315 minutes of League football without registering a goal. Their firepower appeared to be as useful as Kojak's conditioner.

Whatever both managers said at half-time, only one set of players seemed to be listening. Derek Parlane bagged Rangers' first League goal of the season when he pulled one back just four minutes into the second half. Was it to be Shuggygate again from last season when the Icelandic god appeared to have won the game for us in the first forty five only to see the Bhoys pegged back and then defeated by the ninety?

Thankfully, no . . . though it took until fourteen minutes from the end for the Celts to pick up the points when the Tar zinged in a third goal. Big Latch also proved himself a hero when he saved an Alex Miller penalty near the end to make the scoreline an even better one from the green perspective.

First blood to the Bhoys. A point clear of Aberdeen at the top of the table and, more importantly, six ahead of the Govan Select, who sat in the bottom three of the division. We were getting more excited than a hungry Liz Taylor in front of a microwave.

Big Cesar had started convincingly and was marshalling his men like, it has to be said, Caesar on the battlefront. But, of course, like the Roman Emperor, he was urging caution against the Ides. Julius's ides were in March whereas Billy's started in October. And like

Caesar, it was a former friend who plunged the dagger in when Celtic headed through to Pittodrie for a meeting with the Marc Antony that was Aberdeen.

The Dons, under the soon-to-be-famous Alex Ferguson, were keen to whip away the welcome mat from under their former manager's feet and wasted no time in racking up a three-goal advantage before Celtic could strike back with a counter just before half-time. Ten minutes into the second period and it really was all over with a second Joe Harper goal making for a 4-1 reversal. The road back from the Grampians would be a pretty desperate one.

Worse was to follow with defeats from Dundee United and Hearts as well as a 0-0 draw at home to Morton in a match so boring that nobody noticed that Andy Ritchie had gone to sleep – possibly because the crowd beat him to it. We should have seen this coming though, given our European performance.

Eh, what European performance? Okay, there wasn't one but it makes me feel better to fantasise about a continental excursion in 1978-79 rather than to face the unforgivable fact that the only time Celtic ventured out of Scotland this season was in September to play Burnley. And that was in the Anglo-Scottish Cup.

Yes siree, the down-at-heel cousin, surely, of the ill-fated Drybrough Cup was this tournament that invited cross-border competition between teams who only really saw Europe when the wife booked a fortnight in Benidorm. Celtic in the Anglo-Scottish Cup, aka the Texaco Cup, aka meaningless bauble facetiously dressed up as a major prize, it took the biscuit more than McVitie's. In the way that the sins of the father are rendered unto his offspring, Big Jock's last act as Celtic manager was to leave the Celts in fifth place in the Premier Division and, therefore, candidates for the old Anglo-Scottish jamboree.

Billy McNeill, his players and his supporters were being made to don a sackcloth and parade through the streets denouncing the wrongdoings of their forefather by playing against Burnley. If football was considered to be an earthquake, this tie would barely register on the Richter Scale. The TV people weren't even interested.

There was no big match build-up in the press with a pullout souvenir of both teams. Archie Macpherson wasn't looking for panellists' predictions for the *big one* and Jean Paul Gaultier could not have dressed this gig up any better. Apathy, thy name is the Anglo-Scottish Cup. The only certainty was that Celtic would carry a support down to Lancashire for the first leg.

If the Bhoys landed on Mars for an Inter-Galactic Champions League tie against, forgive me, Olympic Mars-eille (ouch), then there would be a Celtic crowd there to greet them. Unfortunately, the tedium and humiliation of being forced to play in this diddy tournament proved too much for some of the support who rioted just after Steve Kindon had put Burnley ahead at Turf Moor.

It was a rarely seen Celtic sight this . . . a baying mob wearing hooped jerseys. Indeed, just as rare as a Celtic side in the Anglo-Scottish. The newspapers seemed to take a healthier interest in the tie after the siege of Turf Moor and this interest was increased when the Bhoys were knocked out of the tournament at Celtic Park a fortnight later. Ah well.

Sure, it was a trophy but nobody could get excited about it. The Clarets, for what it's worth, did go on to win the Anglo-Scottish Cup that year and because of that, they rank alongside those clubs who have picked up the great prizes after having disposed of the Celts. AC Milan, Ajax Amsterdam, Burnley! Did we laugh or cry?

Whilst the Celts were toiling in Lancashire, Big Jock was across the Pennines attempting to revive Leeds United. The initial statements emanating from Paradise when Cesar took control was that Jock Stein would be elevated to a directorship. It sounded like a magnificent gesture for a well-valued employee but, in reality, his role was to oversee the directions of the Celtic Pools. Now, let's not belittle the sterling work that this organisation does to generate pennies for the Celtic cause but Big Jock, The Master, the Architect of Lisbon, selling lottery tickets? Come on. You're 'avin' a laff, ain'tcha? It was like asking Bob Hope to organise the who's-got-the-bonniest-baby competition at Butlins.

It just wouldn't do and he must have mused so when he came out onto the hallowed turf in the East End on the night of his testimonial match. The faithful treated him like God. Hell, God treated him like God! It was a testimonial richly deserved and extremely well organised but for one thing . . . the opposition were Liverpool.

Now, the Big Man's esprit de corps with the Anfield outfit, Bill Shankly, Bob Paisley, et al was a given, but here were Liverpool, the European Champions, being led out by Kenny D. The Merseybeats and their star singer. To the Celtic support, it was like getting an invitation to your ex-wife's wedding. Kenny Dalglish – Kenny Dee of Dee Kop – the artist formerly known as *King.* The Jungle wasn't about to wait at the airport with a bunch of flowers for him. Instead they roared their disapproval whenever Cap'n Ken was on the ball.

Nowadays, the back of the tabloids would be full of the story of Kenny *vowing to beat the boo boys.* Modern players seem to take more vows than a novice nun but Kenny D, ever the professional, just ignored the lukewarm reception and banged in a couple of goals in a 3-2 Liverpool victory.

It probably felt good for Big Jock to be out on the park and involved again so when Leeds United approached him about an Elland Road gig made vacant by Jimmy Armfield, he allowed himself to be persuaded. Brian Clough lasted forty-four days when he was at Leeds. Jock Stein lasted for the exact same number of days. Okay, so he trumped John Paul I by a week and a half in the job, but at least when Big Jock left, it was for the greater good. He was to replace Muhammad Ally in the Scotland dugout.

The good news for Cesar was that he wouldn't have his former manager breathing down his neck. Which was probably just as well since the Celts were in the middle of a League run that saw them go seven games without a win. The euphoria of the derby day cookout was followed by a home defeat to Hibs and Billy McNeill decided that it was time to open the cheque book. He needed somebody with flair. He needed somebody with style. He needed somebody with a perm!

Oh yes, a new epidemic was sweeping the land and footballers were not immune. Men were perming their hair – hunners o' them. Most footballers spent their leisure time playing golf, losing heavily on the ponies or endlessly pushing pennies over in the pub for charity but now they could be seen, sitting in Salon De Chez Jean, rollers tightly wound into their hair, flipping through Cosmopolitan magazine with their female counterparts. It started with World Cup duo Alan Rough and Asa Hartford, then quickly spread like an ammonia rash.

You were likely to bump into one of them now in Boots the Chemist checking out the self-heating conditioning treatments available for chemically-damaged hair. It was a sight to behold when a seasoned internationalist like Joe Jordan tapped you on the shoulder and asked what you would recommend for root nourishment and that shiny bounce in his tired mane.

Watching teams coming out of the tunnel for a big match, you almost expected to hear Archie Macpherson muse lyrically like the girlie adverts: *Now, one of these midfield generals is wearing Silvikrin hairspray for that firm, but natural hold. Can you tell which one it is?*

Hairy-arsed fitba' players were carrying Afro-combs around with them in their back pockets. Where would it all end? Davie Provan had a perm. He also had a great deal of talent and was Cesar's first big signing for his Hoops when he moved from Kilmarnock in September for £100,000. From the brass tips of his polished pointers, through his tight-fitting beige cords, tucked-in cheesecloth shirt right up to his curly magnificence, he was, every inch of him, a late '70s footballer.

The talk was that he looked like *The Professionals'* Ray Doyle.

The talk was also that he was to replace the Professional Celt, Johnny Doyle. Cesar thought talk was cheap, though, and it would be with Doyley rather than without him that Celtic would take the challenge to Rangers.

The Davester made his debut against Partick Thistle when he assisted a goal and won a penalty in a 3-2 Celtic win. He also looked to have eased in nicely for a gratifying 2-1 victory away to St Mirren. Unfortunately, this was the overture before that less than magnificent seven without a win.

He scored his first goal for the club against Hibs in the middle of November and was joined on the sheet by another new bhoy, Murdo MacLeod. Wee Murdie thought a permanent wave was an elongated hand gesture and if his cords were tight, it was only because of the bulging quadriceps underneath them.

As a style icon he was more akin to *Ally* MacLeod but he could lay claim to being the fittest man at Celtic Park for many a year and had a shot of such ferocity that nets should have been reinforced with steel wire. Cesar had picked him up from Dumbarton, which was appropriate. Murdie was as sturdy as a rock and even more reliable. He tackled like a rhino, sprinted like a cheetah, kicked like a stallion and probably swam like a fish. Watching Murdo MacLeod in action was like watching *Animal Magic.*

He was Bodie to Provan's Doyle and together they would offer the Celtic what was missing – a touch of class. And class was what it was all about in the late 1970s. Well, one class anyway. Form 1 Alpha of Grange Hill High School.

Finally, after a childhood spent watching middle-class children's drama series like *The Phoenix and the Carpet* or The *Midnight Garden,* it was time to tune into some modern-day reality when Grange Hill hit the box in 1978. *Flippin' 'eck Tucker!* we chanted as a roll-call of schoolkids, *just like we was,* were set loose on our teatime television screens courtesy of the BBC.

At last. Here was a soapy drama where 'h's were habitually dropped, eyes were frequently rolled and standards consistently challenged. Our heroes were first-formers Benny Green, Alan Humphries and jack-the-lad, Tucker Jenkins. If we weren't egging the lads on to more chaos then we were lusting after the rebel goddess herself . . . Trisha Yates.

No need now to vainly aspire to Felicity Kendal in *The Good Life* or *Blue Peter* presenter Lesley Judd, cool, lazy-mouthed Trisha was the attainable conquest of Grange Hill High School. Tucker knew it too. That's why he held that grudging respect for her even though she was, quite unmistakably, a girl.

When Trisha got involved in Student Action Group or SAG's table-top protest about school uniforms in the canteen, we were right beside her ripping off our brilliant white shirts and lassoing our large-knot ties around our foreheads. When Tucker Jenkins was tanning posh bully Michael Doyle for his evil, racist slandering of good friend Benny, we were haudin' his jaicket. And when arty-farty, right-on, look-I-*know*-these-kids English teacher, Mr Sutcliffe, was trying to get down with the pupils, we were standing at his back drawing chalk penises on his brushed denim Wrangler twin set.

Aunty Beeb was rocked with the controversy of it all when the likes of disgusted Mr and Mrs Cholmondley-Pugh of disgusted Tunbridge Wells sent a disgusted letter in to register their – you guessed it – disgust. But, for once, the channel stuck to its credentials. Indeed, it would see the Turnbridge Wells set and raise it as well when they moved the second series of Grange Hill up to twice a week. Jimmy Pursey and Sham 69 had it sussed: If The Kids Were United, they would never be divided!

Grange Hill was setting out on a run that would last nearly 30 years. Which seemed almost as long as John Travolta and Olivia Newton John had been at number one with *Summer Nights.* Thankfully, the Boomtown Rats brought that little episode to a close when they hit the top spot with *Rat Trap.* Bob Geldof and the rest of the rodents celebrated that achievement by ripping up a photograph of Livvy and JT as they performed their new wave classic on Top of the Pops. It was all about runs now.

Rydell High's sweethearts had been at number one for nearly two months. With a 1-0 home win over Partick Thistle, Celtic brought their own miserable title campaign run to a halt. Thank God we still had our incomparable, relentless fourteen year run in the League Cup to fall back on. Which brings us rather neatly to the Scottish League Cup Final of 1978-79 . . .

Eh – we weren't in it. Flippin' 'eck Tucker! It had finally happened. There was a League Cup Final that didn't have the name Celtic on the ticket. A run that had started on 8 August 1964 with a 0-0 draw against Partick Thistle came to an unsavoury end the week before Christmas 1978 in a tawdry semi-final versus the Govan Select.

When the Celts kicked off that sequence of finals Harold Wilson was settling into Downing Street as the first Labour Prime Minister for over a decade, flares were for distress signals at sea and Manfred Mann were about to replace The Beatles at the summit of what was quaintly known as the *Hit Parade*. Even in those days, the League Cup was viewed as the least relevant of the domestic trophies so it seems appropriate that The Manfs smash-hit 45 was entitled *Do Wah DIDDY DIDDY!*

By the late '70s, its stock was higher than the ill-fated Drybrough or Anglo-Scottish Cup, but there wasn't much in it. Still, the perception was that Celtic *always* contested the final of the tournament in the same way that England and Australia always play out the Ashes. Up until that not-so-festive semi-final it had been business as usual, although some of the scalps on the way to the penultimate stage of the competition were fairly impressive.

I've already mentioned the smothering of the Jute City challenges with aggregate victories over the Tayside clubs of 6-1 (Dundee) and 4-2 (United). The shock of the next round was the Steelmen coming through from Motherwell to win 1-0 at Paradise. Big Latch had been outstanding in this one. That is, Dave Latchford of Motherwell.

The Lanarkshire side had obviously been impressed by Peter the Great in the Celtic goal so they decided to go out and get their very own Latchford. Big brother Dave was picked up from Birmingham City as the last line of defence. He must have enjoyed the family bragging rights after this one, although a 4-1 second leg pummelling meant that if there was to be a Solihull Sulk, it wouldn't be coming from younger sibling Peter.

Montrose made things a bit more than interesting when it took super-cool penalty taker Andy Lynch to squeeze a 1-1 draw away at Links Park in the first quarter-final tie. That result hyped up the box office a bit for the second leg but the big news was that Danny McGrain was fit to play in his first home competitive game for more than a year.

Danny the Beard, as he would now be known, was back among the faithful and played the captain's part with two assists in a 3-1 win. And so to Hampden.

Tommy Burns had been playing some outstanding football with a left foot so educated that it had a degree. His sublime pass to Doylie had the Celts one up in ten minutes. Alas for TB, his tongue appeared to be as unstoppable as his pinpoint passing and so he was sent off a quarter of an hour later for persistently complaining, loud and large, to the linesman when the Govanites were awarded a penalty kick.

Celtic were reduced to ten men in a game against Rangers. Remember this sentence . . . I'll be asking questions later in the season. Alex Miller was the next to see red when he was removed from the action after a second bookable against Doyley. When the Hoops went ahead for the second time a few minutes later, it seemed like time to log on for another League Cup Final shift. And then Colin Jackson of Rangers scored. Once again – remember this phrase for that questionnaire further on.

In extra-time, Derek Johnstone, the DJ from 1970, came back to haunt the Hoops in a Hampden League Cup encounter. He sclaffed a shot across the Celtic bows with about seven minutes to go. Had the big Gov hit it with a frying pan it could not have been any more ridiculous, but somehow it rolled away from Roy Baines in the Celtic goal and walloped off young defender Jim Casey and into the net.

An own goal winner. An own goal winner versus the Govan Select. An own goal winner versus the Govan Select in the semi-final of a major trophy. It's fair to say that the unfortunate Casey would have to get Uncle Ben to refer him to a psychiatrist for counselling (and if you don't get *that* one, ask your parents!) *Oh My Lord!* as Boney M were crooning as the refrain to *Mary's Bhoy Child.*

The League Cup may have had a certain sentimental value for Cesar. He had been the first Celtic captain to lift the trophy in eight years when he led the Lion Cubs to victory in 1965 and he was still the last Celtic skipper to get his hands on the cup back in 1974. He would have wanted desperately to extend that tradition, particularly because it was Aberdeen in the final. What an opportunity to reply to the ribald chanting from the Dons' support after that 4-1 mauling at Pittodrie in October by winning his first silverware as a manager at their expense.

It was not to be and with that Govan reversal being followed up by a 1-1 draw with Dundee United and a 1-0 defeat by Morton to an Andy Ritchie penalty down in Greenock, it was beginning to look like a bleak midwinter.

The Talented Mr Ritchie's penalty had arrived in the eighty-eighth minute of a tight, frost-bitten showdown and meant that, from the last twenty-two points available, the Hoops had picked up a mere seven. Hardly the form of champions.

As Christmas rolled around, Billy's Bhoys were fifth in the table, which is where they had finished the season before. The only good news was that there was only four points between themselves and leaders Dundee United whilst their city rivals enjoyed a mere one point advantage over them. Still, the perception was that the Celts were running out of petrol. Then again, everybody was!

Yet another fuel crisis, that staple of the 1970s' economy, was upon us with a tanker drivers' dispute leading to a serious shortage of the precious liquid and panic buying at the pumps. Streets were blocked as everything from a Rolls Royce to an Austin Allegro queued endlessly around the forecourts of the nation trying to squeeze the last of the juice into their tanks. It was a time to consider giving up the car and taking to the streets with the latest craze . . . skateboarding.

The stockings of Christmas 1978 had to be mighty sturdy to handle the prerequisite, must-have toy, a skateboard from Santa. It was difficult to truly appreciate this mania as the skateboard only seemed to serve any purpose when going downhill. The rest of the time involved the mind-numbing necessity of having to paddle the board with a free foot. What's more, you couldn't really travel to the match on one. Fuel crisis or not, you just didn't see shed-loads of Celtic supporters skateboarding their way through the byways and highways of Scotland bound for Paradise. You might just have got done for eating a Macaroon Bar in a built-up area. Bring back the shift-stick Chopper.

If we were looking for gas, there was always a heap of it emanating from the radio airwaves. Radio Clyde 261 introduced the football fan phone-in at the start of season 1978-79. The beauty of this concept was that it was so bleedin' obvious! Instead of just moaning to other supporters about the referee, the line-up, the tactics, the pies and all this permed hair in the modern game, you could be on air, broadcasting to the west coast of Scotland about it.

The show was hosted by Richard Park, whom Big Jock had once referred to mischievously as *Ibrox* Park, given his alleged penchant for all things red, white and blue, and the panel of experts included uber-egghead Bob Crampsey, uber-ego Gerry McNee and the very youthful, yet even then uber-bald, Chick Young. At last, there was a golden opportunity to cross swords with the men who reported on the game as well as voice your disapproval at your lazy midfield general. There was but one king of the format and his name was James Sanderson.

This Scottish journalist was as direct as a Gestapo order with twice the ferocity. A loquacious man, he had the encyclopaedic sporting knowledge of co-panellist Bob Crampsey but, unfortunately, the high-register whining voice of a Scottish Peter Lorre. When the Sandman really went off on one, there wasn't a dog in all Christendom who couldn't detect his top-of-the-range pitch and would howl accordingly. He was interested in one thing – getting bums on seats.

To be fair, James Sanderson had identified that, with so many other distractions on offer as well as the burgeoning television dollar that was shaping football coverage, there were fewer and fewer people going to the games. You may well have wanted to vent your spleen at Mr Sanderson for his withering appraisal of your star centre-forward and stout defence of the referee who declined to award your team three stonewall penalties over the ninety minutes but if you hadn't actually paid to get in then your critique counted for nothing.

Were you at the game? he would ask with all the conviction of a Nuremburg lawyer scenting the guilty blood of a war criminal. Unless you answered in the affirmative then you were wasting his time. *Eh, Naw. I had to go to ma maw's funeral,* just didn't cut it with the Sandman. As a rule, funerals were over by lunch, which left you ample time to get to the ground before kick-off.

Suffice to say, the airwaves would have been crackling with the sound of disgruntled Celtic supporters as 1978 drew to a close. But it was difficult to 'phone in to complain about Celtic performances when they didn't get to play a League match for nearly two and a half months.

Ever since the formation of the Scottish Football League in the late nineteenth century, there has, at regular intervals, been a movement to instigate summer football or, at least, a midwinter break. For Scots, the only problem is that there isn't generally much difference weather-wise between New Year's Day and the Glasgow Fair Fortnight in July. It ain't the Bahamas, so if you were traipsing around in a fashionable Swallow raincoat in January, there was just as much chance it would still be on your back come summer. This was particularly true for the winter of 1978. Johannes Edvaldsson had never seen as much snow and he hailed from Reykjavik, Iceland.

Rumour had it that the Kennedys were going to cancel their ski break in Colorado and head over to Glasgow for a shot on the piste at Rouken Glen. The torrid conditions meant that Celtic played only two matches in January and February, both Cup ties against Montrose and Berwick Rangers. With more call-offs than a Scottish international squad, Big Billy must have been re-introducing his troops to one another every single week. *Hey, Murdo – Davie Provan. didn't we play together for Celtic once?*

Astonishingly, after that dramatic late defeat in Greenock two days before Christmas, the Celts never kicked another ball in League football until 3 March and a home game against Aberdeen. At Morton, we had been preparing for Christ's birthday. When we met the Dons, Lent had just kicked off and it was full steam ahead for Good Friday and the Resurrection. Time flies, eh?

Week upon week would pass with no sign of a let-up on the weather front. Yet, remarkably, it looked as if it was only Celtic who had the problem. Whilst the Bhoys were struggling to get fixtures started, other clubs, notably Rangers and Aberdeen, were forging ahead with games. Justification was sought in conspiracy theories:

Paranoid? Us? No, no. We're happy for Quinn the Eskimo to do our Saturday morning pitch inspection!

The fixtures were piling up like, well, to be honest, corpses in the street. Being British, we liked the idea of pile-ups. So we were happy to watch bags of rubbish being left out on the roads and bodies not being buried and cancer patients not receiving treatment in hospital because of the unofficial strikes that were adding to an industrial chaos. The *real* Winter of Discontent was upon us.

The Labour Government was pleading for a five per cent limit on pay agreements and the unions were struggling to control the plague of wildcat striking. The Prime Minister, Sunny Jim Callaghan, took off for tropical Guadeloupe and an all-important holiday, sorry, summit meeting, with the heads of France, Germany and the USA. As he posed about with Jimmy 'The Teeth' Carter in the Caribbean, the punters back home were wondering about sticking granny on the fire to keep warm.

In one of the great political *faux pas* of the twentieth century, Sunny Jim arrived back in London looking tanned and relaxed and responded to questions about the escalating situation by denying that there *was* any chaos in the country. Margaret Thatcher watched from the sidelines, knuckledusters gleaming, waiting for the right moment . . .

It was all too much for Sex Pistol Sid Vicious, who died from a heroin overdose in New York. Punk Rockers were mourning their loss by phoning radio stations, requesting *Pretty Vacant* and recalling the night the Pistols had played the Marquee Club in London. *Were you at the gig?* – as James 'Anarchy in the UK' Sanderson might have asked.

Such were the quandaries that we beheld whilst waiting for Celtic's season to restart. If we were bored, what were the players doing? Davie Provan would be having his afro conditioned. Danny the Beard would be bench-pressing 120kg in preparation for his first

League match in almost a year and a half. Johnny Doyle would be attending a special anger management course, dedicated to derby matches. And Peter Latchford booked into the *YMCA* with the Village People.

Well, how else could we explain away the mowser that he had fashioned for himself? Yup, that was the big shock when the Bhoys returned to active duty and we all took one look at the burly one's upper lip. He was now Peter *Tach*ford! *Aaaghh!* we cried. *Falling behind in the League and Big Peter's having a mid-life crisis!* Why couldn't he just have gone out and bought himself a colour-coded TR7 instead of this raffish attempt to look like butch Burt Reynolds? Mercifully, Peter the Great was unimpeded by his rakish new image and returned to the kind of form that had us all chanting *Latchford for England!*

To our minds, there was only one Peter to play in goal for Hadrian's XI and it surely wasn't Shilton the Charlatan! As opening games went, at home to Aberdeen was hardly a walk in the park but *what's-it-all-about* Alfie, complete with *his* moustache, scored a fine goal to take the points and set the Hoops on their way. There was also the welcome addition of Danny the Beard for that promised start to a League line-up.

This was the start of a triple header against the Dons as we were down to play them in the Scottish Cup the following week in a tie that eventually went to a replay. It was like wife-swapping. *Right; you come to us, then we'll come to you and then you come to us again, okay?* Except that it wasn't okay. A credible draw at Pittodrie turned into a midweek cup eviction and whittled our trophy options down to one – the Premier League title.

Cesar had reversed some of Big Jock's decisions like bringing back Lemon Lennox from the American wilderness and being rewarded with the goals in a 2-1 win over Motherwell. He now reversed the trend of the Quality Street Kids *leaving* Celtic by asking one of them to come back to the sweetshop.

Victor Davidson sounded like a British movie idol from the 1930s and his first spell at Celtic had promised much but yielded little. Billy McNeill had remembered that promise and signed him from Blackpool at the end of March. The Celtic support remembered Vic, too. They remembered his, shall we say, *enthusiastic* celebration in front of them when he had bagged the winner for Motherwell against Big Jock's failing charges only the season before. The jury was out and remained that way for Vic's second Celtic debut when Hibs won 2-1 at Easter Road.

Still, at least we were playing games, although the week before the journey to Leith had us back in postponement land again. This one was more controversial than Jim Callaghan with a sun tan. The Govan Select were operating out of Hampden as there was work being done over at Ibrox so the Hoops headed for Mount Florida and a vital match. Conditions were actually more Mount *Everest* than Mount *Florida* but referee Brian McGinlay passed the pitch as playable. It was at that point that club officials of the Hampden landlords, Queen's Park got involved to demand that the game be postponed. They felt that the ground was not suitable to handle the crowd. I mean, hadn't it been in April 1970 when more than 130,000 people turned up for that Leeds United match? But hey, what the hell.

Cesar was furious at the call-off but his anger held little sway with the jobsworth at Hampden and nary a ball was kicked. If Big Billy had little confidence in the administration at Queen's Park, then Parliament had even less in the Labour Government. Sunny Jim's outlook reverted to a black thunder when he lost a House vote on the confidence issue and, as a result, a General Election was called. *I Will Survive* sang Gloria Gaynor to the delight of a wealth of future Karaoke stars. *We Don't Think So,* replied the electorate to Jim Callaghan.

It didn't matter how many miles both the Prime Minister and Maggie T covered on the campaign trail, it couldn't match the kind of itinerary that the Hoops undertook in the month of April. Cesar's troops were playing catch-up now and this involved an average of one game every three days. In less than four weeks, they traversed the playing fields in Lanarkshire, Tayside, Grampian, Lothian and Renfrewshire. And that was just the away games. At the end of the month, they had garnered more votes than a Labour MP in Monklands and tallied enough points to talk realistically of a challenge for the title.

In the midst of it all, it looked like the Govan Select could feel the bristle from Peter the Great's new moustache tickling the back of their neck as they lost unexpected points to the doomed Motherwell and the fancied Aberdeen. Yet they possibly felt that they had landed the knockout blow to the Hoops when that re-arranged Hampden fixture in May resulted in a victory for the blue corner.

Every game for Celtic would be the mythical *Cup Final* after this one. We reminded ourselves of the words of St Francis of Assisi,

> *Where there is despair, may we bring hope;*
> *Where there is doubt, may we bring peace.*

Actually, it wasn't us who were reminding the world about the wonders of St Francis. It was Mrs Thatch who, just forty-eight hours before that crucial derby match at Hampden, became the first female Prime Minister in British history. Sunny Jim had gone down with the ship and the erstwhile patron saint of the economy was quoting the actual patron saint of ecology on the steps of Downing St.

We didn't know that St Francis had been voted in the night before as the Honourable Member for Assisi. Then again, Mrs Thatch probably didn't know that the Goodly Francis was a dangerous revolutionary who had turned from his wealthy father to espouse simplicity and poverty. In fact, if he'd been around in 1979, she would probably have told him to come back when he was better dressed and to drop all this socialist nonsense about an equal society.

Cesar was also calling on a few saints. Who was the patron

saint of centre-halves? Roddie the Highlander was injured and his stand-in, the more than able Shuggy from Iceland, also picked up a knock in the Govan Select defeat. Two days after that one, on the Monday, the Hoops were at Firhill for another one of their postponed fixtures.

It was a Bank Holiday which was good news for all the graduates who didn't want to skip class to watch their favourite Jags go head-to-head with the Celtic. Cesar almost contemplated sticking his boots on but, at the eleventh hour, had a brainwave. Stick Tam the Tar McAdam into the middle of the back four. If he could attack a goal, he could also defend one. It was a master stroke comparable with D-Day. The Hoops lost the first goal but re-grouped for a gutsy 2-1 victory and birth was given to a new defensive star.

The Premier League wagon was heading for Dodge City and the end was in sight. Having disposed of St Mirren and Hearts, the Bhoys were facing up to the biggest game of the season and it's not too far-fetched to say one of the biggest games of the Supersonic '70s. The Govan Select were the final act at Celtic Park on Monday 21 May. Right, stats buffs, here's the state of play.

Celtic had clambered to the top of the League sitting on forty six points with one game left. Greigy's Govan had amassed forty three points but had three games to go. Even Thatcherite economics could not distort the figures. A draw or, even better, a win for the Rangers would see them nicely placed to win the title if they could claim some points from Partick Thistle and Hibs. Ooh, the luxury of choice.

For the Bhoys, it was simple arithmetic: win the match, win the title. The media was in a typical froth about it and the week that they had to build the match up was agony for all concerned. Had Maggie T put a tax on clichés, then the tabloids would have been out of business.

ONE GAME AT A TIME! says 'Gers' boss Greig
Mc Neill says DO OR DIE!!
AITKEN VOWS TO AVENGE TITLE HEARTBREAK!
Big Latch – I'VE GOT FREDDIE STARR'S HAMSTER ON MY LIP!
The stakes couldn't have been higher (See, it's contagious!).

On the night of the match it was more than a worry that the Celtic DJ's choice of pre-match entertainment include Roxy Music urging us to *Dance Away The Heartache* whilst we hoped against hope that the Bee Gees *Tragedy* wasn't an omen.

Barry Gibb would have been counting the royalties when Alex MacDonald put the Govanites 1-0 up within ten minutes. Roy Aitken hit the bar and then, just after half-time, Johnny Doyle asked for a refund on that anger management course. Robust challenges on Alex MacDonald were nothing new but the fact that Doyley chose to stick his foot in when the Rangers midfielder was already lying on the ground requiring attention did not play well with referee Eddie Pringle.

The wee man's *tackle* was so late that the fat lady had stopped singing, gone home and was in a bath. As was Doylie – and an early one at that! Despatched from the action and the Celts down to ten men just like the League Cup semi all over again (I told you to pay attention). *We're doomed! Doomed I tell ye!* shouted Private Fraser from the back of the Jungle.

Out on the park, the Bear had one of those Roy of the Rovers moments. You know that one where, even in the tumult of a critical derby match, Roy could hear that one voice in the crowd saying,

It looks like curtains for the Celts this time.

He might be right, but Roy of the Rovers never gives up.

The Bear rallied the troops and fired in an equaliser in the sixty-sixth minute. But even that wasn't enough. Total victory was required. When Gorgeous George made it 2-1 with fifteen to go, it looked as if the perfect ending was on. But the cliché police were out in force again and that adage about a team never being more vulnerable than when they go ahead was spot on again as the Govan Select equalised a mere two minutes after the restart. Bobby Russell got that one and then Colin Jackson went one better when he stuck the ball in the pokie.

Was it the League Cup semi all over again? Nah! This time old CJ had scored an own goal! Gorgeous rapped one in on goal that the Girvan lighthouse got down to and pushed away but only as far as the onrushing, luckless Jackson who could only knock it into the net. *Michael* Jackson couldn't have screamed louder. There were only six nervy minutes to go.

Six minutes between Cesar and his first League title as a manager. Five minutes between Danny the Beard's first title as a captain. Four minutes between Permy Provan and his first title as a player. Three minutes between Lemon's eleventh and final title as a legend. Two minutes between Ten Men winning that title. One minute between Murdo MacLeod and the most celebrated goal of his career.

Cesar would have been urging wee Murdie to smash one towards the Outer Hebrides or, at least, the back of the Celtic End when he lined up a shot from all of twenty yards out. The Dumbarton Rock was not about time wasting though. He just pulled back his foot and in the glorious words of Archie Macpherson . . . *Let flyyyyyyyyyy!*

And to think they wrote songs about Woodstock! If ever there was a case for picking up the geetar and recalling one of the great festivals of the twentieth century then it was worth getting all musical about the night Murdo MacLeod flashed the ball past the Girvan Lighthouse in the Govan goal to crown the Celts as champions with a 4-2 scoreline. When the whistle blew, anything in a green and white shirt embraced like VE Day.

In his time, Cesar had done it all, seen it all and could tell you all about it. But how high on his list of achievements would be the lifting of the League Championship in his first season as manager of Celtic? The Supersonic 70s had opened with Cesar's extra-time tragedy in the European Cup Final against Feyenoord. It closed with his Celtic side fighting off postponements, red cards, fatigue and the pressure of following on from The Master to net as worthy a title as any that had gone before in the Grand Old History.

As he looked around the stadium, he may well have paused to think of the changes since 1970. The fashions that had seen Bertie Auld start the decade with a brylcreemed, fighter pilot hair slick and Davie Provan end it with a shoulder length, shaggy perm. Of Danny McGrain, still so young back then that his shaving routine involved putting milk on his chin and getting the cat to lick it off. He now had a full face of fuzz and no feline. Of the rest of the Beard's Quality Street Gang pals made up of Big Geordie, Wee Luigi, King Kenny and the Quiet Assassin now reduced to one, Victor Davidson.

Of the thrilling, if flawed, European specials like the Dixmaster's missed penalty against old flames Inter or the Battle of Paradise in 1974 against the Athletico Butchers' Union. Of choppers and skateboards; Bolan and Bowie; Wilson and Thatcher; Elvis and Vicious; of nine-in-a-row and now ten men winning the League.

Supersonic and Sensational!

Supersonic Pin-Upz!

Dixie Deans

John *Dixie* Deans confused me. That's difficult to understand since his primary function was to score goals and he did that so often that there could be no doubts as to who he was in the Celtic frontline. He confused me because, for a frighteningly long time, I actually thought that he was Dixie Dean, the revered hit-man who played for Everton in the 1930s.

Cut me some slack here. When the Dixmaster was in his pomp at Paradise, I was barely ten and clearly arithmetic wasn't to be my major. But I used to marvel at how well Dixie had looked after himself so that he could be up and about thirty-odd years after his Merseyside peak and still be a viable threat in front of goal. There was also a vague resemblance if you compare Dean to the early Dixie who played for Motherwell. Anyway, to be honest, I couldn't have cared if he *was* in his sixties when he played for the Hoops – the point was, he was banging them in good style.

Big Jock nipped in under the radar to pick Dixie up from Motherwell in autumn 1971 when the striker was serving a six-match ban. It's a bit of a myth that Dixie was *trouble.* He'd enjoyed the odd fracas out on the park but he was hardly a Kray twin.

The Dixmaster didn't look like a top striker. He sported a hairstyle (if that's not too loose a term to describe it) that didn't appear to have been cut properly since Sergeant Pepper was a Private and his sideburns could have auditioned for Great Expectations. Also, the only time you would see the word *athlete* and *Dixie* in the same sentence was when he was treating his foot with anti-fungal powder. Make no mistake about it though – this guy was a Prince amongst goals scorers.

He possessed clever feet, had a deceptive turn of pace (no, not over the first two yards) and if he'd been sent out onto the park to play Blind Man's Bluff, he would still have ended up facing the opposition goal, menacing the penalty box.

A succession of Hibernian goalkeepers probably still wake up in the middle of the night shouting *No, no, no not Deans again!* Perhaps one of Dixie's ancestors was maltreated by somebody from Leith a long time ago, such was the vengeance that he took out on the Hibs' rearguard.

The Dixmaster was an instinctive predator who could sniff out a chance like a gas leak and a prolific scorer with the keenest of keen eyes for a goal. I don't care how good the graphics get in the twenty first century Fifa video games, no computer will ever be able to score the belter that Dixie Deans served up as his second offering in the 1972 Scottish Cup Final!

If he were a '70s pop group, he'd have been Slade. Firmly working class, yet pure showbiz and laced with a golden talent for being at the top of the charts. *Cum On Feel the Noize* mighty Dixmaster!

Ronnie Glavin

It wouldn't be entirely surprising if Ronnie Glavin was in the habit of sending a weekly bouquet of roses to Pat Stanton. The surprise introduction of the Edinburgh legend to the Celtic side of

1976-77 freed up the G-Man to exploit his finest season in the Hooped jersey.

His transfer to Celtic was so long in the process that you can probably buy it in a boxed set now to watch over a quiet weekend. He finally arrived in Paradise in November 1974 and, for a while anyway, hinted at the player that he could be, if given an opportunity in the Celtic midfield. Some supporters may have recalled him from the Partick Thistle shock troops in the 1971 League Cup Final although, like most traumatic events, earthquakes, hijackings etc, it's usually difficult to remember a face in such a crisis.

Big Jock lodged his contribution at the back of his mind for future reference and would have fancied the chance of developing Ronnie G's talent when he checked in that season. Sadly, the Big Man's accident in the summer of 1975 meant that he would have to wait a year to really bring out the best in his £80,000 midfielder.

STM

Sean Fallon asked the G-Man to defend a bit more rather than attack when he had sole control of team affairs for the season. To Ronnie, de*fence* was what you put around de *garden* and his game suffered as a result.

The transformation to a goal-scoring midfielder came to fruition in the glorious final triumphs of Jock's last double season and Ronnie G was a standout in an excellent Celtic side. Like many of that team, he felt the loss of King Kenny the following season and despite finishing second overall scorer for the Hoops that year, he still only managed to bag nine. To put the campaign into perspective, he was squeezed out by Shuggy Edvaldsson and the Iceman's less than mammoth tally of ten.

He was less and less of a feature in Cesar's inaugural year in the Celtic dugout with just ten League outings and three goals to his credit. He left for Barnsley in June of 1979 to become a Yorkshire icon second only to Arthur Scargill.

In the Hoops, he witnessed the best of times and the worst of them as well but will forever be remembered for his plundering raids in Big Jock's penultimate season. Oh, and a hairstyle that needed to be treated with WD40 before you could get a comb through it.

If he was a '70s pop artist he would be Peter Frampton. His career looked to be going stratospheric in the middle of the decade and there were some brilliant solo performances but he would only really enjoy a brief moment in the Top 10.

Come on G-Man . . . *Show Me The Way!*

Peter Latchford

The burly Brummie was the greatest thing to come out of the Midlands since William Shakespeare . . . eh, eventually. Big Jock tended to regard goalkeepers like suppositories; they were a necessary evil but a pain in the ass!

Latch arrived at Celtic Park, on loan, towards the end of the 1974-75 season and was pitched in to a side that was in the process of losing the League title for the first time in ten years. He became the fourth Celtic goalie in as many Scottish Cup Finals when he played against Airdrie for Cesar's last hurrah.

I well remember *Shoot!* magazine running a scurrilous item entitled, *Celtic's Goalkeeper – Woeful and Wonderful!* not long after Latch had signed on full time and taken up residence as the Hoops' number one. As a headline, it left little to the imagination and I always hoped that our new English goalie had his subscription to another comic like *Tiger* or *Whizzer & Chips*. It can't be denied that the early days of his Celtic career were, shall we say, inconsistent, and his first full season was the barren campaign of 1975-76, but he little deserved the snide reportage of a once venerable magazine.

Arguably the Big Man's thick Brummie accent was a bit of a problem when it came to communicating with his defence. A scurrilous rumour once suggested that when he was dressing up for a night out in the mid-70s with his missus, Latch asked for her advice on a delicate matter of dress sense. When he said, *Kipper tie?* Mrs Latch replied, *Yes, thank you. Milk and two sugars please!*

But, like so many players in that Celtic side of the following season, Latch seemed to grow into his role and by the finish of it was looking like he could hold the position down for years. *Latchford for England!* was the cry for a few seasons and it wasn't one laced with irony. There was already a Latchford featuring for Hadrian's XI and he was the striker, beardy Bob, Peter the Great's brother.

Latch's international CV records a miserly two caps at under-23 level whilst some other goalie, also called Peter, represented his country a zillion times. Talk about injustice . . . where's Amnesty International when you need them? He was the Celtic Supporters Association Player of the Year in 1978 in recognition of the fact that the Big Brummie's contribution had kept an unpalatable season from lurching into the grave.

Sartorially, he tended to be a bit on the sloppy side with a succession of rumpled goalie tops and what appeared to be a pair of gardening gloves on his hands. But his mitts were a sacred item throughout his Celtic tenure and if he did fancy pruning his begonias on a day off and then keeping the gloves on for a big match, who were we to argue?

The best Celtic goalkeeper since Ronnie Simpson and when

you consider the competition, that's no mean statement. If he was a '70s pop group, who else but the Electric Light Orchestra? Big, brash, colourful, at his best as an ensemble and Midlands to the core . . . a real *Wild West Hero!*

Johannes Edvaldsson

An Icelandic superstar long before Bjork was the Sugarcube glint in a mid-Atlantic eye, Johannes Edvaldsson was the ultimate unknown quantity when he checked in to Celtic Park in the close season of 1975. The first thing to do was to give him a nickname with more of a Scottish twang to it. After all, didn't the royal butler address Prince Charles as *Johannes* when he brought in his breakfast?

STM

The Celtic support alighted on *Shuggy.* Down-to-earth, universally acceptable and easier to chant when the Iceman was turning it on. The second question was where to play Shuggy? Was he a defender, midfielder or a striker? Actually, he was all three and sometimes in the one game. The Iceman was so versatile in his many guises that Mike Yarwood almost issued a writ against him and he was a finer utility than a Zanussi dishwasher.

He kept the door locked at the back with a succession of back four partners, drove the midfield forward like a Sherman tank and on one memorable occasion, had the Celts 2-0 up against the Govan Select at half-time, operating as a centre-forward.

His goal celebrations were famously understated as he always seemed unsure what to do after he'd hit the back of the net. Generally, he would run forward a couple of steps and then leap awkwardly up to a height of eight inches with his two hands clenched like he was lifting a set of dumb-bells above his head. It wasn't exactly a samba around the corner flag but, then again, Shuggy was way too sophisticated for all that nonsense.

His greatest season was Big Jock's final double-winning campaign of 1976-77 when his very presence in a Celtic jersey would sometimes be enough to cause what Arthur Montford would call a *stramash* in the stomachs of the opposition. Shuggy did succumb to the Latch 'tache disease in 1979 but this fashion disaster didn't stop him from playing an integral part in one of the most important Celtic-Rangers derby matches of the Supersonic '70s when ten-men-won-the-league.

He had a bigger cult following than film director David Lynch although if you were making a flick about his career, expect Shuggy to write, direct, produce and star in it all at the one time. Apparently it says *Jack of all Trades* on his passport and if it doesn't, then it certainly should!

If he were a '70s pop star he would be Mike Oldfield. Cool, calm, collected and able to master four million instruments at the one time – including those Tubular Bells!

Johnny Doyle

It would be unfair to think that Johnny Doyle will be best remembered as a Celt because of the undoubted tragedy of his premature death in 1981. His legacy is worthy of more.

Doylie would have walked all the way from Somerset Park, Ayr to Glasgow to merely have a trial for Celtic. All supporters love to see a guy out on the park *living the dream* and if Johnny Doyle hadn't been playing for Celtic then he would definitely have been in the Jungle, roaring them on.

In the near-mercenary state of the game in the twenty-first century when the fans tire of seeing the latest millionaire *kissing the badge,* Doylie would have been regarded as an anachronism for the

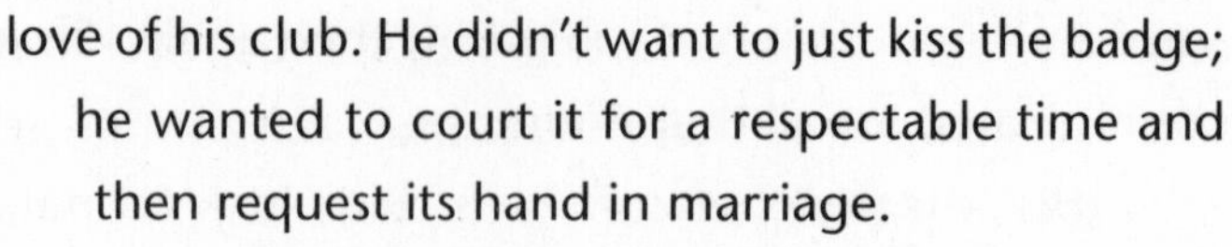

love of his club. He didn't want to just kiss the badge; he wanted to court it for a respectable time and then request its hand in marriage.

He's probably the only player Celtic ever signed at an airport and would certainly have been higher than any of the Boeing 737s taking off that afternoon when he put his signature on the contract.

There were the comic moments – being sent off for misdirecting a cross straight off a referee's napper in 1977 was a particular favourite – and he certainly got more pumped up than Marlon Brando's airbed when he was confronted with a match against the Govan Select. But, it was comforting to know, in that week leading up to a derby match, that you weren't the only Celtic supporter who could barely eat his bacon and eggs in anticipation of the first whistle. Wee Johnny would have been feeding the scraps to his dog as well.

He was a buzz-bomb of a player, a tormented sea of unrelenting energy and yet he regarded training as the boring part of his job. Perhaps, Johnny only thought of himself as a main stage performer rather than one dedicated to the tedium of rehearsal?

He played for the Hoops on 180 occasions and you can bet the housekeeping on the fact that, if you brought up one of those games at random, he could recite chapter and verse on what had happened over the ninety.

His misfortune was to follow on from Jimmy the Jink Johnstone, so comparisons were inevitable, and arguably the arrival of Davie Provan in 1978 suggested that his place in the Celtic line-up was on a shaky peg. Yet, Doylie never lost faith in his ability and in all of the great moments in Big Jock's final years and the successes of the early Cesar reign, there was wee Johnny taking an active part in the celebrations.

Only in 1979, when his dismissal from the pitch in the more-crucial-than-we-can-explain game that decided the Premier League title, did Doylie have to be fetched out onto the park to rejoice with his fellow supporters at the final whistle. The wee man was distraught at the thought that the Celtic faithful would hold it against him if ten men had not won the League. Johnny, ye hardly knew us.

The man had green and white blood and, were he alive today, Johnny Doyle would have been one of those ex-players who greeted you in the hospitality section on a match-day. And he'd be wearing a scarf and would have been worth every penny! If he were a '70s pop group he would be the Sensational Alex Harvey Band. Energetic, passionate, committed and above all, one o' wur ain! Vambo!

Joe Craig

Hollywood beckoned for Joe Craig. It helped that he bore more than a passing resemblance to *Rocky* star, Sylvester Stallone, but the story of a former car mechanic who, only three years after turning pro, plays a starring role as his team secures a League and Cup double is straight out of the Cecil B. De Mille stable.

Of course, such a bio-pic would have ended with Joe coming on as a substitute for his Scotland debut and scoring a goal with his first touch. That would have been the moment when the battered, blood-spattered Joe would have risen above his jubilant team-mates and the Tartan Army to cry *Adriannnnnnn!!* at the top of his lungs. Sadly, there was to be no sequel.

Indeed, arguably his next film outing would have been the Rocky Horror Picture Show as within a year and a bit, he was offloaded to Blackburn Rovers. For some reason, Cesar was not a fan of Joe's rumbustious style.

The moment of his deterioration could be dated back to 10

August 1977 when King Kenny abdicated to become a Merseybeat. Naturally, he wasn't the only loser in that deal. Ronnie G, what's-it-all-bout Alfie, hell, Big Jock and indeed Celtic FC were never really the same after the transfer. But, Joe could argue that the immediate impact of that taxi for Liverpool, was that he was bereft of the man who fed him his goals like he was the King's favourite corgi at chow-time. Lewis without Martin; Morecambe without Wise. Rocky had lost his Adrianna.

Still, there was the fragrant memory of that momentous season when his sixteen League goals and a more than impressive seven in the Scottish Cup paved the way for a Double celebration. Joe had two crucial strikes to subdue a hard-working Blue Bonnets Dundee side in the semi-final that year and it was his finish against the *ye-can-stick-yer-TV-cameras-where-the sun-don't-shine* Hibs on 16 April that clinched the Premier League title with four games to go.

As a consequence, the name of Joe Craig is placed on that list of Celts through the years who count such as Bobby Lennox, Jimmy Johnstone, Kenny Dalglish, Tommy Burns, Tommy Johnston and Shunsuke Nakamura amongst their ranks as the players whose goal completed a League triumph.

And none of that illustrious crew could have sorted out the burning clutch on your Nissan Bluebird either! If Rocky Joe was a '70s pop star he would be David Soul. A brooding, menacing yet sensitive slice of Hutch beefcake who enjoyed a brief, startling success then failed to sustain it when his Starsky left . . . *Let's Have A Quiet Night In, Adriannnnnnnn!!*

Davie Provan

The bhoy with the bubble cut. Davie P was Cesar's big gamble in September 1978 when he splashed out the first six-figure fee in Hoops history to bring him to Paradise from Kilmarnock. If the £120,000 price tag sat uncomfortably on the shoulders of the probin' Provan, it didn't show. Then again, very few things ever looked out of place draped over his wiry, yet muscular frame.

Davie swept into Celtic Park as the best dressed man in Kerrydale Street and with a magnificent perm that would not have looked out of place in Blaxploitation-era flick, *Cleopatra Jones*. He was so up-to-the-minute that you could set your watch by him.

The good news was that he was equally as stylish on the park. Davie's personal strengths included a Buddhist-like devotion to physical fitness which he combined with an ability to torment a defence before releasing a killer pass into the path of any number of Celtic strikers.

Strong, skilful, talented and blessed with a supreme self-belief, he would enjoy a successful Celtic career and alongside Cesar's other first-season purchase, Murdo MacLeod, would form a duo who could claim to be extremely influential in the glories that came the club's way right through until the mid-1980s.

And yet, for all the late '70s posturing, Davie P harked back to a different age of Brylcreem, rattles and Pathe newsreels with his predilection for keeping his socks rolled around his ankles like a pair of dozing vipers. At a time in the game when the lower limbs were considered a legitimate target for tackles from behind, in-front or just plain scything, it took a certain amount of bravery to sport this look.

Of course, these particular vipers would be equally as deadly when spurred to action. His boundless energy and derring-do were a potent factor on the night of the ten-men and in the crushing eight-games-in-one-month that was the April build-up to that fantastic finale to the Supersonic '70s.

It's little surprise that, given his innate intelligence and a penchant for expressing trenchant opinions regardless of reputation, Davie P has enjoyed a post-grad career in the media world. Well, I guess when you've trained a couple of poisonous reptiles to lie dormant over your calves, then getting into the snake-pit of the Fourth Estate would hold little fear.

Like a select band of his Hooped brethren, Davie Provan would have been a first-pick in any Celtic side and his enforced retirement, due to illness, at the relatively active age of thirty one in 1987 has to be viewed as a tragedy for both the supremely fit outside-right and the Bhoys.

In old money, he was the Number '7' link between Jimmy the Jink and a guy called Larsson who we were to hear about in later years. Had Davie Provan been a '70s pop group then he would have been, well, hell, take your pick!

The disco-beat of the Bee Gees? The hairdos of Earth, Wind and Fire? The right-on '70s laidback cool of Fleetwood Mac and their *Rumours*? Let's just settle for Roxy Music. A full range of talent allied to a stylish groove and in lead singer, Bryan Ferry, a worthy adversary for Davie P's coolest-man-of-the-moment title. What a fight it would have been for the shampoo and conditioner in *that* backstage dressing room!

The end of *The Supersonic 70s!*
Celtic will return in *The Electronic 80s!*